The Collect in the Churches of the Reformation

SCM STUDIES IN WORSHIP
AND LITURGY

The Collect in the Churches of the Reformation

Edited by
Bridget Nichols

scm press

© The Editor and Contributors 2010

Published in 2010 by SCM Press
Editorial office
13–17 Long Lane,
London, EC1A 9PN, UK

SCM Press is an imprint of Hymns Ancient and Modern Ltd
(a registered charity)
St Mary's Works, St Mary's Plain,
Norwich, NR3 3BH, UK

www.scm-canterburypress.co.uk

All rights reserved. No part of this publication may be reproduced,
stored in a retrieval system, or transmitted,
in any form or by any means, electronic, mechanical,
photocopying or otherwise, without the prior permission of
the publisher, SCM Press.

The Authors have asserted their right under the Copyright,
Designs and Patents Act, 1988,
to be identified as the Authors of this Work

British Library Cataloguing in Publication data

A catalogue record for this book is available
from the British Library

978 0 334 04207 5

Typeset by Regent Typesetting, London
Printed and bound by
CPI Antony Rowe, Chippenham SN14 6LH

Contents

Acknowledgements   vii
Preface   ix
Contributors   x
Abbreviations   xiii

Introduction   1
  Bridget Nichols

1. The Collect in English: Vernacular Beginnings   9
  Bridget Nichols

2. The Collect in the Church of Sweden following the Reformation   28
  Nils-Henrik Nilsson

3. The Anglican Collect   50
  Donald Gray

4. The Use of Collects in the Methodist Church in Britain   67
  John Lampard

5. The Collect in the United Methodist Church and its Antecedents   83
  Karen B. Westerfield Tucker

6. The Collect in American Lutheran Liturgical Books: *Evangelical Lutheran Worship* (2006)   106
  Frank C. Senn

7 Between Form and Freedom: The History of the Collect
   in the Reformed Tradition   123
      Paul Galbreath

8 Written Prayers in an Oral Context: Transitions in British
   Baptist Worship   139
      Chris Ellis

9 Collects and Lectionaries   157
      David Kennedy

10 Special Collections   178
      Michael Perham

11 The Collect: A Roman Catholic Perspective   197
      Alan Griffiths

Index   217
Index of Collects   229

Acknowledgements

We are grateful to all authors and publishers of copyright material quoted in the essays in this book, and in particular for permission to reprint the following:

The Alternative Service Book 1980: extracts from *The Alternative Service Book 1980* are copyright © The Central Board of Finance of the Church of England 1980; The Archbishops' Council, 1999, reproduced by permission.

The Book of Alternative Services: material excerpted from *The Book of Alternative Services* of the Anglican Church of Canada © 1985 by the General Synod of The Anglican Church of Canada. Used with permission.

Book of Common Order: extracts from the *Book of Common Order* © Church of Scotland 1940 are reproduced by permission of the Office of Worship and Doctrine, Mission and Discipleship Council, Church of Scotland.

The Book of Common Prayer, 1662: extracts from *The Book of Common Prayer*, the rights of which are vested in the Crown, are reproduced by permission of the Crown's Patentee, Cambridge University Press.

Book of Common Worship 1993: extracts from the *Book of Common Worship* of The Presbyterian Church (USA) which originally appeared in *A New Zealand Prayer Book: He Karakia Mihinare o Aotearoa* © Church of the Province of New Zealand, 1989, are reprinted with the permission of the General Secretary. Extracts which originally appeared in *Uniting in Worship*, prepared by the Assembly Commission on Liturgy © 1988, are reprinted by permission of the Assembly of the Uniting Church in Australia.

Walter Russell Bowie: extracts from *Lift Up Your Hearts* (Macmillan, 1939) used by permission of the Abingdon Press.

ACKNOWLEDGEMENTS

Common Worship: Services and Prayers for the Church of England: extracts from *Common Worship: Services and Prayers for the Church of England* (Church House Publishing) are copyright © The Archbishops' Council, 2000, and are reproduced by permission.

Evangelical Lutheran Worship: extracts from *Evangelical Lutheran Worship* © Augsburg Fortress Publishers, 2006. Used by permission.

Forward Movement of The Episcopal Church: extracts from *Prayers Old and New*, 5th edn (Forward Movement, 1943) reproduced by permission of Forward Movement Publications.

Fred Gealy: collect by Fred Gealy and the prayer for the Day of Pentecost © 1989 the United Methodist Publishing House. Used by permission.

Methodist Worship Book: extracts from the *Methodist Worship Book* (Methodist Publishing House, 1999) © 1999 Trustees for Methodist Church Purposes. Used by permission.

Janet Morley: extracts from *All Desires Known* (London: SPCK, 1992 and 3rd edn, 2005). Used by permission.

Opening Prayers: Scripture-related collects for Years A, B & C of The Sacramentary: excerpts from *Opening Prayers* (Canterbury Press, 1997) © 1997 International Committee on English in the Liturgy, Inc. (ICEL). Used by permission.

A Prayer Book for Australia: extracts from *A Prayer Book for Australia* © Broughton Publishing Pty Ltd, 1995. Used by permission.

The Roman Missal: excerpts from the English translation of *The Roman Missal* © 1973 and 2010, International Committee on English in the Liturgy, Inc. (ICEL). All rights reserved. Used by permission.

Steven Shakespeare: extracts from *Prayers for an Inclusive Church* are reproduced by permission of SCM-Canterbury Press.

David Silk: extracts from *Prayers for Use at the Alternative Services* (Mowbray, 1980) are reproduced by permission of the copyright holders, the Continuum International Publishing Group.

Society of St Francis: extracts from *Celebrating Common Prayer* (Mowbray, 1992) are reproduced by permission of the copyright holders, the Continuum International Publishing Group.

George Timms: collects from *The Cloud of Witnesses*, reproduced by permission of The Alcuin Club and Canon Martin Draper.

United Methodist Book of Worship: prayer from the *United Methodist Book of Worship: The Order for the Consecration of Bishops* © 1979 by Board of Discipleship, the United Methodist Church, © 1992 by The United Methodist Publishing House. Used by permission.

Preface

The suggestion that the collect in the Churches of the Reformation deserved attention in its own right came from James Leachman OSB and Daniel McCarthy OSB. I am grateful to them for pointing in this direction, and to the many people who have offered encouragement as this collection of essays took shape.

I am particularly grateful to the wonderful group of liturgists who readily agreed to contribute chapters, delivered their manuscripts on time, and patiently answered the editor's questions.

Thanks are due to Dr Anthony Russell, Bishop of Ely while the book was in progress, for regarding liturgical projects as legitimate chaplain's duties and for his interest in the work. I hope he will enjoy reading it in retirement.

Mary Matthews, Editorial Manager at SCM Press, copy-editor Hannah Ward, and proof reader Linda Crosby have given invaluable help in shaping the text for publication. This is greatly appreciated.

Dr Natalie K. Watson, Senior Commissioning Editor at SCM Press, has advised, guided and encouraged at every stage. Her confidence in a finished product has been far more valuable than she knows.

Contributors

Chris Ellis has been pastor of West Bridgford Baptist Church, Nottingham, since 2006. Previously Principal of Bristol Baptist College, he has also ministered in various churches in England and Wales. He has co-edited the last two Baptist Union worship books, most recently *Gathering for Worship: Patterns and Prayers for the Community of Disciples* (2005), contributed to *The Oxford History of Christian Worship* (2006) and *The New SCM Dictionary of Liturgy and Worship* (2002), and is the author of a number of prayers and hymns. His books include *Approaching God: A Guide for Worship Leaders and Worshippers* (2009), *Gathering: Spirituality and Theology in Free Church Worship* (2004), and *Together on the Way: A Theology of Ecumenism* (1990).

Paul Galbreath is Professor of Worship and Preaching at Union Theological Seminary and Presbyterian School of Christian Education in Richmond, Virginia. He is the author of *Leading from the Table* (2008) and *Doxology and Theology* (2008).

Donald Gray is Canon Emeritus of Westminster. He has been President of the Society for Liturgical Study since 1998, and was President of Societas Liturgica 1987–89. He served on the Church of England Liturgical Commission from 1968 to 1986 and was a member of the Joint Liturgical Group from 1969 to 1996. Since 1987 he has been Chairman of the Alcuin Club. He has contributed to a number of liturgical publications and is the author of *Earth and Altar* (1986); *Ronald Jasper: His Life, His Work and the ASB* (1997); *Percy Dearmer* (2000); *Memorial Services* (2002); *The 1927–28 Prayer Book Crisis*: Part I (2005), Part II (2006).

CONTRIBUTORS

Alan Griffiths is Canon Theologian of St John's Cathedral, Portsmouth, and Director of Studies for the Permanent Diaconate in the Roman Catholic Diocese of Portsmouth. He is the author of *We Give You Thanks and Praise: The Ambrosian Eucharistic Prefaces* (1999).

David Kennedy is Vice-Dean and Precentor of Durham Cathedral, and a member of the Liturgical Commission of the Church of England. He has taught liturgy at The Queen's Foundation in Birmingham (an Anglican-Methodist Theological College) and supervises graduate students in the Department of Theology and Religious Studies of the University of Durham. He is the author of *Using Common Worship: Times and Seasons: All Saints' to Candlemas* (2006); *Using Common Worship: Times and Seasons: Lent to Embertide* (with Jeremy Haselock, 2008); *Eucharistic Sacramentality in an Ecumenical Context: The Anglican Epiclesis* (2008).

John Lampard is a Methodist minister living in Walthamstow, East London. He was a member of the liturgical committee which produced the *Methodist Worship Book* (1999), and is currently a member of the Worship and Liturgy Resource Group. He has a number of publications on funeral liturgy and practice, including *Go Forth Christian Soul* (2005), and is Vice-Chair of the ecumenical Churches Funerals Group.

Bridget Nichols is Lay Chaplain to the Bishop of Ely. Her publications include *Liturgical Hermeneutics* (1996) and 'Liturgy as Literature' in Andrew Hass, David Jasper and Elizabeth Jay (eds), *The Oxford Handbook of English Literature and Theology* (2007).

Nils-Henrik Nilsson is Vicar of Adolf Fredrik's Parish in Stockholm (Church of Sweden). He taught liturgy and ecumenism at the University of Lund, Sweden, from 1982 to 1988, and was Secretary for liturgy at the national level of the Church of Sweden from 1989 to 2006. From 1998 to 2000 he was Secretary of the Liturgical Commission and of the Lectionary Commission. His most recent publications include a commentary on the new Lectionary, *Evangelieboken i gudstjänst och förkunnelse* [*The Lectionary in Worship and Preaching*] (2003), and an investigation of the theology of worship, *Gudstjänsten och vi själva* [*Worship and Ourselves*] (2005).

CONTRIBUTORS

Michael Perham was a member of the Church of England Liturgical Commission through the 1980s and 1990s and played a key role in the development of *Common Worship*, particularly its Calendar, Lectionary and Collects. He has been successively a parish priest in Dorset, Canon Precentor in Norwich, Dean of Derby and since 2004 has been Bishop of Gloucester. He writes and lectures about worship and spirituality and his many books include *A New Handbook of Pastoral Liturgy* (2000) and, more recently, *Glory in our Midst* (2005).

Frank C. Senn is Pastor of Immanuel Evangelical Lutheran Church, Evanston ILL. Dr Senn was Assistant Professor of Liturgics in the Lutheran School of Theology, Chicago, from 1978 to 1981. He has taught courses at the University of Chicago Divinity School, the University of Notre Dame, and at Concordia University in Illinois. He is a past President of the North American Academy of Liturgy and of the Liturgical Conference. He is the author of nine books, most recently *The People's Work: A Social History of the Liturgy* (2006).

Karen B. Westerfield Tucker is Professor of Worship in the School of Theology at Boston University. She taught on the faculty of Duke University in North Carolina from 1989 to 2004, and chaired the World Methodist Council's Committee on Worship and Liturgy from 1996 to 2006. Currently she is the President of Societas Liturgica, and Editor of *Studia Liturgica*. The author of *American Methodist Worship* (2001), she was most recently co-editor with Geoffrey Wainwright of the *Oxford History of Christian Worship* (2006).

Abbreviations

ADK	Janet Morley, 1992, 3rd edn, 2005, *All Desires Known* [Movement for the Ordination of Women, 1988] London: SPCK.
APBA	The Anglican Church of Australia, 1995, *A Prayer Book for Australia*, Alexandria, NSW: Broughton Books.
ASB	Central Board of Finance of the Church of England, 1980, *The Alternative Service Book 1980*, London: SPCK; Colchester: Clowes; Cambridge: Cambridge University Press.
BCP	*The Book of Common Prayer* (Church of England, 1662).
BCP 1979	The Episcopal church of the USA, 1979, *The Book of Common Prayer*, New York: Church Hymnal Corporation.
BCW	Presbyterian Church (USA), 1993, *Book of Common Worship*, Louisville KY: Westminster John Knox Press.
CCP	Society of Saint Francis, 1992, *Celebrating Common Prayer*, London: Mowbray.
CLC	Central Board of Finance of the Church of England, 1997, *The Christian Year: Calendar, Lectionary and Collects*, London: Church House Publishing.
CLP	Comme le prévoit.
CoW	Martin Draper (ed.), 1982, *Cloud of Witnesses*, London: Collins.
CW	Archbishops' Council of the Church of England, 2000, *Common Worship: Services and Prayers for the Church of England*, London: Church House Publishing.
CWDP	Archbishops' Council of the Church of England, 2005, *Common Worship Daily Prayer*, London: Church House Publishing.
ECUSA	Episcopal Church of the United States of America (now The Episcopal Church).
ELCA	Evangelical Lutheran Church in America.
ELCiC	Evangelical Lutheran Church in Canada.

ABBREVIATIONS

ELW	ELCA and ELCiC, 2006, *Evangelical Lutheran Worship*, Minneapolis MN: Augsburg Fortress Press.
ER	F. E. Brightman, 1915, *The English Rite*, 2 vols, London: Rivingtons.
ICEL	International Commission on English in the Liturgy.
ICET	International Commission on English Texts.
ILCW	Inter-Lutheran Commission on Worship.
JLG	Joint Liturgical Group.
LBW	Lutheran Church in America, Board of Publications, 1978, *Lutheran Book of Worship*, Minneapolis, MN and Philadelphia PA: Augsburg Publishing House.
LCMS	Lutheran Church-Missouri Synod.
LHWE	Central Board of Finance of the Church of England, 1986, *Lent, Holy Week and Easter*, London: Church House Publishing; Cambridge: Cambridge University Press; London: SPCK.
LSB	Lutheran Church-Missouri Synod, 1982, *Lutheran Service Book*, St Louis MO: Concordia Publishing House.
LW	Lutheran Church-Missouri Synod, 1982, *Lutheran Worship*, St Louis MO: Concordia Publishing House.
MSB	Methodist Church of Great Britain, 1975, *Methodist Service Book*, London: Methodist Publishing House.
MWB	Methodist Church of Great Britain, 1999, *Methodist Worship Book*, Peterborough: Methodist Publishing House.
OP	ICEL, 1997, *Opening Prayers: Scripture-related collects for Years A, B & C of The Sacramentary*, Norwich: Canterbury Press.
PHG	Central Board of Finance of the Church of England, 1991, *The Promise of His Glory*, London: Mowbray.
PIC	Steven Shakespeare, 2008, *Prayers for an Inclusive Church*, Norwich: Canterbury Press.
RCL	Consultation on Common Texts, 1992, *Revised Common Lectionary*, Norwich: Canterbury Press.
SBH	*Service Book and Hymnal of the Lutheran Church in America*, 1958, Minneapolis MN: Augsburg Publishing House; Philadelphia PA: United Lutheran Publishing House.
TEC	The Episcopal Church (formerly ECUSA).
TLH	Lutheran Church-Missouri Synod, 1941, *The Lutheran Hymnal*, St Louis MO: Concordia Publishing House.

Introduction

BRIDGET NICHOLS

The persistence of the collect form in the Churches of the Reformation and in the Reformed tradition speaks of a continuing allegiance to one of the treasures of their common heritage. It also shows the resilience and vitality of a form of prayer which, at its best, has survived translation, revision and differences in theological approach to present the petitions of the assembly with grace, dignity and restraint.

That might be all that needed to be said, were 'the collect in the Churches of the Reformation' as innocuous a generic description as it sounded. But 'collect', 'Churches' and 'Reformation' are three nouns with large hinterlands. Which Churches of the Reformation are being considered, and why? How did they approach the matter of the collect when they came to devise their own orders of worship? What is the distinctive claim of the collect as a linking device among church traditions? The present collection of essays is shaped by these questions, and authors who are practitioners as well as liturgists explore them armed with the experience of leading worship, serving on the liturgical decision-making bodies of their Churches, writing new material, and teaching liturgy.

Three Reformation lineages, identified with Luther, Calvin, and the English Reformers who drew on multiple influences as they engaged with their own volatile domestic scene, have been taken into account. The Lutheran stream is represented by chapters on the Church of Sweden and the Evangelical Lutheran Churches in America and in Canada. The Calvinist stream is treated in a chapter on the Presbyterian Church (USA). A chapter on the Anglican collect examines the English stream. Their descendants in subsequent generations are represented by treatments of the Methodist Church in Britain and on the other side of the Atlantic, the United Methodist Church. Immediately, things become less simple, and this is not unrelated to the migratory tendencies of the collect. John Lampard describes how British Methodism grew out of the Church of England, but looked to the service book provided by John Wesley for the early colonists in North America who did not continue to use *The Book of Common Prayer*. Karen Westerfield Tucker explains that the United Methodist Church, which brought together a number of earlier Churches, has embraced a heritage that is by no means entirely British.

Many other candidates could have been chosen. English-speaking provinces of the Anglican Communion other than the Church of England have produced some fine collects in recent revisions and their achievement receives attention in chapters by Donald Gray and David Kennedy. The Church of Scotland offers another expression of liturgical work in a Calvinist idiom. Paul Galbreath refers to some of its earlier history as a fascinating parallel to developments in Geneva and Strasbourg. 'Lutheran' describes a number of Churches whose liturgies are by no means identical. Even within the United States, two distinct Lutheran Churches exist. Yet a book that attempted to accommodate all candidates would have offered opportunities only for superficial consideration of questions of usage and identity. It might also have excluded the situation of the Free Churches. In a chapter on the British Baptist Church, Chris Ellis tells how a Church formed, in part, in reaction against the liturgical rigidity and prescriptivism of the Church of England has understood its worship. Central to this narrative is the honoured position given to extempore prayer inspired by the Spirit. Recently, however, there has been a trend away from suspicion of any previously composed material towards a growing appreciation of the role such texts might play in worship, alongside spontaneous prayer.

The function of the collect

It would be difficult to improve on Michael Perham's beautifully succinct definition of what a collect should do: 'However brief a collect is, it has to draw together the prayers of the Church for the Church, for the whole company of those united by prayer.' This aspiration has been worked out in different ways over hundreds of years. For that reason, it has seemed important to begin by taking seriously the transition from the Latin service books and prayers of the Late Middle Ages to the use of vernacular forms, for common prayer in the vernacular fulfilled one of the major ambitions of the sixteenth-century Reformers. In chapters tracing the process in England and in Sweden, Bridget Nichols and Nils-Henrik Nilsson discuss two reforming endeavours. Both begin with a close eye on Latin examples, but where the Church of Sweden, even in its most recently revised Gospel Book, has continued to consult traditional Latin models, successive Church of England and other Anglican revisions have been less and less concerned with fidelity to an original language. Other interests, as Donald Gray and Michael Perham describe, have taken precedence.

All of the chapters dealing with particular church traditions and, very importantly, the chapter on Collects and Lectionaries, address the function of the collect as a liturgical unit. Anglicans have understood the collect of the day to have two principal positions in worship – as the prayer that concludes the entrance rite or gathering and precedes the Liturgy of the Word at the Eucharist, and as one of the closing prayers in the daily offices. Perhaps less familiar to contemporary worshippers are the six *BCP* collects, one or more of which is 'to be said after the Offertory, when there is no Communion', and the two collects at the end of the *BCP* Litany. More prayers in collect form appear among the *BCP*'s 'Prayers and Thanksgivings upon Several Occasions', paralleled in present-day sets of occasional prayers like those in *Common Worship*'s 'Other Prayers'. Collects are also to be found in the Ordinal and in the occasional offices of baptism, confirmation, marriage, the visitation of the sick, and burial or cremation. Finally, in a development that is novel in Anglican experience, the psalms in *Common Worship Daily Prayer* are followed by short prayers, a number of them in the form of collects.

This summarizes the working experience of only one Church, and even here the position of the collect is not entirely straightforward. There is, for example, less and less certainty as to whether the collect formally concludes the eucharistic entrance rite, or serves to introduce the readings. The situation of other Churches is well described by Nils-Henrik Nilsson, John Lampard, Karen Westerfield Tucker, Frank Senn and Paul Galbreath. Their chapters do not merely express a wide variety of views on the role of the collect, changing over time, but also challenge the assumption that the collect has always enjoyed a place in liturgical worship as of right. Methodist worship has valued the freedom of extempore prayer, and the use of service books has not been compulsory, though the collect has gradually become a more familiar feature of church life. Lectionary revision has been a significant inducement to expand existing resources and compose new collects. Lively creativity in response to a three-year lectionary has been evident in the Evangelical Lutheran Church in America and the Evangelical Lutheran Church in Canada, as Frank Senn shows. Paul Galbreath introduces a different dimension in his account of Calvin's use of the collect as a prayer for illumination, opening the minds and hearts of worshippers to the proclamation of Scripture. Here, too, there has been variation, and Churches of this family today exhibit the diversity permitted in the Reformed Churches' dual allegiance to form and freedom in worship.

Chris Ellis describes something entirely different in the experience of the British Baptist Church. Conscientious avoidance of previously composed prayers as potential impediments to the work of the Holy Spirit has recently given way to a growing awareness of the use such prayer might have in Baptist worship. Personal spirituality remains a central concern, but the value of a form that sums up extemporary utterances or gathers the needs submitted for the prayer of the assembly has been recognized. In considering what the collect should do as it enters a tradition in which it has had no previous claim, Ellis adds a helpfully self-conscious reflection to the individually nuanced analyses of the classic collect structure provided by Donald Gray, Frank Senn and Paul Galbreath. Here is a fresh voice reminding us that, before all else, the collect should be 'theologically grounded in the nature of God'.

Collects in relation

The survey of different Churches' understanding of the function of the collect has made it clear that in public worship collects live in relationship to other components of liturgical rites. Few of these relationships can have received more attention than the interplay between collects and lectionaries. Donald Gray gives an early example in the failed *Liturgy of Comprehension* of 1689, whose compilers amplified the scriptural content of the *BCP* collects. This was a good intention with ungainly results. Since the second half of the twentieth century, ecumenical determination to find a common way of reading Scripture has promoted awareness of and affection for collects, and much excellent writing has been produced in response to the Joint Liturgical Group's two-year lectionary, and subsequently to the three-year cycle of the *Revised Common Lectionary*. Donald Gray underlines the important work of the Joint Liturgical Group. David Kennedy's chronological examination of collect-writing in step with lectionary design, particularly in the period since the establishment of the JLG in 1967, shows how a common mind on the way the Bible should be read in church has encouraged different Churches to look to one another for models

INTRODUCTION

as they have embarked on revision. His chapter demonstrates comparative liturgy at its best, and in addition, complements the historical discussions of Senn and Galbreath with textual examples from the 1993 *Book of Common Worship* of the Presbyterian Church (USA) and *Evangelical Lutheran Worship* (2006).

Several contributors point out that praying and singing often have a significant partnership. Discussions of Methodist, United Methodist, and especially Baptist, worship take up this theme in relation to hymnody. John Lampard gives examples of prayers inspired, at least in part, by the hymns of Charles Wesley and others. Karen Westerfield Tucker shows that the converse has also been true, and that some of Wesley's hymns carry distinct echoes of *BCP* collects. In those Baptist Churches where singing has been admitted in worship, the hymnal has often occupied the place that would have been assumed by fixed forms of prayer in other settings, and Chris Ellis presents some of Isaac Watts's hymns as instances of this exchange. The chanting of prayers themselves is mentioned only once. Nils-Henrik Nilsson describes how the translators of Swedish vernacular prayers have striven to achieve rhythms that would allow them to be sung to traditional chants. The significance of this for liturgical composition in general is surely far greater than brief mention might suggest. Testing new texts for use in public worship for their singability would be a powerful means of detecting rhythmical infelicities and controlling excessively prosaic tendencies.

A third relationship takes us outside the liturgical gathering itself. This concerns the collect and domestic life. Frank Senn notes that, long before the church orders of North American Lutherans included collects, these prayers were included in the vernacular hymnals brought by European and Scandinavian immigrants and would have been better known at home than in church. John Lampard sees this kind of household piety continuing to this day among British Methodists, thanks to the inclusion of collects in the annually published *Methodist Prayer Handbook*. Far more people purchase this resource than the *Methodist Worship Book*, and its contribution to household devotion can be determined from its buoyant sales figures.

Finally, it would be wrong to ignore the contextual relationship between collects and the culture inhabited by the people who pray them. This dimension has arguably touched the Churches most powerfully in challenging them to re-examine their liturgical language with a genuine commitment to acknowledging the presence of women. The call for inclusion has drawn attention to specific forms of unintentional exclusion, notably the use of an entirely masculine language for God and the failure to incorporate the experience and spirituality of women into the imagery and frame of reference of texts used in worship. The Churches have taken different pathways towards inclusion. On the one hand, there is the 'soft' revision of the Church of Sweden's collects, discernible mainly in the much reduced presence of overtly masculine terminology in addressing God. On the other hand, there are more adventurous approaches, which employ a new range of images as well as finding alternatives to words like 'Lord', 'Father' and 'almighty'. The Presbyterian Church (USA) and the Evangelical Lutheran Churches in America and Canada are to be found at this end of the spectrum.

But it is writers who are not constrained by synodical bodies and liturgical committees who have had greater freedom to explore the possibilities of liturgical language. No contemporary collection, it seems, has been more influential than Janet Morley's *All Desires Known*, first published in 1988 and reprinted in 1992. Her work is given a prominent place in several chapters, and it is clear that her prayers have neither dated nor ceased to speak freshly to the concerns of Church and world. Reasons for this must be sought in the quality of the writing – its thoroughgoing fidelity to Scripture, its appreciation of lectionary themes (the JLG scheme at that time), its imaginative range, and its refusal of gimmickry and other kinds of excess verbal baggage. The book was revised in 2005, in conformity with the *Revised Common Lectionary*'s approach to the Church Year and, while retaining the original prayers, it is now a rather different shape from the original edition.

Morley's work is a more general reminder that the officially authorized service books of the Churches might not be the first place in which to look for collects. Michael Perham finds a good deal of evidence in the Church of England alone to suggest that they have not enjoyed a monopoly of the genre for some time. New collections have most often been motivated by a perceived need for prayers to meet needs or honour occasions where no provision exists in official collections. It is to the credit of bodies charged with revising the official resources that they have looked to these pieces of 'private enterprise' and found opportunities for drawing some of their material into wider use in the Churches. Perham welcomes the fact that gifted composers are flourishing and singles out some notable examples of writing that stretch the boundaries of the collect form without compromising its ability to represent the whole assembly.

INTRODUCTION

A view from outside the Churches of the Reformation

It is particularly fitting that the final chapter in a collection that follows the fortunes of a style of prayer first known in fifth-century Rome should come from a Roman Catholic author. Alan Griffiths writes of the revisions that the English-speaking Roman Catholic world has seen since the Second Vatican Council mandated translation into the vernacular. He vividly describes the drive towards finding an appropriate language and register for prayers translated from Latin. The process has been very different from revision exercises in other Churches, because it has been governed by strict instructions on the faithful rendering of Latin texts. These principles have themselves been revised, in step with changing linguistic and translation theories.

Griffiths depicts a Church learning from itself, and learning from other traditions. The sparse style of the 1973 ICEL collects, at times over-fastidious in avoiding some of the robust imagery of collects in the post-Vatican II *Missale Romanum*, is now giving way to a form that returns to complex sentences and richer metaphors as the ICEL translation of the 2002 *Missale Romanum* moves towards approval. The discussion is positioned so neatly on the cutting edge that, at the time of writing, the Holy See had not granted the *recognitio* for the new translation. Permission to reprint some of its collects in this book had to wait upon this official endorsement. Yet this chapter is much more than a guarantee that the whole collection is up to date: it is a fascinating insight into the way new collects come into being, how considerations of accuracy, expressiveness, rhythmic grace and literary elegance are weighed, and how useful it is for Churches engaged in the process of revision to have models to consult.

Griffiths is optimistic that what is emerging in the latest ICEL enterprise signals a thoroughly ecumenical approach to translation itself. It is also a compelling illustration of the fact that collects capable of speaking to a contemporary Church and continuing to speak to future generations of worshippers cannot simply be produced in sudden moments of inspiration. The best examples are more likely to be crafted by people who have prayed with Scripture and studied the tradition of Christian prayer. His hope for a 'common Christian collect heritage in the future' speaks not just of a single form of prayer, but of a mutual recognition, regard and search for unity, grounded in 'a hearty desire to pray'.[1]

---

[1] *BCP* collect for the Third Sunday after Trinity.

I

The Collect in English: Vernacular Beginnings

BRIDGET NICHOLS

When does it make sense to speak of 'the English collect'? A small number of medieval and early Reformation examples of prayers in collect form can certainly be produced from Books of Hours or Primers.[1] Yet these do not constitute a substantial body of generically similar texts, and it is not until 1549 that a full set of collects for Sundays and holy days, together with the fixed collects for the King and for Morning and Evening Prayer, the Litany, and the Funeral Service, is found in English.

It is conventional to treat these prayers as the work of Archbishop Thomas Cranmer (Archbishop of Canterbury 1533–56). This is something of an enigma. He left no working papers containing draft versions, and it is known that he was assisted by a committee of divines. Not all commentators are as unhesitating as Geoffrey Cuming in seeing his hand in the whole set.[2] But even those who will not go as far as claiming Cranmerian authorship for the collects outright have agreed that the balance of probability lies very much towards establishing him as the translator of a number of Latin collects of the Sarum rite for the new Prayer Book, and the composer of collects for occasions where no model existed, or where the existing model was not adopted. Other-

---

1 The Primer collects are excellently discussed in Geoffrey Cuming, 1998, *The Godly Order*, Alcuin Club Collections 65, London: SPCK. See especially pp. 25–57. Cuming offers a more general view of Cranmer's liturgical enterprise in 'Thomas Cranmer: Translator and Writer', in D. Jasper and R. C. D. Jasper (eds), 1990, *Language and the Worship of the Church*, London: Macmillan, pp. 110–19.

2 Cuming's essays on Cranmer in *The Godly Order* and *Language and the Worship of the Church* are premised on the assumption that the collects are Cranmer's work.

wise, it becomes very difficult to explain their consistency of style, their economy of expression, and in the case of those that are translations or adaptations of Latin originals, their skilful negotiation between two languages, and their deft adjustments of content to conform to Reformation doctrinal precepts.[3]

This chapter approaches the question of identifying the English collect with two aims in mind: first, to provide a sketch of the material already available in English and familiar to those closely involved in liturgical reform in the 1530s and 1540s; second, to provide a survey of the way in which the characteristics of the full set of collects published in 1549 evolved. A short survey cannot offer the level of detail that would be possible in a longer study. Instead, it tries to select examples for discussion whose points of interest find frequent echoes in other collects.

English as a language of prayer

From around 1200, Anglo-French, the form of French spoken in England, began to vie with Latin as 'a language of written record'.[4] It also became the language in which much of civic life was conducted, and was the only vernacular language used in schools before 1349. Up to this point, English had been a language for addressing inferiors, but from the mid-fourteenth century, notable changes occurred. Parliament was opened by English speeches for the first time in 1362, the same year in which English began to be used in the law courts.[5] In the field of education, Oxford University Statutes of 1389 required gram-

---

3 Gordon Jeanes, 2008, *Signs of God's Promise: Thomas Cranmer's Sacramental Theology and the Book of Common Prayer*, London and New York: T&T Clark, p. 11; F. E. Brightman, 1915, *The English Rite*, 2 vols, London: Rivingtons, vol. I, p. lxxvii; Ian Robinson, 1988, *The Establishment of Modern English Prose in the Reformation and the Enlightenment*, Cambridge: Cambridge University Press, p. 82. Bryan Spinks is more cautious in 'Treasures Old and New: a look at some of Thomas Cranmer's methods of liturgical compilation', in Paul Ayris and David Selwyn (eds), 1993, *Thomas Cranmer: Churchman and Scholar*, Woodbridge, Suffolk: Boydell Press, pp. 175–88, p. 175.

4 Hans Frede Nielsen, 2005, *From Dialect to Standard: English in England 1154–1776*, Odense: University Press of Southern Denmark, p. 14.

5 Margaret Deanesly, 1920, repr. 1966, *The Lollard Bible*, Cambridge: Cambridge University Press, p. 205; Nielsen, *From Dialect to Standard*, pp. 17–18.

THE COLLECT IN ENGLISH: VERNACULAR BEGINNINGS

mar masters to teach in English as well as French.[6] This describes the situation of written language.

Oral language was a different matter. The Victorian editor of *The Lay Folks' Mass Book*, a popular medieval manual for the use of lay people attending the Mass without the benefit of any knowledge of Latin, claimed that by the middle of the twelfth century, French was the language of private prayer in England.[7] He qualified this by distinguishing between the higher echelons of society who spoke French, and the growing class of people who 'spoke English as a rule, and had not only learnt to speak it, but think and pray in it, as their mother tongue'.[8] Recent research suggests, however, that from the twelfth century, English was the vernacular of everyone born in England, with the likely exception of the royal family, who continued to contract dynastic marriages with European royal houses. Most people, except for the lower classes (who spoke only English), would have been bilingual, though learning French by instruction, rather than as a mother tongue.[9] On this evidence, personal prayer in English is likely to have been a much more democratic phenomenon than earlier commentators imagined. It was for this group that the mid-twelfth-century *Lay Folks' Mass Book*, composed by a canon of Rouen, was translated into northern English about 1300.[10]

The Lay Folks' Mass Book is not a translation of the Mass, but a set of rubrics and devotions for every part of the Mass except the administration of communion. Most of these are in simple rhyming couplets, which are an obvious aid to memory.[11] The rubrics are copious, giving instruction as to when worshippers should cross themselves, stand, or say the Lord's Prayer. They also give a stage-by-stage account of what the priest will be doing. The parallel material often provides a profound spiritual meditation. Some of the texts (the Lord's Prayer and Gloria in Excelsis, for example) are paraphrases, since the scribe does not believe it necessary to provide English words when the Latin versions should be known by heart. The Creed, on the other hand, is

---

6 J. A. H. Moran, 1985, *The Growth of English Schooling 1340–1548: Learning, Literacy and Laicization in Pre-Reformation York Diocese*, Princeton NJ: Princeton University Press, p. 40.

7 F. E. Simmons (ed.), 1879, *The Lay Folks' Mass Book or the Manner of Hearing Mass . . . & Offices in English according to the Use of York*, London: Early English Text Society, p. xlix.

8 Simmons, *Lay Folks' Mass Book*, p. li.

9 Nielsen, *From Dialect to Standard*, pp. 13–14.

10 Deanesly, *Lollard Bible*, p. 212.

11 Simmons, *Lay Folks' Mass Book*, p. xxviii.

explained in rhyme.[12] The book was in use in English, from the time of its translation to about 1450.[13]

Alongside this was the family of books of private devotion known as Books of Hours or Primers. Designed for the use of lay people, these usually contained the Little Hours of the Virgin (short offices developed in monastic houses and recited in addition to the main offices of the day and night) together with the gradual psalms, the penitential psalms, the Litany of the Saints, and the Office of the Dead or *Dirige*.[14]

Manuscript Primers had included some English prayers, but such books were available mainly to wealthy owners. The advent of printing made possession of a Primer possible for a much wider range of people, and by 1529 English material had begun to be included in the *Sarum Horae*, a popular Primer produced by the French printer François Regnault.[15]

A new direction was set by the *Hortulus Animae* of the Lutheran sympathizer George Joye (1530). This offered translations of the canticles (Magnificat, Benedictus and Nunc Dimittis), whose phraseology is demonstrably influential in later Primers. William Marshall's Primer of 1535, published just after the break with Rome, when conditions for the dissemination of Reforming material were more favourable, adopted Joye's renderings and what Diarmaid MacCulloch calls their 'evangelical radicalism' unaltered.[16] Many of them survived into the First Prayer Book of Edward VI. Another more conservative trend, starting with Robert Redman's Primer of 1535, produced different readings of the canticles, corresponding to the text of Tyndale's New Testament.[17] These, too, were to have an influence on the First Prayer Book.

---

12 Deanesly, *Lollard Bible*, p. 212.

13 Deanesly, *Lollard Bible*, p. 213.

14 See Eamon Duffy, 2006, *Marking the Hours: English People and their Prayers 1240–1570*, New Haven and London: Yale University Press, pp. 5–6. See also Charles Butterworth, 1953, *The English Primers 1529–1545*, Philadelphia: University of Pennsylvania Press, and Edgar Hoskins, 1901, *Horae Beatae Mariae Virginis or Sarum and York Primers*, London: Longmans Green.

15 Duffy, *Marking*, p. 126.

16 Diarmaid MacCulloch, 1996, *Thomas Cranmer: A Life*, New Haven and London: Yale University Press, p. 335.

17 Cuming, *The Godly Order*, pp. 27–8. Duffy gives a less neutral account of the Reforming Primers, describing Marshall's Primer, for example, as 'aggressively protestant'. *Marking*, p. 147.

THE COLLECT IN ENGLISH: VERNACULAR BEGINNINGS

The devotional habits of ordinary people may not have been as radically affected as this steady stream of new texts suggests. For alongside the Reformed models, Sarum Primers and Books of Hours continued to be used. Surviving pre-1534 Catholic books show evidence of strategic deletions. The book trade responded to the times by removing the Pope's name, as well as indulgenced prayers and images of Thomas Becket, from all newly printed Sarum Primers.[18]

In general, the proliferation of Primers after 1534 does not seem to have caused much anxiety to the authorities. On the other hand, access to vernacular Bible reading occasioned serious concern. Reports of dissent arising from the public reading of Scripture in English led to a Proclamation for the uniformity of religion in 1536, limiting the reading or preaching of the Bible or New Testament to curates or graduates in the Universities of Oxford and Cambridge, and those holding a licence to preach. No one else was to read Scripture, silently or aloud, in church during divine service or the Mass. That time was to be used 'in reading or praying with peace and silence' (one assumes that reading matter was a Primer).[19]

Thinking must have changed quite rapidly, however, for later in 1536, Thomas Cromwell, the King's Vicegerent, issued directions for a large Bible in English to be set up in church where parishioners could easily read it. Furthermore, the clergy were to help their parishioners to learn an article of the paternoster or Creed by heart each Sunday until they had committed the whole text to memory in English. After this, they were to introduce the Ten Commandments.[20]

The last of the Reforming Primers, and the only one to carry official approval, was *The King's Primer*, issued in May 1545. This was henceforth to be the only permitted text, and no other forms were to be used. In an injunction printed at the beginning of the Primer, Henry VIII set out its educational purpose. His particular concern was for young people, who were customarily 'taught the Pater noster, the Ave maria, Crede, and .x. commaundementes all in Latin and not in Englishe, by meanes whereof the same are not brought up in the knowledge of their faith, dutye and obedience'.[21]

---

18 Duffy, *Marking*, p. 158.

19 D. Wilkins, 1737, *Concilia Magnae Britanniae et Hiberniae ab anno MCCCL ad annum MDXLV*, 4 vols, London: R. Gosling, F. Giles, T. Woodward & C. Davis, vol. 3, p. 811.

20 Wilkins, *Concilia*, vol. 3, p. 815.

21 Butterworth, *English Primers*, p. 257. The full text of The King's Primer is printed in T. A. Lacey (ed.), 1932, *The King's Book or a Necessary Doctrine and Erudition for any Christian Man, 1543*, London: SPCK.

He sought to dispose of the 'dyversitie of primer bookes that are nowe abroade' and instead 'to have one uniforme ordre of al such bokes throughout all our dominions, bothe to be taught unto children, and also to be used for ordinary praiers of al our people not learned in the Latin tong'.[22] Schoolmasters were exhorted to 'teache this Primer or boke of ordinary praiers unto [their pupils] in Englishe'. Children were to be instructed in this way until they reached 'competent understandying and knowledge to perceive it in Latin'.[23] No evidence exists to prove that an English Prayer Book was already in view at this time, but if a strategy of preparation was being introduced, the familiarization of young people with a repertoire of prayers in the vernacular would have played a useful part.

Cranmer and English prayers

Cranmer himself seems to have been composing prayers in the vernacular at least as early as 1539, according to the reports of some of his Reforming contemporaries. Unfortunately, their remarks contain no hint as to the nature or content of these prayers.[24] Then, on 11 June 1544, as hostilities with Scotland and France persisted and a campaign in France seemed imminent, the King wrote to the Archbishop, expressing a wish that general processions should be held to intercede for 'the miserable state of all Christendom'.[25] These were to be in English, since attendance at processions had been markedly lax, possibly because people could not understand the Latin prayers. The letter (which F. E. Brightman believed to have originated from Cranmer's pen) comes with 'certain godly prayers and suffrages in our native English tongue'. Henry asks that the processions should become a part of regular practice rather than a short-term expedient, and that Cranmer should enforce them in the Province of Canterbury. By the time the Mandate for this had been issued (18 June), the Litany and its prefa-

---

22 Butterworth, *English Primers*, p. 257.
23 Butterworth, *English Primers*, p. 257.
24 MacCulloch, *Thomas Cranmer*, p. 224. Gordon Jeanes takes up MacCulloch's point here, noting that it was reported to Conrad Pellikan in Zurich that Cranmer was composing *orationes* in English. Jeanes accepts MacCulloch's reading of 'prayers', rather than 'discourses', for *orationes*. Jeanes, *Signs*, p. 67.
25 J. E. Cox (ed.), 1846, *Miscellaneous Writings and Letters of Thomas Cranmer*, Parker Society, Cambridge: Cambridge University Press, p. 494.

tory Exhortation had already been printed. In 1545, it would replace the Sarum Processional altogether.[26]

MacCulloch comments that '[i]ts wonderfully sonorous language conceals the fact that, like all Cranmer's compositions, it is an ingenious effort of scissors and paste out of previous texts'. Much of the material originates in the Sarum rite, though specific mention of the saints has been reduced only to Mary. Marshall's Primer of 1535 had included a prototype which exerted further influence.[27] The characteristic identified by Cuming as Cranmer's 'psychological need . . . to use someone else's work as a starting point' was beginning to emerge.[28]

Ian Robinson maintains that '[i]t was in the Litany of 1544 that Cranmer, already in his mid-fifties, first showed his hand as a liturgist and developed his sense of the rhythms of spoken English'.[29] A frequently quoted letter from Cranmer to Henry later in that year gives a fascinating insight into the principles he was already applying to the task of producing vernacular liturgical texts. The occasion was a project for developing an English Processional for festal days in response to another royal request. The Archbishop writes:

> I have translated into the English tongue, so well as I could in so short time, certain processions, to be used upon festival days, if after due correction and amendment of the same your highness shall think it so convenient. In which translation, forasmuch as many of the processions, the Latin, were but barren as meseemed, and little fruitful, I was constrained to use more than the liberty of a translator: for in some processions I have altered divers words; for by cause the matter appeared to me to be little to purpose, or by cause the days be not with us festival-days; and some processions I have added whole, because I thought I had better matter for the purpose, than was the procession in Latin: the judgment whereof I refer wholly unto your majesty . . .[30]

'More than the liberty of a translator.' This modest remark alludes to an armoury of techniques available to Cranmer, which he would employ fully later. The result was a set of liturgical texts in an ecclesiastical register, which nevertheless drew on resources native to the

---

26 Brightman, *The English Rite*, vol. I, pp. lix–lx.
27 MacCulloch, *Thomas Cranmer*, p. 328.
28 Cuming, 'Thomas Cranmer: Translator and Writer', p. 112.
29 Robinson, *Modern English Prose*, p. 85.
30 Cox, *Miscellaneous Writings and Letters of Thomas Cranmer*, p. 412.

English language. Yet it remains a challenge to explain how he progressed from a few prayers at the conclusion of the Litany to a full set of English collects in a matter of four years, in addition to undertaking other liturgical work (such as the 1548 *Order of Communion*) and the heavy responsibilities of State.

Towards the collects

The work that the producer of the 1549 Prayer Book collects would have had constantly to hand was the Sarum Missal. In considering how – and in some cases whether – to render its *orationes*[31] in English, the translator would have had in mind not only matters of language and style, but also the representation of Reformed doctrine. Even where the translation is apparently exact, very slight nuances may have entered the English text. The search for a generic term probably presented little difficulty. 'Collect' is used in its current sense as early as 1225, and occurs in wills and devotional books in the fifteenth and earlier sixteenth centuries.[32]

The Primers had given Cranmer a number of clues as to how a collect might be shaped. In some cases, they had even provided words and phrases that he would adopt into the Prayer Book of 1549. But this accounts for a small percentage of the total set. Cuming points out that

> [t]he collects in the Primers do not play as important a part in the prehistory of the Prayer Book as do the canticles. Only a few of the collects in the Prayer Book appeared in any of the Primers. Since the Primers are based on the Hours of the Blessed Virgin Mary, the collect for the Annunciation is normally present, and so are the collects of Whitsunday and Trinity Sunday. The more traditional Primers included a number of collects for saints' days, but the majority of these days and their collects were not carried on into the Prayer Book.[33]

---

31 The Sarum Missal uses *oratio* or *oratio ad collectam* to describe what we know as the collect.
32 *Oxford English Dictionary*, 2nd edn, 1989, Oxford: Oxford University Press, online edition.
33 Cuming, *The Godly Order*, p. 49.

Cuming's examination shows that, in addition to those already mentioned, the second and third collects of Evensong, the second collect after the Litany, the collects for the Second and Fourth Sundays after Trinity, the collects for the Feasts of Saint John the Evangelist and Saint Michael and All Angels, and the collect included in the burial service can be found in Primer sources. Thus, of 84 collects for Sundays and holy days in the Prayer Book, only 7 have an earlier English form.[34] Of the other 77 Sunday and holy day collects, 24 (the majority of saints' day collects, together with collects for the First and Second Sundays in Advent, Quinquagesima, Ash Wednesday, the First Sunday in Lent, the third collect on Good Friday, the Second Sunday after Easter, and the Sunday after the Ascension) are new. The rest are translations or adaptations.

The improvements made to the Primer collects in their Prayer Book form are striking, not so much for originality of expression, for the reviser sticks closely to the substance of the original, but for remarkably effective adjustments. The collect for the Fourth Sunday after Trinity provides an excellent illustration of reference to the Latin text, with simultaneous attention to existing English translations. Cuming offers two versions from Primers of 1535 and 1540:

> O God the protector of al that truste in ye withoute whome nothynge is of value, nothynge is holy, multiplye thy mercy on vs, that thorowe thy gouernaunce & guydynge we may so passe in temporall goodes, that we lese not the eternall. By Chryst oure Lorde. (Redman's Primer, 1535)

> O God defender of all that trust in the without whom nothynge is stronge nothynge holy multiply ouer vs thy mercy that thou beynge gouerner and leder, we may so passe temporall felicyte that we lose nat eternall, graunt thys for Jesu Christe the Lordes sake which with the and with the holy gost lyueth and regneth God for ever and ever. Amen. (Grafton and Whitchurch's Primer, 1540)[35]

The Sarum text reads:

> Protector in te sperantium Deus sine quo nichil est validum: nichil sanctum: multiplica super nos misericordiam tuam: vt te rectore

---

34 Cuming, *The Godly Order*, pp. 51–6.
35 Cuming, *The Godly Order*, p. 54.

te duce sic transeamus per bona temporalia vt non amittamus eterna.[36]

The First Prayer Book of Edward VI has this translation:

God, the protector of all that truste in thee, withoute whom nothing is strong, nothing is holy: increase and multiply upon vs thy mercy, that, thou being our ruler and guide, we may so passe through things temporal, that we finally loose not the thynges eternall.[37]

The 1549 reading has remained faithful to the Sarum text, yet has learned from its two English predecessors the advantages of using nouns rather than participles ('ruler and guide' rather than 'thorowe thy gouernaunce & guydynge'), and then of using words with fewer syllables and placing strong stresses strategically ('ruler and guide' rather than 'gouerner and leder'). It has also recognized the importance of concreteness in place of abstraction. The simple addition of 'the thynges' to provide a noun associated with the adjective 'eternall' grounds the prayer in the reality of items tangible enough to be lost.

This argues for some reference to the *bona temporalia* ('good things of this world') of the Latin. Yet the English collect does not adopt the specific identification of *good* things as distinct from other things. Instead, it expands the reference to the whole of material mortal existence, managing in this way to suggest not a contrast between earthly and heavenly riches, but a whole eschatological picture of the peril of the soul that concentrates on earthly things, and thereby loses its eternal salvation.

There are other noteworthy Cranmerian touches. *Multiplica*, a single Latin imperative, becomes the doublet 'increase and multiply', easing the rhythm and giving a sense of accumulation towards abundance.

---

36 The text of this collect is taken from Brightman, *The English Rite*, vol. 2, p. 474. Brightman used the 1534 edition of the *Missale ad usum ecclesie Sarisburiensis* (Paris: Regnault, 1534). The Collects of the Sarum Missal are also given in Martin Dudley, 1994, *The Collect in Anglican Liturgy: Texts and Sources 1549–1989*, Collegeville MN: Alcuin Club/Liturgical Press, 1994, pp. 45–54. Dudley uses the 1916 edition of the Sarum Missal by J. Wickham Legg.

37 Brightman, *The English Rite*, vol. 2, p. 474. Brightman takes the texts of the English collects from Edward Whitchurch's edition of *The Book of Common Prayer and Administration of the Sacraments* (London, 1549), though pointing out that the different editions of the book offer a number of textual variants.

'Finally' is a solemn and important adverb, newly inserted to remind worshippers of the judgement which even the elect will not avoid.

This example shows that the translator's task is to some extent predetermined. The prayers should not be any longer than their originals than is absolutely necessary to convey the thought coherently in English. They may emulate the literary devices (particularly alliteration and parallelism) used in the Latin prayers, but in ways suited to English. The English collect should also be rhythmically well balanced. As Stella Brook pointed out in an influential work on the language of the Prayer Book, an indigenous rhythmic pattern develops in written English out of the stress-patterns of ordinary English speech. This is the consequence of 'the spacing-out of strong stresses by a varying number of unstressed or weakly stressed syllables'.[38] Admiration of the rhythmic excellence of Prayer Book prose should take account of the fact that it was composed primarily to be read aloud by the clergy and heard by churchgoers.[39]

The same linguistic and poetic considerations apply to collects for which there are no interim forms in the Primers, although in these cases it becomes possible to retrace some of the steps that the translator took in developing an English prayer from a Latin original. Two Sunday collects from the Trinity cycle offer particular instances of characteristics which recur through the whole set.

The Sixth Sunday after Trinity (Sarum)

Deus qui diligentibus te bona invisibilia preparasti, infunde cordibus nostris tui amoris affectum, vt te in omnibus et super omnia diligentes, promissiones tuas que omne desiderium superant consequamur.
(*ER* 2, p. 480)

The Sixth Sunday after Trinity (1549)

God, whiche hast prepared for them that love thee, *suche* good things *as* passe al mans vnderstanding: Powre into our heartes *such* love toward thee, *that* we, louing thee in all things, may obteyne thy promises which excede all that we can desire.
(*ER* 2, p. 480)

---

38 Stella Brook, 1965, *The Language of the Book of Common Prayer*, London: André Deutsch, p. 68.
39 Brook, *Language*, p. 69.

Several features of this example are noteworthy. The invocation, 'God', shows a translator facing an initial decision. The 1549 translator's practice varies, and some collects begin in this way, while others begin 'O God', which reflects the two syllables of *Deus*. While 'God' is a completely exact translation of *Deus*, it falls rather harshly and abruptly on a modern English ear. The editors of the 1662 Prayer Book uniformly adopted the smoother 'O God', suggesting that, even then, the longer form was more comfortable to the inheritors of more than a century of worship in English.

While the Latin *bona invisibilia* is elegantly placed and acts as an almost exact counterweight to *qui diligentibus*, the English translator cannot follow the original in closing the sense unit neatly with a verb (*preparasti*). The solution is to render 'those good things which we cannot see' by '*such* good things *as* pass man's understanding'. This is something of a masterstroke, taking advantage of a familiar English construction – the such/as pairing. The prayer then enacts the attempt to define a quantity or quality that resists definition, because it will always exceed the capacity of the human imagination to contain it.

A different form of balanced construction follows in the petition, 'Pour into our hearts *such* love . . . *that* we . . .'. This expresses the loving response to divine love articulated in the Latin prayer, but with a subtle nuance of longing in the indefinite quantity of 'such' that goes well beyond material desires, though it can only be vaguely quantified as 'loving thee in all things'. The theme of love responding to love, and its superiority to the desire for worldly things, is continued through the prayer in 'love', 'love' and 'loving'.

The Latin text is more emphatic about how we might love God, with its *in omnibus et super omnia*. But the 1549 translation chooses only to reproduce 'in all things', wisely recognizing that to add 'and above all things' would unbalance the neat parallelism between 'in all things' and 'all that we can desire'. In 1552, the text was revised to read 'above all things', though still avoiding the Latin doublet. Modern versions, such as that offered in the Church of England's *Common Worship*, have restored the full Latin phrase, 'in all things and above all things', to the disadvantage of the rhythmical flow of the earlier English text.[40] The effect is a rather pedantic underlining of the sense.

---

40 The Archbishops' Council of the Church of England, 2000, *Common Worship: Services and Prayers for the Church of England*, London: Church House Publishing, p. 411.

THE COLLECT IN ENGLISH: VERNACULAR BEGINNINGS

The Twelfth Sunday after Trinity (Sarum)

Omnipotens sempiterne deus: qui abundantia pietatis tue et merita supplicum excedis et vota, effunde super nos misericordiam tuam: vt dimittas que conscientia metuit: et adijcias quod oratio non presumit.
(*ER* 2, p. 502)

The Twelfth Sunday after Trinity (1549)

Almightie and everlastyng God, whiche arte always more ready to heare then we to praye: And arte wonte to geve more then eyther we desyre or deserue: Powre down vpon vs the aboundance of thy mercy, forgeuing vs those thinges wherof our conscience is afraide, and geuyng vnto vs that that our prayer dare not presume to aske.
(*ER* 2, p. 502)

This collect offers an outstanding illustration of attention to the innate possibilities of English for this kind of subject matter, as well as an excellent working example of the way in which a text could be theologically rewritten in the act of translation.

Showing a preference for the concrete and personal over the abstract, Cranmer does not render the relative clause ('qui abundantia pietatis tue et merita supplicum excedis et vota') by something like 'who in the abundance of your fatherly goodness exceed both the merits and the acts of devotion of those who pray to you'. Instead, we gain a glimpse of the human face of God, 'always more ready to hear than we to pray', and in the habit of giving 'more than either we desire or deserve'. A similar coloration can be seen on the Tenth Sunday after Trinity, where the Latin petition, 'Pateant aures misericordiae tue dominus precibus supplicantium' ('Let the ears of thy mercy, O Lord, be open to those who pray to you') is translated, 'Let thy merciful eares, O Lorde, be open to the prayers of thy humble seruauntes' (*ER* 2, p. 494). The neatly ironic contrast between the actions of hearing and praying suggests that God is always ready to grant our prayers, and that the only impediment to this is our negligence. The clause is almost replicated in structure by the next one, with 'more' loosely linking the two. Here, the use of alliteration neatly associates 'desire' and 'deserve'.

Cranmer has eliminated the idea of personal merit and of the invariable efficacy of prayerful acts. The God portrayed here is not a God who rewards good works, but a God of profligate grace. Salvation by grace alone was a message actively promoted and the liturgy was a natural vehicle for communicating this to the greatest number of people.

When it came to composing collects in English, Cranmer might have allowed himself a rather freer hand. One commentator speculates that, given the style of late medieval devotional manuals and Primers, much of the Prayer Book might even have emerged in rhyming verse.[41] Instead, he stayed close to the form that was evolving in the translations, though turning to Scripture for inspiration in a way that would not have been possible when translating. Advent 1 and 2 refer to the Epistle, as does Sunday next before Lent (Quinquagesima). The third collect of Good Friday is a pastiche of the Ash Wednesday collect, Ezekiel 33.11 (also part of the Absolution at Matins and Evensong), the Litany and John 10. The Second Sunday after Easter reflects both the Epistle and the Gospel. Compositions for saints' days refer to the lections where there is tangible and particular material to be mined, though there are exceptions, like the collect for Saint Andrew's Day, which relies on a legend of the saint's life. The collect provided for Saint Mark's Day, replacing one that requested the saint's intercessions, goes rather further than the Epistle itself (Eph. 4.7ff.) to make its polemical point clear. Whereas the Ephesians are urged to grow to maturity in Christ and not to be like children, 'wauering and caried about with every winde of doctrine', the collect prays that 'we be not, like children, caried away with every blast of vayne Doctrine' (*ER 2*, p. 580).

Where a Latin collect has been rejected, it is always worth looking at it alongside its English replacement. The First Sunday in Lent offers a useful demonstration.

The First Sunday in Lent (1549)

O Lorde, whiche for our sake, diddest fast fortye days and fortie nightes: Geve us grace to vse such abstinence that our fleshe beyng subdewed to the spirite, we may euer obey thy godly monicions, in righteousnes, and true holynes, to thy honour and glory: whiche livest and reignest. &c.
(*ER* 1, p. 294)

In this example, the initial idea of Jesus' 40-day fast comes from the day's Gospel, recounting his temptation by Satan in the wilderness (Matt. 4). Yet instead of continuing this in an explicit way to reflect the

---

41 Robinson, *Establishment*, p. 82.

temptations of the devil, the writer changes course. In part, this is an allusion to the Epistle (2 Cor. 6.1ff.), which presents bodily affliction and persecution as sources of spiritual strength. But it is also a decisive inversion of the thought of the rejected collect of the day in the Sarum Missal:

> Deus qui ecclesiam tuam annua quadragesimali observatione purificas: presta familie tue vt quod a te obtinere abstinendo nititur: hoc bonis operibus exequatur. Per dominum.
> (ER 1, p. 294)
>
> [O God, who cleanse your church by the yearly forty-day observance: grant to your servants that what they strive to obtain from you by fasting, they may continue to pursue through good works.]

The Latin prayer proposes a theology of grace obtained by works. A Reformed Church could not entertain this idea, and so the governing image becomes Christ's fasting for us. Human beings can and should follow this example by disciplining their bodies towards an enhanced life of the Spirit, and thus a much more secure obedience to God. But they will not achieve their own salvation.

This has been only the briefest introduction to the practical business of creating prayers in an English voice, an exercise in illustrating principles rather than a systematic analysis. Always, the temptation is to attempt to enter the mind of Cranmer. Yet, if we follow Cuming's hint, he produced the collects fairly quickly, and may not have regarded them as the pinnacle of the Prayer Book achievement, even though they have become its definitive component in the eyes of many devotees.[42]

Reception of the First Prayer Book of Edward VI

Although the new Prayer Book did not assume its status in law until Pentecost on 9 June 1549, the laborious nature of sixteenth-century printing required that it be with the printers much earlier in the year. Three printers were permitted to undertake the printing and the first copies were ready by 7 March.[43] A statute governing the book's implementation required that it be put into use within three weeks

---

42 Cuming, *The Godly Order*, p. 56.
43 Robinson, *Establishment*, p. 87. Two London printers and a Worcester printer were engaged for this task.

of purchase, if copies had been acquired before the official inaugural date of 9 June. Contemporary evidence confirms that several London churches adopted the new provisions almost immediately.[44] The fact that the Prayer Book was introduced in some places several months before it became mandatory suggests that, at least in London, there was little sense of compulsion and a significant measure of active enthusiasm.

This should not be taken as a general indication of the reaction. Brightman records the responses of fellow divines to the new Prayer Book's publication. He identifies three groups – those who readily acquiesced; those who were not entirely content but hoped the Book represented an interim measure to be improved in due course; and those who 'deplored and rejected it, from opposite points of view'.[45]

The exiled Strasbourg Reformer Martin Bucer wrote home to fellow ministers soon after his arrival in England in the spring of 1549 to take up the Regius Chair of Divinity in Cambridge to report his observations. He had some misgivings about the survival of such ceremonial apparatus as vestments and candles under the new dispensation, but assured the Strasbourg clergy that his English colleagues 'affirm that there is no superstition in these things, and that they are only to be retained for a time, lest the people, not having yet learned Christ, should be deterred by too extensive innovations from embracing his religion'. He was, however, very pleased to hear services in English, commenting approvingly that '[i]t much refreshed us ... that everything in the churches is read and sung in the vernacular tongue, that the doctrine of justification is purely and soundly taught, and the eucharist is administered according to Christ's ordinance, private masses having been abolished'.[46]

Stephen Gardiner, the imprisoned Bishop of Winchester, was opposed to the Prayer Book, but managed to identify, particularly in the Order for Holy Communion, much that clergy not in sympathy with the liturgical changes of the Reformation could use in good conscience. This led to a vituperative exchange between him and Cranmer.[47]

---

44 Thomas Lathbury, 1858, *A History of the Book of Common Prayer and Other Books of Authority*, Oxford and London: John Henry & James Parker, p. 27.

45 Brightman, *The English Rite*, vol. 1, p. cxlii.

46 H. Robinson (ed.), 1846–47, *Original Letters Relative to the English Reformation*, 2 vols, Cambridge: Parker Society, pp. 535–6. The letter is quoted by MacCulloch, *Thomas Cranmer*, pp. 411–12.

47 Brightman, *The English Rite*, vol. 1, pp. cxliv–v; MacCulloch, *Thomas Cranmer*, pp. 485–9.

Gordon Jeanes describes the book's reception as 'mixed' and, as far as the popular response was concerned, 'unfavourable'.[48] In some areas of the country, particularly Devon and Cornwall, there were heated reactions. Cranmer responded to a schedule of objections to the replacement of Latin with English, removal of prayer for the dead, withdrawal of English Bibles and other changes in a rather patronizing archiepiscopal letter.[49] His insistence on the use of English embodies a central aspiration of the Prayer Book:

> For all the whole that is done should be the act of the people and pertain to the people, as well as to the priest. And standeth it with reason that the priest should speak for you, and in your name, and you answer him again in your own person; and yet you understand never a word, neither what he saith, nor what you say yourselves? The priest prayeth to God for you, and you answer *Amen*, you wot not whereto. Is there any reason herein? Will you not understand what the priest prayeth for you, what thanks he giveth for you, what he asketh for you? Will you neither understand what he saith, nor let your hearts understand what your own tongues answer?[50]

Some reluctance to abandon the Latin forms of service for the Prayer Book evidently persisted, for a Royal Proclamation of Christmas Day 1549 required all other service books 'the keeping of which should be a let [obstacle] to the said book of common prayers' to be handed in to be destroyed.[51] Jeanes's examination of parish registers and episcopal articles of enquiry makes a persuasive case for a gentle return to older practices, such as elevation, reservation of the Sacrament, blessing of the font on Easter Eve, and baptisms on days other than Sundays.[52] He remarks tellingly that '[p]eople's worshipping patterns were not going to change overnight, and it is by no means clear how well prepared congregations, or even the clergy, were for this innovation'.[53]

This likely lack of widespread preparation and consequent local discontent and disobedience gives a clue to the gap between the official aspirations of the Prayer Book project and those for whom it was to be

---

48 Jeanes, *Signs*, p. 221.
49 Thomas Cranmer, 'Answers to the Fifteen Articles of the Rebels, Devon, Anno 1549', in Cox, *Miscellaneous Writings*, pp. 163–87.
50 Cranmer, 'Fifteen Articles', p. 169. This is the answer to the Third Article.
51 Wilkins, *Concilia*, vol. 4. pp. 37–8.
52 Jeanes, *Signs*, p. 221.
53 Jeanes, *Signs*, p. 222.

the sole formulary for worship. The resonant propaganda statement of the book's Preface is often invoked:

> And where heretofore there hath been great diversitie in saying and synging in churches within this realme: some folowyng Salsbury vse, some Herford vse, some the vse of Bangor, some of Yorke, & some of Lincolne: Now from hencefurth, all the whole realme shall have but one vse. And if any would iudge this waye more painfull, because that all thynges must be read vpon the boke, where as before, by the reason of so often repeticion, they could saye many things by heart: if those men will waye their labor, with the profite in knowledge, whiche dayely they shal obtein by readyng upon the boke, they will not refuse the payn, in consideracion of the greate profite that shall ensue therof.[54]

What is harder to gauge is whether lay people thought that the 'greate profite' entailed in becoming worshippers capable of sharing in the understanding of the clergy outweighed the losses. Eamon Duffy concedes that the Prayer Book 'preserved the basic pattern of parochial worship, matins, Mass and evensong', but maintains that the most serious transformation was in 'lay experience of the Mass'.[55] Cuming suggests that the Prayer Book's components and the shape (if not the ritual performance) of its services had not in fact departed very far from its Sarum predecessor, since it was politically expedient 'to retain at any rate an outward appearance of continuity'. At the same time, he admits that 'the sound of the English language in the new rite must have destroyed most of the traditional flavour that is apparent to the reader'.[56] Serious alterations to ritual and language, even to create worship in a language that worshippers understood, would have had a disproportionate impact on the experience of churchgoers. If the object had been to create a particular kind of community – a national church – bound by a national liturgy that eloquently expressed its Reformed identity – then this was not apparent to the first generation of Prayer Book users.[57]

---

54 Brightman, *The English Rite*, vol 1, p. 36.
55 Duffy, *Stripping*, p. 464.
56 Cuming, 'Thomas Cranmer: Translator and Writer', p. 111.
57 The use of the vernacular to create community is excellently treated in relation to Lollardy in Ruth Evans, Andrew Taylor, Nicholas Watson and Jocelyn Wogan-Browne, 1999, *The Idea of the Vernacular: An Anthology of Middle English Literary Theory 1280–1520*, Exeter: University of Exeter Press, pp. 314–30.

Conclusion

It is in this context that we must imagine the reception of the new collects, and it would be anachronistic to impute contemporary notions of literary and liturgical appreciation to sixteenth-century English worshippers. They encountered these prayers Sunday by Sunday, and if they attended the offices of Matins and Evensong during the week, they heard the Sunday collect repeated. But for the most part, lay people did not own copies of the Prayer Book and would not have been able to refer to the collects as a consecutive body of texts.

Later generations have made the judgements to which we now tend to refer. These concur on the general elegance of Cranmer's liturgical prose, his readiness to use other people's words or to recycle his own, and the invariable improvements he achieved on those occasions. The achievement was at times uneven. Yet in discovering how to adapt traditional patterns from Latin sources into English usage, and to exploit the possibilities of his own language, he and his colleagues established an idea that has persisted, not only in the English-speaking Provinces of the Anglican Communion, but also in the Churches of the Reformation.

2

The Collect in the Church of Sweden following the Reformation

NILS-HENRIK NILSSON

Introduction

The Church of Sweden grew from the medieval Roman Catholic Church of the 1520s. The Swedish Reformers, Olaus Petri (1493–1552) and his brother Laurentius Petri (1499–1573), both studied in Wittenberg under the young Martin Luther at an early stage of the German Reformation. Olaus Petri later worked at the Church of Saint Nicolas, Storkyrkan, in Stockholm, close to the king and the government of the nation. He took the initiative in the production of new liturgical books in Swedish. His brother Laurentius was appointed Archbishop of Uppsala in 1531 and was consecrated in September of that year. Until his death in 1573, he worked on the consolidation of the Reformation in Sweden.

The Lutheran Reformation was carried out in quite a gentle manner as far as liturgical changes were concerned, and the main structure of the worship services was retained, although in Swedish translation. In 1529, the Manual (the book containing orders of services for baptism, marriage, the churching of women, sick communion including anointing, commendation of the dead, funeral and preparation for death for those sentenced to execution) was published in Swedish and 1531 saw the first Order of Mass in Swedish. In 1536, a meeting of the leading churchmen took the decision to strive for the celebration of the Swedish Mass, the *Swecana Missa*, in all cathedrals and in other churches where the circumstances would permit this.[1] A Swedish translation of

---

1 Christer Pahlmbad, 1998, *Mässa på svenska* (The Mass in Swedish), Lund: Arcus förlag, pp. 42–50. The transition from the Latin to the Swedish Lutheran Order of Mass seems to have taken place gradually. The Latin language was also retained in worship for a long time.

the whole Bible was published in 1541. The active participation of the congregation in the service was emphasized through celebrations in the vernacular and the congregation was expected to participate in the singing of hymns. The Mass was to be celebrated every Sunday. The basic structure of the liturgical year was retained, as were the lectionary and the building blocks of the collects. Some parts of the Mass which were difficult to translate continued to be used in Latin. The use of vestments was also retained and, as was previously the custom, the chasuble was handed over to priests at their ordination to the priesthood.

Aspects that were heavily reworked or altogether removed were the Roman canon of the Mass and the petitions for intercessions of the saints. Revision of the canon was the work of Olaus Petri, whom one commentator has described as 'the only Protestant Reformer of the sixteenth century who had a liturgical sense drawn from the ancient sources' ['le seul Réformateur protestant du 16e siècle qui ait eu un sens liturgique puisé aux sources anciennes'[2]]. Some feast days of the liturgical year were also abolished, particularly commemorations of relics, but all major saints' days, such as the feasts of the apostles and the more prominent saints' days, were kept as public holidays and days for worship. It was only in 1772 that a more thorough reduction of the number of saints' days was carried out, and then for the primary purpose of decreasing the number of days off from work in order to further the productivity of the nation and not for any theological reasons.

The collects were among those elements of the liturgy that were gradually translated into Swedish, though the vernacular version retained the same linguistic structure that had been used in the period prior to the Reformation. Throughout the centuries, this structure has offered the possibility that the collect might be sung by the priest. Only during the twentieth century have clear changes to the content of the collects begun to be introduced, and these will be discussed below.[3]

---

2 Dom Louis Bouyer, 1966, 'La Préface et le Sanctus', *La Maison-Dieu* 87, pp. 97–110, p. 104.

3 A summary of the liturgical changes that have taken place in the Scandinavian countries from the Reformation until today is available in Nils-Henrik Nilsson, 2006, 'The Lutheran Tradition in Scandinavia', in Geoffrey Wainwright and Karen B. Westerfield Tucker (eds), *The Oxford History of Christian Worship*, Oxford: Oxford University Press, pp. 422–35.

Sources and research

The sources available for a closer study of the developments of the collects in the Church of Sweden are medieval missals and breviaries, as well as the church service books and the proposed revisions of the service books that were published after the Reformation. Following the Reformation, the collects were published in the so-called Gospel Book, together with the biblical readings appointed for each Sunday and a special prayer based on the Gospel, which summarized the main thoughts of the Gospel passage appointed for each Sunday.

The term 'Gospel Book' refers to a liturgical book arranged according to the Sundays and holy days of the liturgical year. Each Sunday and holy day has a collect (and from 1983 onwards, two alternatives in Sweden), biblical readings (from 1862 more biblical readings besides the medieval Epistle and Gospel) and up until 1983 in Sweden, also a concluding Gospel-based prayer. It is particularly in the Lutheran Churches in Scandinavia that such Gospel Books exist.

At the Reformation, the designation *collecta* was first used, and after that the designations 'the collect' (*kollekt*) and 'the prayer of the collect' (*kollektbön*) were adopted. In the Gospel Book that was adopted in 2002, this prayer is designated 'the Prayer of the Day' (*Dagens bön*), which was the proposal of the working group charged with preparing this revision.[4] Several other Churches (for example Lutheran churches in the USA and Germany) use the designation 'the Prayer of the Day' (*Dagens bön*) for the collect. In this chapter, the designation 'collect' will be used throughout.

The first Gospel Book in Swedish was published in 1544, but there is no copy of that version in existence today. The earliest surviving Gospel Book was published in 1562.[5] Revised editions, including the

---

4 Compare the designation *oratio de ipsa die pertinens*. Geoffrey G. Willis, 1968, *Further Essays in Early Roman Liturgy*, London: Alcuin Club Collection 50, p. 105.

5 The primary source used to follow the collects throughout history is the medieval Roman Missal in various versions, for example *Missale Upsaliense*, and various versions of the Breviary, for example *Breviarium Lincopense* in the edition of Knut Peters (Lund: Laurentius Petri sällkapets urkundsserie, 1950–58), as well as *Breviarium Strengense*. These sources show substantial agreement on which prayers have been used and translated into Swedish. The 1562 Gospel Book is published in facsimile by Arthur Malmgren, 1965. It forms volume II of *Fyra svenska reformationsskrifter* (Four Swedish Reformation Writings), Malmö: Malmö Ljustrycksanstalt, 1965.

collects, appeared in the years 1628, 1862, 1921, 1942, 1983 and 2002 and were adopted for use by the Church of Sweden.

Some of the standard works on the evolution of the liturgy in Sweden contain a few pieces of information about the development of the collect,[6] but there have been very few attempts at a close study of the use and development of the collect in the Church of Sweden. It is usually in connection with revisions of the ecclesiastical liturgical books that this issue has been studied. Unfortunately, the committees that have been charged with the task of proposing liturgical changes have only very rarely motivated their proposals in printed form and have not made any written comparisons with previous collects. A picture of these developments can be obtained through a study of the proposals for new books and the minutes of the meetings of the Church Assembly, where such proposals have been considered, but only the latest working group has provided extensive motivations for their proposals in print, as well as descriptions of how these relate to previous collects.[7]

The current Swedish Gospel Book is to some extent an exception with regard to the report on the work on the collects and their relationship to their Latin predecessors. When the Church of Sweden Governing Body and the Church of Sweden General Synod had carried out their revisions on the proposals from the year 2000, the General Synod took the decision in 2002 to adopt a new Gospel Book with revised collects and readings for the services. On the basis of the motivations given by the Gospel Book Revision Group, the chairman and the secretary of that Group were able to publish a more extensive commentary

---

6 Edvard Rodhe, 1923, *Svenskt gudstjänstliv: Historisk belysning av Den svenska kyrkohandboken*, Stockholm: Svenska kyrkans diakonistyrelses bokförlag. Also by the same author, 1917, *Studier i den svenska reformationstidens liturgiska tradition*, in Uppsala: Uppsala universitets årsskrift 1917, Teologi. IAOT Hellerström, 1954, *Liturgik*, 3rd edn, Stockholm: Svenska kyrkans diakonistyrelses bokförlag. Carl-Henrik Martling, 1993, *Svensk liturgihistoria*, Stockholm: Verbum. Nils-Henrik Nilsson, 1994, *Gudstjänst i Svenska kyrkan, En praktisk handledning*, Stockholm: The Church of Sweden.

7 The Church of Sweden, 2000, *Evangelieboksgruppens förslag till Den svenska evangelieboken*, Uppsala: Svenska kyrkans utredningar (SKU 2000:4). The Church of Sweden, 2000, *Motiveringar*, Uppsala: Svenska kyrkans utredningar (SKU 2000:5). This group had the task of providing a review of the collects and the readings in the lectionary of the Church of Sweden. The present author served as secretary to that group. Works listed here provide a presentation of the wording of all the collects from the Reformation up until today, and also clarify what changes have been made as well as what the Latin originals were behind the prayers translated into Swedish.

on the new Gospel Book in 2003, which also includes comments on the changes to the collects.[8]

A significant contribution to research on the collects in the Church of Sweden was made in 2008 in an essay on the discipline of practical theology at Lund University. In June that year, Dan Nässelqvist presented an investigation of the collects in the Swedish Gospel Books 1562–2003. He had also undertaken an analysis of the changes to the collects and the reasons behind them. This is the most extensive piece of research that has so far been made on the collects in the Church of Sweden. The results of this investigation will be taken into account in this chapter.[9]

Usage and changes up until 1921

During the Middle Ages, Sweden received missions from England and from the Holy Roman Empire, then under the heirs of Charlemagne. After 1066, influence from England decreased. This affected the content of the missals and breviaries that were used. Scholars have discussed the extent to which any influences from the English liturgical tradition can be traced, for example in the Skara Diocesan Missal and Breviary. It has been assumed that when Olaus Petri was working on the translation and adaptation of the liturgical books for the Lutheran Church in Sweden, his primary source of reference was the medieval material from the diocesan traditions nearest to Stockholm: Uppsala, Strängnäs and maybe Linköping. He also made use of German material from the early period of the Lutheran Reformation as a background for his work of translation and adaptation.[10]

The collects retained their traditional place and shape in the Swedish Mass. With few exceptions, the Swedish translations followed their Latin originals closely. It is mainly with regard to the petitions for intercessions by the saints and to the references to the merits of fasting that changes have been made.

---

8 Lars Olov Eriksson and Nils-Henrik Nilsson, 2003, *Evangelieboken i gudstjänst och förkunnelse*, Stockholm: Verbum.

9 Dan Nässelqvist, 2008, 'Kollektbönen i svenska evangelieböcker 1562–2003: En analys av förändringar och deras orsaker', Lund: Examensarbete i praktisk teologi. Lunds Universitet (unpublished study).

10 Yngve Brilioth, 1951, *Nattvarden i evangeliskt nattvardsliv*, Stockholm: Svenska kyrkans diakonistyrelses bokförlag, pp. 331 and 336 (A. G. Hebert (tr.), 1930, repr. 1965, *Eucharistic Faith and Practice, Evangelical and Catholic*, London: SPCK).

The transition from medieval orders of services in Latin to Lutheran orders in the vernacular was allowed to take a long time. This was particularly true of the sung parts of the Mass. Even though a decision was taken in 1536 to move on to Swedish, the old liturgical books remained in use for a considerable period. The material that has been preserved shows how texts in Swedish and instructions for singing the Swedish texts were gradually written into the books.[11]

The first editions of the Mass in Swedish only contained one collect, and later only a few collects, in translation. In an Appendix to the Mass, another 16 collects were added for ordinary Sundays, but these were not appointed to any specific Sundays. Yet another 15 collects were added in 1537, this time appointed to particular feasts. The Hymnal that was published in 1553 (*A little Song Book for use in the Churches*) contained a complete series of collects, which were introduced into the 1557 Order of Mass.[12]

The tenacity of the view that the traditional way to use the collects should be retained is made clear by the so-called Vadstena Articles of 1552. They prescribe that, should the priest wish to use more than one collect, this would be permitted and the collect *de tempore* (collect of the day) should always be used first. The 1571 Church Order also provides the opportunity to use more than one collect. That Church Order prescribes that, if the priest wishes to use more than one collect, he may do so, as long as the collect that is *de tempore* or *de festo* is read first.[13] During the following century the use of several collects seems to have disappeared.[14]

In the Hymnal of 1553 mentioned above, the series of collects from Advent until and including Pentecost corresponds to the collects in the Latin Missal, with one exception. The Latin collect for the First Sunday in Lent is omitted because it highlights the meritorious character of Lent,[15] and the collect for the Fourth Sunday after Trinity has replaced

---

11 Pahlmblad, *Mässa på svenska*, pp. 57–8. On p. 66 the author notes how the text of the Preface and the Words of Institution from the 1537 Mass in Swedish, complete with music, have been written into a copy of the New Testament as a gloss, and that ten intonations to the Gloria and a series of collects have been added at the end of the book.

12 Rodhe, *Svenskt gudstjänstliv*, p. 78.

13 Sven Kjöllerström, 1971, *Den svenska kyrkoordningen 1571*, Lund: Håkan Ohlssons Förlag, p. 91.

14 Rodhe, *Svenskt gudstjänstliv*, p. 78.

15 The collect for the First Sunday in Lent in *Breviarium Lincopense* and in the old *Missale Romanum*: *Deus, qui Ecclesiam tuam annua quadragesimali observatione purificas, praesta familiae tuae, ut quod a te obtinere abstinendo*

it. Both these Sundays thus have the same collect, although the wording of the translation is different. The collect prescribed for the First Sunday in Lent comes from the Appendix of the 1531 Order of Mass and was translated from Latin by Olaus Petri. In the 1553 Hymnal, Archbishop Laurentius Petri translated the prayer in his own way. Easter Sunday, too, has an additional collect besides the collect translated from the Latin, of which Laurentius Petri is assumed to be the translator.[16] That collect, which provides a short résumé of salvation history, is introduced with the words, 'O Almighty, Eternal God, who at this time brought Thy people out of Egypt through Moses . . .'.

The translations made by Olaus and Laurentius Petri and how they found their way into the Swedish Mass are also mentioned by Eric Esskildsen Yelverton in his book *The Mass in Sweden*. He refers to the anomalous use of two different translations of one and the same collect for a period on two Sundays and describes the changes that were made to solve this problem.[17]

It is worth noting that Easter Sunday in particular became the object of the Reformers' interest. Easter Sunday is the model for every Sunday. In the Swedish Mass, this is expressed in the linking of the Words of Institution with the Preface for Easter Sunday, thus constituting a prayer that is reminiscent of a Eucharistic Prayer. The text in the Swedish Mass had no anamnesis or epiclesis and no other mention of the sacrifice of Christ other than his death and resurrection. The

---

nititur, hoc bonis operibus exsequatur. Per Dominum etc. Not even the first Gospel Books in Sweden follow the wording of the Latin prayer, nor does the Catholic diocese in Sweden.

16 Rodhe, *Svenskt gudstjänstliv*, p. 80.

17 Dissatisfied with the wording of this prayer, he (Laurentius Petri) substituted for it the sixth collect in the small cycle of collects contained in the supplement of Olaus's 1531 Mass: medieval collects were provided for the Twenty-first to the Twenty-fifth Sundays after Trinity, and the scheme was complete. The Archbishop then discovered that the collect he had selected from Olaus's supplement was his brother's rendering of the collect for the Third Sunday after Trinity in the medieval missal which he himself had already used for the same Sunday: thus by an oversight the same collect had been made to serve two Sundays, the Third and the Twentieth after Trinity. The error was removed by the device of omitting the collect for the Third Sunday after Trinity, and displacing the collects from the Fourth to the Twenty-fourth Sundays, so as to fill up the gap: a new collect was written for the now vacant Twenty-fourth Sunday, and the collect for the Twenty-fifth Sunday brought the series to a conclusion. Yelverton, 1920, *The Mass in Sweden: Its Development from the Latin Rite from 1531 to 1917*, London: Henry Bradshaw Society, 1920, pp. 55–6.

Easter Preface was put together with the Institution narrative, not as a reading from the Bible, but as words directed to God the Father. The intention was that this prayer should be used every Sunday.[18]

For the collects used on the Sundays after Trinity, the 1553 Hymnal follows the prayers found in *Breviarium Strengense*, which are the same as in *Breviarium Lincopense* and *Scarense* (but not in *Upsaliense*). The only deviation is the omission of the collect for the Nineteenth Sunday after Trinity. It is difficult to find any reason for this today. It was replaced by a collect for the Third Sunday after Trinity that had been translated into Swedish from *Missale Upsaliense*. This translation was found in the Appendix to the 1531 Order of Mass.[19]

A manuscript in Latin from 1569, written by Archbishop Laurentius Petri, shows how the collect was intended to be used during the Reformation period. In this manuscript he writes about the shape of the divine office and thus mentions the collects. At First Vespers, he says, the collect should be recited in Latin, but at Second Vespers and Second Compline, it should always be said in the vernacular, as well as at Matins and Mass 'according to the current translation'. This should be done 'with regard to the nowadays more common presence of the laity'.[20]

Laurentius Petri also writes that the person who will read the collect should use the ordinary liturgical greeting, *Dominus vobiscum*, together with the exhortative invitation, *Oremus*, in Latin to precede the Latin version of the collect, but he should use Swedish to introduce the collect translated into Swedish. However, if the reader of the collect is not yet ordained to the priesthood, he should omit the greeting *Dominus vobiscum* in accordance with common practice. He should only say *Oremus* and then continue immediately with the collect.

The Archbishop underlines the importance of proper preparation, including having read through the collect before the service. The person who reads the collect should be attentive, so that he can bring it to its conclusion in a suitable and appropriate manner. There are different forms of endings, and anyone who does not pay attention to this may stumble over the words and thus betray his negligence.

In addition, Laurentius Petri mentions the various endings used for the collects: 'Through Jesus Christ, Thy Son our Lord, who with

---

18 Nils-Henrik Nilsson, 1997, 'Eucharistic Prayer and Lutherans: a Swedish perspective', *Studia Liturgica* 27 (2), pp. 176-99.

19 Rodhe, *Svenskt gudstjänstliv*, p. 81.

20 Nat. Fransén, *Ärkebiskop Laurentius Petri d. ä:s gudstjänstordning* (*Ordo Officiorum Ecclesiasticorum*), Stockholm 1927, pp. 26-7.

Thee lives and reigns in the unity of the Holy Spirit, God for ever and ever'; but sometimes also 'Through the same Jesus Christ, our Lord . . . etc.'. Sometimes the following form is used: 'Who with Thee lives and reigns'; or 'Our Lord Jesus Christ . . . etc.'; or even 'Our Lord Jesus Christ, who with Thee . . . etc.'. When the prayer is addressed to the Son, it ends in the following way: 'Who with God the Father and the Holy Spirit lives and reigns . . . etc.'; or 'who with the same God the Father . . . etc.'. Again, when the Holy Spirit has already been mentioned in the collect itself, this is reflected in the words: 'the same Holy Spirit'.[21]

Laurentius Petri says that such differences become apparent to the attentive reader, either because of grammar itself, or from the notes that are usually appended to the book of collects.[22] From what is mentioned, it is obvious that special books containing collects and notes on how they should be applied were in use at that time.

The Archbishop then continues by mentioning that, since improved collects in Latin as well as in the vernacular have been available in Swedish Gospel Books for some time, the lectors may follow these, whether it is a matter of reading the collects *de tempore* or *de sanctis*. He therefore considers it quite unnecessary to issue further instructions.

In subsequent sections of this manuscript, the Archbishop surveys the entire liturgical year and states which antiphons, introits, graduals, hymns, versicles and other material should be used for the various offices and at Mass. This list also stipulates which form of the introductory words for the collect should be used. It is interesting to note that he sometimes quotes the introductory words in Latin and sometimes in Swedish. From this fact we can probably conclude that a complete transition into Swedish had not yet taken place, although the collects had been available in Swedish for some time in the published edition of the Swedish Gospel Book.

Another conclusion from Archbishop Laurentius Petri's writing is that there must be no negligence with regard to the collects. Every

---

21 Per Dominu[m] notrum Jesu[m] Christum filium tuum, qui tecum viuit et regnat, in vnitate Spiritus sancti Deus, per o[m]nia secula seculorum. Alias vero sic: Per eunde[m] Dominu[m] nostrum J. Ch. Etc. Rursus quandoq[ue] in hunc modum tamen: Qui tecum viuit et regnat, aut: Dominu[m] nostrum Jesum Christum etc. aut etiam: Dominus noster Jesus Christus, qui tec[um] etc. Quando ad Filium dirigitur oratio sic: Qui cum Deo patre et Spiritu sancto viuis [et] regnas etc. Vel: Qui cum eode[m] Deo patre etc. Quando vero in Collecta prius facta e[st] mentio Spiritus sancti, inseritur vocula (eiusde[m]) dicendo Eiusdem Spiritus s[an]c[ti]. Fransén, p. 28.

22 'Vel notula quæ in libris Collectarum fere ascribi solet.' Fransén, p. 28.

word is significant and their performance during the liturgy should be well prepared by the priest or the lector. This gives a hint that the translation process from Latin into Swedish was also undertaken with great care. It was not a matter of abandoning the medieval inheritance, but rather a question of rendering the Latin original in Swedish, word by word, as long as it did not militate against the Lutheran conception of the faith.

For the greatest part of the period following the Reformation the collect has been sung. The 1531 Order of Mass envisaged a said Mass, but when the practice of singing the Mass was resumed, the collect was normally sung to the old recitation tune. Said collects were also used. The instructions from the eighteenth and nineteenth centuries stipulate that the priest should say or sing this prayer.[23] During the twentieth century said collects have become normal practice, although examples of sung collects on special occasions can be found. The introductory salutation is sung in most cases. The collect ends with the congregational 'Amen' – said if the prayer is said and sung if the prayer is sung.

The 1562 Gospel Book included Epistles and Gospels for the Sundays and holy days from the First Sunday of Advent until and including the Twenty-sixth Sunday after Trinity as well as for 19 'excellent Solemnities and Holy Days', of which seven have their own collects. These Sundays and holy days are Saint Andrew's Day with a collect for a Feast of the Apostles, Saint Thomas' Day with a reference to the collect for Saint Andrew's Day, Saint Stephen's Day with the collect for a celebration of a martyr, Saint John the Evangelist with a reference to Saint Andrew's Day, Holy Innocents with a reference to the collect for Saint Stephen's Day, the Feast of the Conversion of Saint Paul, with a reference to Saint Andrew's Day, Candlemas (the Presentation of the Lord in the Temple, also known as the Purification of the Blessed Virgin Mary) with its own collect, Saint Matthias' Day with a reference to Saint Andrew's Day, the Feast of Our Lady in Lent (The Annunciation) with its own collect, Saint Philip and Saint James' Day with a reference to Saint Andrew's Day, the Feast of Saint John the Baptist with its own collect, the Feast of Saint Peter and Saint Paul with a reference to Saint Andrew's Day, the Feast of the Visitation of Our Lady to Elizabeth, with a reference to the Feast of Our Lady in Lent, Saint James' Day with a reference to Saint Andrew's Day, Saint Bartholomew with a reference to Saint Andrew's Day, Saint Matthew's Day with a reference to Saint Andrew's Day, the Feast of Saint Michael and All Angels with

---

23 Rodhe, *Svenskt gudstjänstliv*, p. 79.

its own collect, Saint Simon and Saint Jude with a reference to Saint Andrew's Day and the Feast of All Saints with its own collect.

Following these special Sundays and holy days, there are some general Epistles and Gospels without any collects that seem to be intended for use in services on yet other days during the liturgical year. The Gospel Book ends with a couple of Epistles and Gospels for special days of prayer.

In the period leading up to 1772, when the great reduction of holy days took place, a large number of holy days were celebrated during the year, besides those appointed in the Gospel Book. The Epistles and Gospels appointed in the Gospel Book could, for example, be used during the Rogation Days following the Fifth Sunday after Easter – Rogation Sunday – which were public holidays. Other holy days that were also public holidays, although not mentioned in the Gospel Book, were the so-called red-letter days because they were marked in red in the published calendars. In the calendar for the year 1598, the following days are marked in this way: Saint Mark, Saint Erik, Saint Mary Magdalene, Saint Olov, Saint Laurence, Saint Luke the Evangelist and Saint Nicolas. Calendars from the first part of the seventeenth century also include Saint Anthony, Saint Fabian and Saint Sebastian, Saint Gregory, Saint John and Saint Paul, Saint Margaret, Saint Anne, the Beheading of Saint John the Baptist, Saint Martin, Saint Barbara and Saint Lucy. The Feasts of the Assumption of Our Lady and of the Birthday of the Blessed Virgin Mary were celebrated as holy days for a long time. The principle was the keeping of the feasts to which markets were traditionally attached (*festa fori*) in order to celebrate these days with a service of worship and a sermon. The feasts that were only kept by the priests (*festa chori*) and which were not anchored in public tradition were abolished.[24]

A newly written collect for Good Friday was introduced in the 1628 Gospel Book. Previously, the 1562 Gospel Book had, in accordance with medieval practice, referred to the collect for Palm Sunday. The 1628 Gospel Book omitted the old medieval collect for Easter Sunday and only the newly written version, which had been included since 1553, remained. During the seventeenth century, new collects for the additional Sundays, the Twenty-sixth and Twenty-seventh after Trinity, were introduced.[25]

---

24 Carl Henrik Martling, 1993, *Kyrkans år och dagar*, Stockholm: Verbum, pp. 50–1.

25 Rodhe, *Svenskt gudstjänstliv*, pp. 80–1.

The 1553 Hymnal included a number of collects for saints' days (*de sanctis*). They are collects for the Feasts of the Purification of the Blessed Virgin Mary, the Annunciation and other Feasts of the Blessed Virgin Mary, Saint John the Baptist, for the angels, the common of the apostles, the martyrs and the saints ('in die purificationis, in die annuntiationis et aliis festis b. virginis, de s. Iohanne Baptista, de angelis, de apostolis, de martyribus, de sanctis collecta generalis'). The Swedish translations of these prayers have deviated considerably from the original for reasons indicated above. As a consequence of the omission of the feasts of the apostles as holidays and days for worship in 1772, the collect for the common of the apostles (*collecta de apostolis*) was omitted from the Gospel Book.[26]

It is also worth noting how teaching about the collects was conducted during this period. The standard textbook on liturgy that was used for a long time for candidates for the priesthood includes a paragraph on the collect. The book is entitled *Historiska anmärkningar om Kyrko-Ceremonierna* [*Historical Notes on the Church Ceremonies*] and was written by the Dean of Växjö Cathedral.[27] It was printed in several editions, the first in 1762, the second in 1783 running to 800 pages, and the third in 1838. The third edition was supplemented with the changes that had been included in the Church Service Book, which had been adopted in 1809.

The author first describes in comparative detail the background to the salutation that precedes the collect, supported by evidence from the Bible and the Church Fathers. In the next paragraph he expounds the background to the exhortation 'Let us pray', by giving examples from the New Testament and from Saint John Chrysostom.[28]

About the collect itself, the author says that the *collecta* is read or sung by the priest. The word *collecta* and its meaning have to do with the prayer that the priest used to say in the past as a summary or a gathering up of all the previous prayers. Here follow references to Justin, Tertullian and Saint Augustine. He refers to Gelasius, the Bishop of Rome, in the year 493, who was apparently the first to bring some order to the collects. He also claims that it is from Saint Gregory

---

26 Rodhe, *Svenskt gudstjänstliv*, p. 81.

27 Sven Baelter, 1838, *Historiska Anmärkningar om Kyrko-Ceremonierna så wäl Wid den offentliga Gudstjensten som andra tillfällen hos de första Christna, och i Swea Rike; i synnerhet Efter Reformationen till närvarande tid, tredje upplagan*, Örebro: N. M. Lindhs Boktryckeri.

28 Baelter, *Historiska Anmärkningar*, p. 234.

the Great (Gregorius Magnus), who was Pope in the year 600, that we have learnt most of the collects that we now use.[29]

The textbook continues by stating to which person of the Holy Trinity these prayers are usually addressed and how they should end. The following paragraph expounds the meaning of the congregational *Amen*.[30]

How the collects have changed from 1921 onwards

It is very clear that the changes were only minor up to 1921. The medieval use of the collects was continued in the form that the Lutheran Reformers gave them.

In the 1921 Gospel Book, the series of collects was revised in accordance with the Latin texts. On some points changes were made. The collect for New Year's Day was revised, since the character of this day had been changed to focus more on the beginning of a new year than on the circumcision of Christ. At the revision, motifs were however brought in from the old tradition. The old collect for Easter Day, which was omitted in 1628, was reinstated, but this time for use on Easter Monday, although with the possibility that it could also be used on Easter Sunday itself. Whit Monday, which had previously lacked a collect of its own, was now given its own collect by the reinstatement of a translation of a prayer for that day previously found in *Missale Upsaliense*.[31]

The Feast of the Transfiguration of Christ, which is celebrated in the Church of Sweden on the Seventh Sunday after Trinity, has been given a new collect in the 1921 Gospel Book, based on motifs from the old tradition. Previously, the collect for the Seventh Sunday after Trinity had been used on this day. That collect was now placed as an alternative for the Fifteenth Sunday after Trinity, and the old collect for the Fifteenth Sunday after Trinity became an alternative for the Eighth Sunday after Trinity. The old collect for the Eighth Sunday after Trinity in turn became the alternative on the Ninth Sunday after Trinity. These moves took place in order to make a clearer connection between the collect and the theme announced in the rubrics on the respective Sundays. In several cases the wording of the collects was also considered in the proposals for the 1921 Gospel Book, in order to make a

---

29 Baelter, *Historiska Anmärkningar*, pp. 235–6.
30 Baelter, *Historiska Anmärkningar*, p. 236.
31 Rodhe, *Svenskt gudstjänstliv*, p. 81.

better agreement with the thematic rubrics which were introduced at that time.[32]

The committee that worked out the proposals for the 1921 Gospel Book stressed that they had without exception returned to the medieval Latin texts and compared them with the texts in published editions of the Gospel Book from the sixteenth century onwards. They had found some variations in the sixteenth century, but the agreement was almost total between the 1695 and the 1862 editions. The principle followed by this committee was to take Swedish medieval material as the starting point. The revision was considered primarily as a linguistic one, and the committee made the changes described above in order to achieve a better agreement between the prayers and the themes for the days. Even so, the priests among the membership of the 1920 Church Assembly reacted against the adaptation of the collects, which they thought had gone too far in relation to the content of the biblical readings. They believed that uniformity in accordance with the expressions of the biblical translations was not desirable, and that the liturgical language ought to be allowed greater freedom to retain 'ecclesiastically conventional expressions of noble character'.[33]

The Church Assembly supported the views of the clerical members, and the changes to the collects adopted in the 1921 Gospel Book were therefore not as far-reaching as those suggested in the proposal. The new Gospel Book was published with a Foreword that spoke of generations who had long ago composed prayers and affirmed an intention to preserve what devout fathers have created. Here is 'a testimony to our affinity with these generations who have gone before us as well as with the Christian community in other places'.[34]

When the preparations began for a new Church Service Book in 1938, there was also talk of a sensitive revision of the 1921 Gospel Book. Some of the collects were considered to have significant value, whereas others were thought to be poor and of meagre content. A linguistic revision was needed on the basis of the Latin text but the purpose of this would be to make the collects better suited to fulfilling the prayer needs of modern worshipping congregations. At the same time, 'the liturgical tradition which links our church to the Universal Church of ancient times as well as of the future' was underlined. The

---

32 Rodhe, *Svenskt gudstjänstliv*, p. 81.
33 Nässelqvist, *Kollektbönen i svenska*, p. 11.
34 Nässelqvist, *Kollektbönen i svenska*, p. 12.

collects should by and large 'be kept unchanged but should be . . . subject to a linguistic revision'.[35]

The group that was charged with working on the Gospel Book found, however, that the collects in the 1921 Gospel Book deviated strongly from the Latin originals. The working party thought that this was caused partly by changes made by the reformers when these prayers were first translated, and partly by influences from rationalism and pietism. They therefore sought to create a closer agreement with the original texts that would express more of the original force of these prayers.

When the proposal for a new Gospel Book was presented to the 1941 Church Assembly, a heated debate on the shape of the collects arose. Voices were raised, claiming that the proposal had gone much further than a sensitive revision would entail. On the other hand, there was also talk of 'artistic inspiration and fresh originality'. Some wanted to carry out an even more thorough revision, while others sought to achieve closer continuity with the original versions. One of the bishops wanted 'greater links with the Sunday'. In the Church Assembly, a more restrained view won the majority vote, which retained most of the collects in continuity with the old tradition.

The Foreword to the 1942 Gospel Book stresses that the collects are used in common with the universal Church. They unite the different parts of the Church, the great majority of them having been used since the introduction of Christianity into Sweden.[36]

By 1968, some quite extensive work towards a renewal of the Church Service Book had begun. The work on a new Gospel Book was carried out in close collaboration with the group that was working on the Church Service Book. Within the framework of these undertakings, an alternative series of collects was presented in 1974. After the subjection of these prayers to a wide variety of views and a revision undertaken by one of the bishops, the 1975 Church Assembly took the decision to permit the use of this revised series of collects as an alternative to the collects found in the 1942 Gospel Book until a new Gospel Book had been adopted and put into practice.

The proposal for a new Gospel Book that had been submitted in March 1979 only contained one series of collects, built on the previously presented series of prayers. These were not constructed according to the medieval tradition. Although the proposal did not include any

---

35 Nässelqvist, *Kollektbönen i svenska*, p. 13.
36 The Church of Sweden, 1942, *Den svenska evangelieboken*, Stockholm: Svenska kyrkans diakonistyrelses bokförlag, pp. 5 and 11.

motivations for the shape of the collects, an unspoken principle stipulated that the collects should be linked to the themes of the Sundays.

The proposal was severely criticized. Another working group charged with reworking it was therefore appointed in 1980, and a new proposal was presented in 1981. (In the same year, a new translation of the New Testament was published, and the Church of Sweden accordingly required a new revision of the readings in the Gospel Book.) The proposal made by that working group was intended to meet both lines of criticism by making the existing series of collects from the 1942 Gospel Book the second series of prayers, while the previously proposed prayers were to become the first series of collects in the Gospel Book. With regard to the series of collects in continuity with the old tradition, the working group suggested changes to some generally worded prayers to give them a more specific link to the theme of the Sunday. No less than 25 newly written prayers were proposed as part of that series – a third of the total number.[37]

During the debate in the Church Assembly, demands were again raised that the collects should follow the Latin originals more closely. A revision of the prayers included in the revised series, with an eye to classical structure, took place to ensure that they agreed more closely with the received tradition. It was also thought that this series should be the first in the Gospel Book and the newly written alternatives should be the second series. However, most members of the Church Assembly took the view that it is the content of the biblical texts that should govern the form of the prayers.[38]

The Gospel Book that was adopted for use in 1983 has two series of collects: the first series, which is structured on older tradition, and a new series, which is formed on the original proposals of the Revision Committee for the Church Service Book.

In the Gospel Books that were adopted for use in 1983 and 2002 another alternative series of collects was inserted besides the old series. The practice of using more than one collect had disappeared as early as the sixteenth century and therefore the two collects that are now appointed for each Sunday should be considered as alternatives to one another. The first series of collects follows the traditional structure and can be sung. The second series of collects is newly written and gathers up various thoughts from the Bible readings appointed for that Sunday, forming them into a prayer.

---

37 Nässelqvist, *Kollektbönen i svenska*, p. 16.
38 Nässelqvist, *Kollektbönen i svenska*, p. 16.

Here a shift in the use of the collect can be seen. The move has been away from a more general prayer that ended the introductory part of the Mass towards a prayer that leads into the readings of the biblical texts and that is given the function of introducing these readings. This shift has to do with the changes to the content of the Gospel Book that have taken place since the nineteenth century. In the 1862 Gospel Book two additional annual series of texts for preaching, one for the Sunday Mass and one for the Sunday Evening Prayer, were introduced in addition to the old Epistle and Gospel for each Sunday. The intention was that the Church of Sweden would have a triennial cycle of texts on which to preach. The old Epistle and Gospel should always be read. Thus in the first year of the cycle, the old Gospel should be the starting point for the sermon; in the second year, the second series of texts for the High Mass should be read from the pulpit and should provide the starting point; in the third year, the sermon should be based on the third series of texts for the Sunday High Mass. This arrangement, with a triennial cycle of texts providing a basis for the sermon, continued until 1983.

This complementary addition of the biblical texts available in the Gospel Book was made for educational reasons, in order to provide a greater variety in the choice of biblical texts that formed the basis for the sermon. The choice of texts that were added to the old biblical readings was thematically governed according to the content of the original Gospel for the day. In this way, the content of new biblical texts had a theological and educational link to the original readings. As a consequence, it was considered that a special theme for the sermon was appropriate for each Sunday and holy day.

In the 1921 Gospel Book, this conception received visible expression in the form of a thematic rubric, which was added following the rubric stating the name of the Sunday, and placed above the collect. As an example of this, the cycle of Advent collects might be mentioned – the First Sunday in Advent: 'The Coming of the Lord to his Church', the Second Sunday in Advent: 'Wait for the Day of the Lord', the Third Sunday in Advent: 'The Forerunner of the Lord', etc. With this, clear attempts began to be made to influence the content of the collects and to adapt them in order to improve their agreement with the perceived theme of the Sunday. How this happened will be described below.

The preparations for the 1942 Church Service Book show two clear tendencies with regard to the collects. By and large, a restorative intention prevailed, which implied a return to medieval originals and a desire to stress that the Church of Sweden was part of the worldwide catholic

Church. This should be clearly expressed in the liturgical texts, music and performance. At the same time, the strengthening of the themes of the Sundays continued.

In the 1983 Gospel Book three complete series of biblical readings have been inserted, providing a three-year lectionary with an Old Testament reading, an Epistle and a Gospel for each year. Below the name of each Sunday, a theme is again given for each Sunday and holy day. The demand for a collect that clearly connected with the theme of the day and the biblical texts had by then become so strong that a second series was worked out and included in the Gospel Book. The first series of collects is structured more or less on the model of the medieval originals, while the second series is new, written for the purpose of connecting with the theme of the Sunday.

It was already clear as the 1983 Gospel Book was approved that it would last only for a short period. A new translation of the Old Testament was under way, and was received in 1999.

In order to make a revision of the Old Testament readings and continue the work of producing a new Gospel Book, the Church of Sweden Governing Body appointed a group of people who were charged with the task of working through the material and of presenting a proposal. This proposal was presented to the Church of Sweden Governing Body in the year 2000 and was revised by the General Synod Committee on Worship. Following extensive responses to referrals, it was finally approved by the 2002 Church of Sweden General Synod. The new Gospel Book, with its revised series of collects, was brought into use on Advent Sunday in the year 2003.

The work that led to the current Gospel Book included a proposal that was sent out for consultation, with a request for comments. The group that worked on the proposal made an attempt to lessen the strong thematic character of the Sundays, since the stress on the theme of the Sundays had often led to sermons that were more about the subrubric of the Sunday than about the content of the biblical texts. The theme appointed for each Sunday and holy day was removed in the proposal and replaced by a short quotation from one of the biblical readings for the day.[39]

The working group also undertook extensive work on the collects, with the expressed purpose of structuring the first series on medieval

---

39 The Church of Sweden, 2000, *Evangelieboksgruppens förslag till Den svenska evangelieboken* (Gospel Book Group's proposal for the Swedish Gospel Book). Motiveringar, Uppsala: Svenska kyrkans utredningar SKU 2000:5, pp. 30–2.

originals and of linking the second series to the content of the biblical passages.[40] In collaboration with the Institution for Classical Languages at Lund University a complete investigation was made of the medieval originals behind the Swedish collects and of the way in which these had been translated into Swedish. There is a report on how the medieval texts, Sunday by Sunday, have been treated in the various Swedish Gospel Books in an appendix to the proposal for a new Gospel Book, in which the working group also reports on its motivations for the changes suggested. Here the group shows how the proposed revised series of collects has been structured on the basis of the old tradition.

The responses from the referrals expressed almost complete support for the view that the first series of collects should be expressed in accordance with the medieval material (98.7 per cent supported that general proposal) and the second series should reflect the biblical texts (91.6 per cent). There was a lesser degree of support for the abolition of the familiar system of using thematic sub-rubrics for each Sunday (59.2 per cent). With regard to the proposed form of the first series of collects, there were a number of suggestions for improving the details, although the view was mainly positive.[41]

The task committed to the Gospel Book working group included some work on the issue of a more inclusive style of language. The Church of Sweden Governing Body had included this task in its instructions, following the attention that this matter had received from a number of Church Assemblies. The brief focused on suggestions as to how masculine language might be made less prominent. It was agreed that the working group's remit should also include the collects.[42]

Work on less male-dominated language focused primarily on the introduction to the collects, that is, on the invocation. The Latin originals that had been used in Sweden show only seven different types of introductions. Of these, *Deus*, *Domine* and *Omnipotens sempiterne Deus* constitute 90 per cent of the opening lines. In the 1562 Gospel Book, the number of openings was doubled. After that, between 13 and 17 variants occur in each edition of the Gospel Book. Behind these

---

40 The Church of Sweden, 2000, *Evangelieboksgruppens förslag till Den svenska evangelieboken*. Motiveringar, Uppsala: Svenska kyrkans utredningar SKU 2000:5, pp. 32–4.

41 Eriksson and Nilsson, *Evangelieboken i gudstjänst*, p. 14. Ten per cent of all congregations in the Church of Sweden were asked to give their view.

42 The Church of Sweden, 2000, *Evangelieboksgruppens förslag till Den svenska evangelieboken*. Motiveringar, Uppsala: Svenska kyrkans utredningar SKU 2000:5, pp. 27–30, 33–4.

developments lie the facts that some of the Latin openings have been translated with or without an introductory 'O' ('God' or 'O, God', respectively) and also that some of these opening invocations have been combined to make new forms. In this way *Domine* and *Deus* are combined, for example, in the introduction 'Lord God' or 'O, Lord God'. This form was, until the current edition of the Gospel Book, even more common than the use of both 'God' and 'Lord' taken together.[43]

Up until the publication of the 1983 Gospel Book, the use of '(O,) Lord God' increased slowly, while the use of '(O,) God' decreased. The opening '(O,) Lord' did not occur very often – only in some 4 per cent of the prayers, in comparison with 30 per cent in the Latin originals. In the 1983 Gospel Book, the phrase '(O,) Lord' disappears completely and almost half of the collects in this Gospel Book were introduced by the variant form, 'Lord our God'. On one Sunday, the Latin original began *Omnipotens et misericordis Deus*. Until the 1942 Gospel Book appeared, this introduction was used in two variant forms on two or three Sundays. From the 1983 Gospel Book, one of the shorter variants, 'Merciful God' or 'Merciful Lord', was used as the introduction to the collect on six Sundays.[44]

This tendency, beginning with the 1983 Gospel Book, continues in the proposals presented in the year 2000 and in the current edition of the Gospel Book. On 11 Sundays, variants to the phrase 'God of mercy and comfort' are used. The most common introduction in the 1983 Gospel Book, 'Lord our God', disappeared as part of the work undertaken thereafter and was by and large replaced by the simple 'O, God', which in the current Gospel Book is the dominant introduction to the first series of collects. Other introductions to the first series of collects used today are 'God of grace', 'God of salvation', 'God of heaven and earth', 'God of all goodness', 'God of Life', 'God of Love', 'Holy Trinity', 'O, God of power', and 'Eternal God'.

The Latin originals lacked the use of 'Father' in the invocation. In the 1562 Gospel Book the form 'O, Lord God, heavenly Father' was introduced on one Sunday. In all the following editions of the Gospel Book, the use of 'Father' became increasingly frequent. The 1983 Gospel Book reduced the use of 'Father' in the opening line of the collect to only five Sundays, and the proposals in 2000 reduced its use to only one day in the liturgical year – Good Friday. Following criticism from the responses to the consultations, the use of 'Father' was reinstated in

---

43 Nässelqvist, *Kollektbönen i svenska*, p. 27.
44 Nässelqvist, *Kollektbönen i svenska*, p. 27.

the collects on five Sundays in the current Gospel Book.[45] As a result of views expressed in the responses to the consultation and debates in the General Synod, the use of the concept of 'almighty' in the invocation of the collect has also been reduced to only one Sunday (1 per cent of the collects compared to 25 per cent of the Latin originals).[46]

In this way, the discussion about a less male-dominated form of language has had some impact on the work on the introductory formulations of the collects in the Church of Sweden.

A close investigation shows that about 70 per cent of the first series of collects in the 2000 proposals for a new Gospel Book reveal a clear continuity with the medieval prayers. In the current Gospel Book approved by the 2002 Church of Sweden General Synod, the collects with a medieval original have decreased to 50 per cent of the collects that are now part of the first series of collects in the Gospel Book.[47]

Summary

From this investigation of the use of the collects in the Church of Sweden and the changes made after the Reformation in relation to the Latin originals a few simple conclusions may be drawn.

It is first of all obvious that all the work of renewing the collects has included a strong determination to preserve continuity with the old inheritance and with the worldwide Church. Time and again, it is possible to find affirmative notes in the comments on the work of revision of the Gospel Book, which state that the starting points have been the Latin texts from the Middle Ages and that the desire has been to preserve continuity with the old Church.

In the life of worship within the Church, the use of the collects has preserved the old Latin linguistic structure more or less unchanged, thus keeping open the possibility that this prayer might be sung. Its position has also followed the position of the collect in the Latin Order of Mass, where it is usually said by the priest and follows the introductory salutation. Gradually, however, the collects have come to be perceived as an introduction to the Bible readings, with the particular function of gathering up the theme of the Sunday and the biblical texts into a prayer. This view has clearly gained momentum during the twentieth century, expressed in the comments made on the work

---

45 Nässelqvist, *Kollektbönen i svenska*, p. 28.
46 Nässelqvist, *Kollektbönen i svenska*, p. 28.
47 Nässelqvist, *Kollektbönen i svenska*, p. 47.

of revising the collects by, for example, the Church of Sweden General Synod. The Sundays have increasingly been characterized by a theme, and the demand that this should also affect the form of the collects has gained increasingly strong influence.

Even so, there have been changes made in the course of time. The introductions to the collects first saw an increased use of the address 'Father', not least in combination with 'almighty'. The addresses 'Lord' and 'God' from the Latin originals were used as introductions to the prayers in varied and simplified forms – 'O, Lord God' and others. During the twentieth century and up to this day, changes have taken place with regard to the introduction to the prayers. These changes have not been uniform. The use of the medieval original *Domine* has decreased and finally been omitted in favour of the dominant use of *Deus*. To this has been added a number of variant ways to address God, often with some link to the content of the biblical readings appointed for the specific Sunday.

With regard to the ending of the collects, the medieval endings have by and large been preserved, although the use of more extensive endings with a trinitarian character has been somewhat increased by being appointed to some of the major feasts. The dominant ending is 'Through your Son Jesus Christ, our Lord'.

With regard to the formulated content of the prayers, tension has arisen between the Latin original behind the prayer and the increasingly thematic character of the Sunday, which has been shown here. Altogether, this has resulted in the fact that in the current Gospel Book, only about 50 per cent of the first series of collects have a structure and wording in accordance with their Latin originals.

The purpose of this chapter has been to investigate and study the collect in the Church of Sweden with a particular focus on the way in which the modern collects are related to the medieval collects in Latin. Both the language and the use of the collects in the Church of Sweden from the Reformation until the present have been analysed. During the period of the Reformation, most of the collects were translated over a period of time from Latin to Swedish, in translations closely following the Latin text. These translated collects were in use up until the twentieth century. During this last century many of the collects have been changed to fit the theme of the Bible readings of each Sunday. In the present Gospel Book about 50 per cent of the collects are still built on the Latin texts from the medieval sources.

Translated by Sr Gerd Swensson

3

The Anglican Collect

DONALD GRAY

It can certainly be claimed that there is no more characteristic Anglican liturgical ingredient than the collect. The collect, which derives from a Gallican tradition coming down to us via the Sarum Missal, not only survived any possible major liturgical surgery in the sixteenth- and seventeenth-century compilations but, most importantly, acquired both a status and a tradition in its own right in the Prayer Books of the Church of England, and consequently in the Anglican Communion, which has never been seriously challenged.

The collect, as has been described elsewhere, was inherited from the liturgy of the Western Church and found an honoured and natural place, in the first instance, in the liturgical compositions of Thomas Cranmer.[1] He never seemed to have questioned that this particular form of prayer should not be included in his new forms of service, but delighted in adapting the Sarum form into its Anglican manifestation.

The overwhelming proportion of the collects, which acquired widespread familiarity when they appeared in English in the 1549 Prayer Book, were translations from the Latin, though there are certain notable new compositions provided for the new liturgy. Not least, as though to make a point, the very first two in the liturgical year for Advent Sunday and the second Sunday of that season. Collects have a definitive form in Latin and they assumed a similarly definitive form in the English order. This form of prayer consists of four parts, that is, the Address or Invocation, the Acknowledgement, the Petition, the Aspiration and the Pleading. It has been well said that these prayers have such a consistent and recognizable shape and content that a listener accustomed to the collect form can usually tell, after hearing the opening

---

1 Donald Gray, 2007, 'Cranmer and the Collects', in Andrew W. Hass, David Jasper and Elizabeth Jay (eds), *The Oxford Handbook of English Literature and Theology*, Oxford: Oxford University Press, pp. 564ff.

words, approximately how the prayers will continue, not anticipating the actual words, but sensing the pattern.[2]

For the 1549 Prayer Book Cranmer and his assistants (the seventeenth-century historian Thomas Fuller (1608–61) records that the Archbishop headed up a team of six bishops and six learned divines who shared the labour) provided a collect for each Sunday of the year accompanying the appointed Scripture readings.[3] They also provided a collect for the choice which had been made of red-letter saints' days. These were all 'biblical saints', that is, they were persons found in the New Testament. These collects were almost entirely new compositions because the Sarum collects invariably involved unacceptable invocation of the saints. Similarly, a number of the medieval collects that were retained were revised in order to eliminate the doctrine of merit and to stress the initiative and liberality of God's grace. The new saints' day collects did not ask for the prayers of the person, but instead told something about the saint being so commemorated and prayed for grace to follow the example so set for us.

The Sunday collects made no attempt to condense the teaching contained in the subsequent scriptural readings. That they did this is a suggestion that has rightly been described as 'merely fanciful and not borne out by the facts of the case'. It is also a fancy that has burdened many a sermon that has attempted to make such an association of ideas and themes.[4]

Additionally the compilers used the collect shape at a number of other points in the Prayer Book, notably at Matins and Evensong (entitled Morning Prayer and Evening Prayer from 1552 onwards). These daily services each had, after the Sunday collect, a second and third collect. At Matins they are designated as being 'for peace' and 'for grace'. At Evensong the second collect has no specific attribution, while the third is 'for aid against all perils'. In 'The Supper of the Lorde and the Holy Communion commonly called the Masse' the service commenced with the priest reciting the Lord's Prayer 'with this collect', a prayer widely familiar from its opening line, 'Almighty God, unto whom all hearts be open'. This prayer, which is not the collect for the day or feast, has come to be known as 'the Collect for Purity' and was originally

---

2 J. W. Suter Jr., 1940, *The Book of English Collects*, New York: Harper, p. 69.

3 E. C. Ratcliff, 1976, *Liturgical Studies*, London: SPCK, p. 184.

4 C. L. Felto, 1912, 'Collects', in George Harford and Morley Stevenson (eds), *The Prayer Book Dictionary*, London: The Waverley Book Company, pp. 210–20, p. 210.

said by the priest alone in the vestry. The Holy Communion service is also provided with six further collects, one of which, it is instructed, should be said after the Offering on those occasions when there is no communion (i.e. no distribution of bread and wine). Other prayers in the 1549 Prayer Book might have a similar pattern to the collect, but generally lack the terse and tightly formulaic form of those prayers that are specifically described in the rubrics as 'collects'.

The 1549 Prayer Book had a short life, but the collect provision suffered no harm in its early revision and emerged practically unscathed, apart from a few slight changes of spelling in the book of 1552. The sole exception was the inclusion of a new collect for Saint Andrew's Day, because the 1549 prayer contained information derived from outside Scripture. Neither the book of 1559 nor that of 1604 contained changes in the collects. There were more changes in the book just over one hundred years after the publication of the 1552 Prayer Book, when the Prayer Book of 1662 appeared. These survive to this day.

Here there were a number of amplifications and developments of the 1549/1552 texts (for example Advent 3 and 4, Trinity 2, 11, 18) and some new compositions, probably from the talented pen of John Cosin, who became Bishop of Durham after the Restoration of the monarchy in 1660 (for example Advent 3, Epiphany 6, Easter 4). In the 1662 Prayer Book there are 20 changes or amendments in the *Temporale*, ranging from expansions to the smallest amendment. In the *Sanctorale* there are 16 changes of a greater or lesser degree to Cranmer's work.

So, in England at least, the Prayer Book collect entered a long period of settled life, although the so-called 'Liturgy of Comprehension' of 1689 made some substantial proposals for the revision of the collects. This publication was the result of the official, though unsuccessful, attempt sponsored by the joint monarchs, William and Mary, to alter the liturgy in such a way as to encourage Dissenters to return to the Established Church. Its compilers were particularly concerned that these prayers should reflect the content of the scriptural lections read at the same service. The whole project failed, however, and the proposal died with it.[5]

In the nineteenth century it became the custom for young people to be expected, either at Sunday school or at home, to learn the Sunday collect off by heart. This produced a number of generations in which the Prayer Book collect was a major segment of their Christian vocabu-

---

5 Timothy Fawcett, 1973, *The Liturgy of Comprehension: An Abortive Attempt to Revise The Book of Common Prayer*, Alcuin Club Collections 54, Southend-on-Sea: Mayhew-McCrimmon, *passim*.

lary. The prayers also became a vehicle for devotional studies of various kinds. However, with the onset of liturgical revision, the settled life of the Anglican collect was bound to be disturbed.

In England, stirrings towards change were first seen in what was eventually to be known as the 1928 Prayer Book. There were not many alterations in the collects for Sundays and Festivals, but a number of additional collects were needed for lesser feasts and fasts, which had not hitherto had any particular liturgical provision. However, the new compositions for the lesser feasts did not escape criticism. The liturgical expert F. E. Brightman described them variously as 'awkward and prosaic' and 'incoherent'. In the case of two of the prayers, he pronounced damningly that 'all that can be said of either of them is that they make one shudder'.[6]

There is no doubt that the writing of collects is a specialized art form. If the compilers of the 1928 Prayer Book had not got the literary skill they were in good company. Even the original collects of the Prayer Book tradition have not escaped criticism. While the work on the 1928 Book was in progress, Percy Dearmer, known for his writings on ceremonial and religious music and a member of an erstwhile 'Liturgical Commission' (which was eventually largely ignored and the work completed by the Bishops of the Church of England themselves), wrote:

> Although the collects of the First English Prayer Book are the finest prayers in the language, they are, then, not equally good; but the habit of regarding all 'Prayer Book Collects' as necessarily perfect has almost destroyed that faculty of discrimination which it is very important for the Church, in these times of change, to recover. Some of the original collects show signs of weariness or haste, some fall into a sameness of phrase and idea. Some, following literally their originals in the Sarum Missal, are rather arid.[7]

More recently, one of the leading Anglican liturgical scholars of the second half of the twentieth century counselled a more nuanced approach to the Cranmerian canon of collects. Geoffrey Cuming, in an essay entitled 'Cranmer at Work', gave this as his judgement:

---

[6] F. E. Brightman, 1927, 'The New Prayer Book Examined', *Church Quarterly Review* CIV (1927), pp. 219–52, p. 229.

[7] Percy Dearmer, 1919, *The Art of Public Worship*, London: A. R. Mowbray, p. 159.

> Cranmer has been the subject of much uncritical adulation for his versions of the collects. Sometimes, indeed, he has received credit in popular estimation which was really due to the revisers of 1661. Some of his collects are flat, and one or two downright bad, as he would have been the first to admit: his criticism of his own attempts at translating hymns from the Latin is well known. But considering the lack of good models and probably also the shortage of time (a good collect cannot be thrown off in one sitting), the standard of excellence he maintained is fully worthy of the praise which generations of Englishmen have gratefully bestowed upon it.[8]

This should have served as a timely warning to all modern-day Anglican collect composers. How far that has been heeded is highly debatable. The results, as observed right across the Anglican Communion, are distinctly patchy.

The first Prayer Book for use outside of Britain was that produced for the Protestant Episcopal Church in the United States, and was provided for Congregations in 'Plantations, Missions and Colonies'. The first proposals printed in 1786 reflected, in a number of ways, the topics that had been discussed in England in 1689 at the time of the drafting of the Liturgy of Comprehension. A list was compiled containing 13 points as 'Chief matters proposed for a review . . . stated under the decent and modest form of queries'. They were reproduced in a book entitled *Free and Candid Disquisitions*. One of the proposals asked the question, 'whether our collects, which in the main are excellent, are always suited to the epistle and gospels . . . and whether there is any occasion of using the collect for the day twice in the same service?'[9]

In the event, the compilers of the first American Book of Common Prayer in 1789 did not rewrite the collects to suit the Epistles and Gospels. They were content to do a small amount of what they believed to be modernization of the language. Thus, in the collect for Good Friday, they substituted 'desirest' for 'wouldest'; on the Third Sunday after Easter, 'avoid' for 'eschew'; on Pentecost, 'O God' for 'God'; and 'by sending' for 'by the sending'; on the Second Sunday after Trinity, 'those' for 'them'; on the Ninth Sunday after Trinity, 'are right' for 'be rightful'; on the Eleventh Sunday after Trinity, 'chiefly' for 'most

---

8 Geoffrey Cuming, 1983, *The Godly Order: Texts and Studies Relating to the Book of Common Prayer*, Alcuin Club Collections 65, London: SPCK, p. 52.

9 Marion J. Hatchett, 1982, *The Making of the First American Book of Common Prayer*, New York: Seabury Press, pp. 75ff.

chiefly'; on the Twentieth Sunday after Trinity' which thou commandest' for 'that thou wouldst have done' (1662); on Saint Thomas' Day 'greater confirmation' for 'more confirmation'.[10]

The revision of the first American Prayer Book waited till 1892. This book made an important contribution to the collects by adding an entirely new one for the Feast of the Transfiguration.[11] Other notable changes were occasioned by the necessity of finding new prayers for a set of Epistles and Gospels for a second celebration of Holy Communion at Easter and Christmas.[12] A more substantial revision was authorized in 1928 which was free from the controversies that plagued the abortive English revision of the same date. The American 1928 revision had no bearing on 'such matters of popular clerical or lay interest as the number of candles used on the altar, the kind of vestments, and so forth'.[13]

Then in 1979 there was an extensive and thorough revision, said at the time to be the most substantial piece of Prayer Book revision since 1549. In the 1979 book, approximately half of the collects were from the 1928 Book. Thus around thirty of the 1928 collects were dropped. Some of these, although no longer appointed as collects of the day, were given greater exposure. For example, in an Order for Service for Noonday, the collect for Monday in Whitsun week was employed, and in the Burial of the Dead, the collects for Easter Eve and Trinity 21 were included in those respective rites. Marion Hatchett has provided a detailed listing of their origins in his *Commentary on the American Prayer Book* (1981). Among the 'new' collects were compositions or translations by William Bright (Advent 4; Epiphany 8; Propers 18 and 20), Charles M. Guilbert (Epiphany 1), Massey Shepherd (Epiphany 5; Proper 6), F. B. McNutt (Lent 4), W. R. Huntington (Monday in Holy Week), Frank Colquhoun (Thursday in Easter Week; Proper 9), Armitage Robinson (Proper 1), and Howard E. Galley (Proper 29).[14]

By the time of the 1979 American revision, many other Anglican provinces had also become immersed in the process of liturgical revision and the 1662 Prayer Book as a primary symbol of Anglican

---

10 Hatchett, *Making*, p. 184.

11 H. Massey Shepherd, 1951, *The Oxford American Prayer Book Commentary*, New York: Oxford University Press, p. 247.

12 Marion J. Hatchett, 1981, *Commentary on the American Prayer Book*, New York: Seabury Press, p. 10.

13 H. Boone Porter, 1981, 'Towards an Unofficial History of Episcopal Worship', in Malcolm C. Burson (ed.), *Worship Points the Way*, New York: Seabury Press, pp. 99–115, p. 106.

14 Hatchett, *Commentary*, pp. 163–216.

identity was disappearing. In this process, as can be seen from the 1979 American book, the ancient collects were not believed to be immune to change.

Yet if the Prayer Book of the Church of England was no longer a benchmark for other parts of the Communion, there was always considerable interest in what was happening in England. What they discovered was that the Church of England was deeply involved in a unique venture of ecumenical liturgical co-operation.

The Joint Liturgical Group was formed in 1963 and one of its earliest projects was a basic reconsideration of the calendar and lectionary.[15] The result was a scheme that differed from the Prayer Book in a number of important points. In the first place it was a two-year cycle. Second, it provided three and not two lections for each Sunday: a reading from the Old Testament as well as the Epistle and Gospel. Third, it was thematic, although cautiously emphasizing that the thematic titles were no more than *indications* of emphasis. First, a controlling lection was chosen and then, once the controlling lections were selected, and the indications of emphasis plotted, the allied readings were chosen.[16]

Having completed the lectionary, the JLG turned to providing a set of collects to go with the lections. This was published in 1968. Because of the innovations in the new *Calendar and Lectionary*, they realized that no existing set would do. Yet they also realized that

> many of the existing collects in their traditional Anglican form are of great beauty and are used in non-Anglican Churches also. We have therefore tried to retain what we believe to be the best of them, sometimes on their traditional days, sometimes by rearrangement. Where we could not find any such collect that was particularly suitable to the lections, we have sought other existing collects, and we have drawn a number from the Book of Common Worship of the Church of South India and from various other sources.[17]

---

15 Horton Davies, 1986, *Worship and Theology in England*, Book III, Part VI, *Crisis and Creativity 1965 to the Present*, Grand Rapids MI and Cambridge: Eerdmans, p. 9. Donald Gray, 1997, *Ronald Jasper: His Life, His Work and the ASB*, London: SPCK, pp. 75–8.

16 Ronald C. D. Jasper (ed.), 1967, *The Calendar and Lectionary: A Reconsideration by the Joint Liturgical Group*, London: Oxford University Press, pp. 15–29.

17 Ronald C. D. Jasper (ed.) 1969, *The Daily Office by the Joint Liturgical Group*, London: SPCK and Epworth Press, p. 78.

There was also the problem regarding the style of the collects. Both in their Latin form and in Cranmerian English they 'are of great beauty', the JLG stated. They expressed the belief that any attempt to modernize them, particularly by addressing God in the second person plural, would have a very disturbing effect on their structure. The Group decided to avoid this difficulty by retaining the address to God in the second person singular, and by revising the prayers themselves only very slightly. Because the collects from *The Book of Common Prayer* were so familiar, they thought it best to use them largely unchanged or not to use them at all. But where the collects were drawn from other sources and thus less familiar, they felt free to take greater liberties with them, often by simplifying them, but sometimes by considerable alterations. On the whole, though, they kept the general style of collects. Perhaps, they thought, 'if at some future date the whole office is put into more modern English with the address to God in the second person plural, then the use of the collect form itself will have to be reconsidered'.[18]

The following year the Church of England Liturgical Commission published its own document, *The Calendar and Lessons for the Church's Year*. Acknowledging the work of the JLG, it looked forward to

> the possibility that in the very near future the Church of England and the Free Churches of this country might be able to use the same eucharistic lectionary and the same daily office. This [the Commission said] will be great spiritual gain, and a matter for profound thanksgiving.[19]

In their proposals, the Liturgical Commission said that the new lectionary called for new collects and in general they adopted the provisions of JLG, not least because they had made 'substantial use of the familiar collects of the Prayer Book'.[20] In a small aside, the report contains the faintest echo of a discussion that was current in the 1960s but seems to have fallen away in recent years. This included several questions. Do we need a different collect for every Sunday?[21] The writing

---

18 Jasper, *Daily Office*, pp. 78–9.
19 Church of England Liturgical Commission, 1969, *The Calendar and Lessons for the Church's Year: A Report Submitted to the Archbishops of Canterbury and York, November 1968*, London: SPCK, p. ix.
20 Liturgical Commission, *Calendar and Lessons*, p. 21.
21 Liturgical Commission, *Calendar and Lessons*, p. 21.

of the collects, as we have already noted, is a specialized art form, so are we making undue difficulties for ourselves by attempting to produce over fifty compositions for the year? For instance, could not one superb prayer for Advent, Christmas or Lent serve for a season rather than just one week? And in the long post-Pentecost season could we not choose from the very best of our prayers those that could serve for a little while? Would this not also help to restore the contents of our prayer vocabulary which has been depleted since we ceased to learn the collects by rote, by introducing a little repetition?

While this discussion was proceeding, there were also calls for more thematic prayers to replace the more general collects that had been provided. Such proposals, it would seem, only served to obscure the purpose of the collect as the opening prayer for an act of worship. In this respect it has been maintained that the quintessential Anglican prayer, the Collect for Purity, fulfils all that is needful and necessary by way of prayer at that point in the Eucharist and might very well serve on its own on many occasions.

The proposals of the 1969 report were carried over, to a very large extent, into the 1980 *Alternative Service Book*. This body of prayers contained, in addition to the Cranmerian compositions (both in their original form or modified), prayers deriving from the Church of South India, Frank Colquhoun, Armitage Robinson, the 1972 South African Prayer Book, the 1929 Scottish Prayer Book, Thomas Aquinas, John Cosin and the 1979 American Prayer Book, as well as a dozen or more new compositions by the Commission itself. The *Companion to the Alternative Service Book* summarizes the situation in this way:

> This body of collects is the result of wide consultation with other Churches, Anglican and non-Anglican, both at home and overseas; and most of them are now common property. It is therefore difficult to indicate all the original sources in every case. No contemporary writers can claim the genius of a Cranmer; but the ASB collects do represent a brave attempt to produce a distinctively Western form of prayer which is contemporary in outlook yet faithful to the traditional style.[22]

A typographical decision was made in the printing of the collects in the *ASB* which, it was hoped, would assist their use in worship. 'For the sake of clarity and to assist in public recitations, the collects are

---

22 R. C. D. Jasper and Paul F. Bradshaw, 1986, *A Companion to the Alternative Service Book*, London: SPCK, p. 267.

set out with their various elements on separate lines.'[23] Of the contents and style of the *ASB* collects it must be said that they significantly reshaped the language, function and traditional reference points of the collect. The most significant change was the replacement of the relative clause, which traditionally contained an attribute of Almighty God, with a statement about God, 'often with unfortunate results', it has been observed.[24]

We now take a few random snapshots in order to illustrate the way in which the provinces of the Anglican Communion have tackled the question of the collect in their revised acts of worship. Take Canada for instance. In 1911, the General Synod of the Anglican Church of Canada decided that, because 'through the lapse of some three hundred years many changes have taken place in the world', some 'adaptions and enrichment' of the Prayer Book were justified. In the resulting book, and in further revision in 1959, the collects were substantially retained in the 1662 form.[25] It was not until the appearance of *The Book of Alternative Services*, authorized in 1983, that there was a distinct change of mind. Cranmerian language, they decided, would not do for modern Canada:

> Whatever the source of Cranmer's elegance, it is not characteristic of the English language now. The poetry of our own day tends to be spare, oblique, incisive, relying more on the sharpness of imagery than the flow of cadence. Liturgical language must attempt to speak in its own idiom. The purpose of liturgy is not to preserve a particular form of English address but to enable a community to pray, and that demands struggling with the vernacular.[26]

The resulting collects reflect that point of view. Take the collect for the Second Sunday of Easter, for example:

---

23 Jasper and Bradshaw, *Companion*, p. 267.

24 Bridget Nichols, 2001, 'Collects and Post Communion Prayers', in Paul Bradshaw (ed.), *Companion to Common Worship*, vol. 1, Alcuin Club Collections 78, London: SPCK, pp. 179–224, p. 181.

25 Anglican Church of Canada, 1959, 'Preface to the Canadian revision of 1918, altered in 1959', in *The Book of Common Prayer 1959 Canada*, Toronto: Anglican Book Centre.

26 Anglican Church of Canada, 1985, Introduction to *The Book of Alternative Services of the Anglican Church of Canada*, Toronto: Anglican Book Centre, p. 12.

Almighty and Eternal God,
the strength of those who believe
and the hope of those who doubt,
may we, who have not seen, have faith
and receive the fullness of Christ's blessing,
who is alive and reigns with you and the Holy Spirit,
one God, now and for ever.

A similar process had been taking place in Australia.[27] It was not until 1978 that a Revised Prayer Book was issued 'for use together with The Book of Common Prayer 1662'. In that book there were two series of collects: the One-Year Series, based on *The Book of Common Prayer 1662*, while the Three-Year Series is equipped with the Prayer Book collect and an alternative prayer for each Sunday. All the 1662 collects for Sundays and holy days are used, though not always on the days to which they were originally assigned. The alternative prayers are taken from the English translation of *The Prayers from the Roman Missal, 1973* and were chosen 'to treat the collect as the first component of the Ministry of God's Word', and to 'match' the readings.[28]

A much enlarged volume entitled *A Prayer Book for Australia* came into use in 1995. In this book the provision of collects is considerably expanded. In the introductory matter the compilers state unambiguously what, in their opinion, is the function of a collect. They say of the collects that they are 'the prayers of the collected or gathered community', a different emphasis from the 1978 book. The scheme in this book is quite a complicated one. The collects are set out for each Sunday as a prayer *of the week* (or, in Advent and Lent, of the season) and as three prayers *of the day* (the italics are from the book). The prayers of the day are generally chosen to fit the readings of the three-year cycle of the *Revised Common Lectionary* for years A, B and C. The prayers of the week are more general in content and are intended mainly for use at services when those readings are not used. The prayers of the week may, however, be used at the discretion of the presiding minister when the readings from the three-year cycle are used. The prayers 'for the season' may be used instead of the other prayers provided.[29]

---

27 John Grindrod, 1978, 'The Story of the Draft Book', in Gilbert Sinden SSM (ed.), *When We Meet for Worship*, Adelaide: Lutheran Publishing House, pp. 17–30.

28 Sinden, *When We Meet*, pp. 116–17.

29 Anglican Church of Australia, 1995, *A Prayer Book for Australia for Use together with the Book of Common Prayer (1662) and an Australian Prayer Book (1978)*, Alexandria: Broughton Books, pp. 462–3.

This pattern obviously requires a large number of suitable prayers to serve its needs. The Australian Liturgical Commission cast their net widely to find them. Consequently they have been taken from the *ASB*, the 1989 South African, 1985 Canadian and 1989 New Zealand Prayer Books; the 1973 ICEL collects from *The Roman Missal*; the 1978 *Lutheran Book of Worship* and the *Uniting in Worship* (1988) of the Uniting Church in Australia. Additionally they have utilized 21 prayers from Janet Morley's *All Desires Known* (1992).

Morley's book, in which she tries 'to integrate [her] faith and [her] feminism', contains a complete set of collects for Sundays and major weekday festivals, and a selection of collects for lesser festivals and other occasional uses. She explains:

> Some are closely tied in with the precise stage of the liturgical year; others, while related to the set theme, will also be usable in other contexts and at other times. In most cases, the collect will link more strongly with one or two of the set readings than with the others . . . The collects are designed to have a wide use in church and elsewhere, and their language is deliberately inclusive. However, wherever possible within the constraints of the lectionary, I have picked up images and narratives concerning women, as norms for the Christian life.[30]

In *A New Zealand Prayer Book: He Karakia Mihinare o Aotearoa*, there are also a considerable number of newly written collects to provide cover for both a two- and three-year lectionary – which the book contains. The latter is the Common Lectionary of 1983, the work of the North American Consultation on Common Texts, which in turn derives from the Roman Catholic *Ordo Lectionum Missae* (1969).

For the two-year cycle three collects are provided, one of which is often a modern version of a 1662 collect. The others are much briefer, barely conforming to the traditional collect structure. In the case of the three-year cycle the rubrics say:

> Suitable collects from the two-year series have been suggested, but other collects appropriate to the theme may be selected from any source. Where only one reference to the two-year series is given, the same collect is appropriate for all three years.[31]

---

30 Janet Morley, 1992, *All Desires Known*, London: SPCK, p. xii.
31 Anglican Church in Aotearoa New Zealand and Polynesia, 1989, *A New Zealand Prayer Book, He Karakia Mihinare o Aotearoa*, Auckland: William Collins; London: Collins Liturgical Publications, p. 691.

The Church of Ireland made revisions to the 1662 book in 1878 and 1926. Then in 2004 a new edition was authorized. In this book the lectionary is described as 'The Revised Common Lectionary adapted for use in the Church of Ireland'. An introduction maintains that there are only minor adaptations. For use with these readings two collects are provided. The first is in traditional language and is particularly recommended for use with readings carried over from the 1926 book. The second prayer is in modern language but conforms to traditional collect form. The 26 sources of these prayers are detailed at the conclusion of the Collect Section. They include the work of other Anglican provinces, the Alcuin Club's *Enriching the Christian Year* (1993), as well as prayers by twentieth-century authors such as Charles MacDonnell, Kenneth Stevenson, David Silk, Janet Morley and Brian Mayne.[32]

The Church of England entered the twenty-first century with a new worship book, *Common Worship: Services and Prayers for the Church of England*. There were a number of major changes from the *ASB* of 1980. One that affected the collects was the abandonment of the thematic two-year JLG lectionary and the adoption of a slightly altered version of the *Revised Common Lectionary*. Because of this a point of discussion arose: should the collects be attached to the Sunday names or to the sets of lections? It was decided to associate them with the Sunday names, while not denying their possible relationship to the biblical passages which were chosen for that particular day. This is especially true in the seasons of Christmas and Easter, when a clear connection between collects and readings can be seen.[33]

There was a further important change with regard to the style of the collects. The Liturgical Commission reported to the General Synod that in this new book they had taken the *BCP* collects as their starting point, not those of the *ASB*. The result of this decision, which they had taken after the convening of an Inter-Provincial Group in which representatives of the English, Irish, Scottish and Welsh Commissions shared their ideas, was a revival of the use of the relative clause:

> We have departed from this starting point only with good reason. On as many days as possible, it seems desirable that Anglicans should be using the same collect, even in a slightly different version

---

32 Church of Ireland, 2004, *The Book of Common Prayer and Administration of the Sacraments and the Rites and Ceremonials of the Church according to the Church of Ireland*, Dublin: The Columba Press, p. 337.

33 Nichols, 'Collects and Post Communion Prayers', p. 182.

to accommodate the desire for both traditional and contemporary translations.[34]

In *Common Worship* there are many *BCP* collects because of another decision to provide a variable and seasonal collect after communion in the Eucharist. 'It allows us to draw more widely on the Anglican treasury of collect material,' it was explained.[35]

In preparing this new collection of prayers the difficulties involved in rendering the *BCP* collects in contemporary English were recognized by the Commission. In some cases the *ASB* version was followed, whereas in others they went back beyond the *BCP* to the Latin original. They admitted they had not found it possible to be entirely consistent in stylistic matters. There were examples in which they retained what might be regarded as an archaism that had been removed in another instance. This was justified by declaring, 'We have looked at each prayer individually, with an eye to doctrine, to intelligibility and to rhythm but always aware that many (not all) still have an older translation lodged in their mind.' They believed that the *ASB* had undermined the function the collect had fulfilled in the past as worshippers' 'prayer for the week', yet reckoned that there is still among some Anglicans 'not only a desire to know and memorize the collect, but to associate it with a particular day or week. We have wanted to encourage this use of the collect and to recover this emphasis which brings liturgy and spirituality together creatively.'[36]

When CW came into general use in 2000 it soon became clear that the idealism reflected by the Liturgical Commission in their 1995 statements on collects (though admittedly subsequently approved by the General Synod) was not generally shared across the dioceses. Within months, in July 2001, the Synod passed a motion noting 'criticisms of the collects for *Common Worship*', and in the light of this criticism, they called on the House of Bishops to commission 'additional collects for each Sunday and feast days in the liturgical year in a worthy contemporary idiom'.

Paul Roberts has attempted an explanation of this apparent synodical and liturgical volte-face. He writes:

---

34 David Stancliffe (Bishop of Salisbury and Chairman of the Church of England Liturgical Commission), 1995, 'Introduction' to *The Calendar, Lectionary and Collects: Report to the General Synod July 1995* (GS 1161A), London: Church House Publishing, p. A21.

35 Stancliffe, *Calendar*, p. A19.

36 Stancliffe, *Calendar*, p. A2.

In restoring instances of the relative clause and by adopting a conservative modernisation of the *BCP* originals, the compilers of the *CW* collects had intended to correct an infelicity. However, they had probably not reckoned with the effect of twenty years of using the *ASB* in public worship.[37]

The Commission conducted a consultative process that produced a wide range of criticisms, some of which recurred with considerable frequency. These were: in the collects the syntax was too complicated and archaic; the prayers themselves were too long; and they were bland in the themes, imagery and choice of language. Indeed, 'they end up saying very little, and take a long time to say it, in an unnecessarily complicated way'. It was asserted that the closing doxology only adds to their complexity and length. Finally, the accusation was made that they were frequently inaccessible in certain contexts, for example where children are present in significant numbers, in 'non-book' contexts, and among missionary congregations where there is no background experience of the language of the *BCP*.[38]

The resulting collects are therefore offered as short, simple in syntax, containing vivid and interesting themes and images, and written in an accessible language that ends up saying something clear and distinct. The relative clause is not entirely abandoned, but the need for brevity curtails its use. The vocative is entirely abandoned.[39] It needs to be realized that these *Additional Collects*, as they have been entitled, represent a complete departure from the collects of the *BCP* and are at present unique in the Communion. The hope expressed is that these new prayers 'convey the spirituality of the Anglican collect in a worthy, contemporary idiom complementing the approach of those already contained in Common Worship'.[40] The jury is out on this one.

While such a process of linguistic simplification of the collects is advocated by some, there is also evidence of the advocacy of what

---

37 Paul Roberts, 2006, 'The Additional Collects', in Paul Bradshaw (ed.), *A Companion to Common Worship*, vol. 2, Alcuin Club Collections 81, London: SPCK, pp. 121–7. See also *Report of the Proceedings of the General Synod*, 2003, vol. 34(1), London: Church House Publishing.

38 Liturgical Commission of the Church of England, 2003, *Common Worship: Additional Collects*, Report to the General Synod (GS 1493).

39 Liturgical Commission, *Additional Collects*.

40 Liturgical Commission, *Additional Collects*. See also Archbishops' Council of the Church of England, 2004, *Additional Collects*, London: Church House Publishing.

might be called 'performative matters' concerning them, which have the effect of emphasizing their liturgical importance.

The aim, it would seem, is to underline the place and significance of the collect as primary at the beginning of the Eucharist. Revised Anglican prayer books have adopted the sequence of liturgical events and actions surrounding the collect which can be seen to derive from the General Instruction on the Roman Missal of 1969, which was one of the results of the Second Vatican Council. The sequence decreed in that document consists of four parts: an invitation to prayer, followed by a silence, then the collect itself, concluding with the assent of the congregation given by the acclamation 'Amen'.[41]

Many Anglican provinces have recommended some or all of these elements, but there is no overall Anglican consistency regarding this sequence. In fact, Canada (1962) anticipated Rome. In their book, after the celebrant had bidden 'Let us pray', the rubric continues, 'the community may pray silently. The celebrant then sings or says the collect, after which the people respond, Amen.' South Africa (1989) has just the priest's bidding and the people's response. Australia (1978) also has only the bidding, but in 1995 the silence was added. Order One in *CW* (2000) has all three elements with the possible replacement of 'Let us pray' with 'a more specific bidding'. Ireland (2004) has the presiding minister introducing the collect, then 'allowing a short space for silence'. Wales (2004) has little in the text of the service but has the possibility of all the elements in the accompanying Notes.

USA (1979) and Order Two of *CW* have a preparatory 'the Lord be with you'. This has disappeared from the Roman rite and seems to have lost favour in Anglicanism, where it is no longer a common feature.

The danger surrounding the use of the bidding 'Let us pray' is that the congregation may think they are to change position, particularly if they are standing at this point in the liturgy. It is always a great pity if this ancient bidding is omitted for this reason. *Oremus* is not just an exhortation, it is also an invitation for all to join not only with the immediate assembled community of the faithful, but with 'the whole company of heaven'. It has great significance. That it is followed by a silence emphasizes the solemnity of the moment and the crucial importance of the collect in the liturgy. It is for this reason, some argue, that if any other part of the service is sung the collect should be solemnly sung as well.

---

41 General Instruction on the Roman Missal, in Thomas C. O'Brien (tr. and ed.), 1982, *Documents of the Liturgy 1963–1979: Conciliar, Papal and Curial Texts*, Collegeville MN: The Liturgical Press, 1982, § 1422, p. 476.

All these 'performative' matters add to the dignity and grandeur of this cardinal element of Christian worship. If the main emphasis has been on the collect in the Eucharist, that should not be taken as suggesting any form of casualness regarding its function in the daily office. There also it has a historic and crucial liturgical use in the liturgical tradition of Anglicanism which ought never to be gainsaid.

4

The Use of Collects in the Methodist Church in Britain

JOHN LAMPARD

The use and appreciation of collects in the Methodist Church in Britain over the years has, to say the least, been patchy. At all stages of its history many Methodists, possibly including a few ministers, will have asked the question, what is a collect? This chapter will look at the developments in the use of collects almost entirely from a worship-book angle, although much Methodist worship continues to be of an extempore nature. This means that what is described here is only part of an overall picture.

John Wesley

In England during the eighteenth century a significant minority of Methodists attended their Anglican parish church for their main Sunday service, where they would have been familiar with the collects contained in the 1662 *Book of Common Prayer* (*BCP*). As the new Methodist movement developed, Wesley prepared no formal liturgical material for its distinctively extempore 'Methodist' preaching services held on Sundays, usually outside customary church hours, and on weekdays.

The situation in America was different as there were practically no Anglican churches where new Methodist communities were springing up. British Methodists were travelling or emigrating to America as members, evangelists or church-planters, so John Wesley determined that there was a need for written liturgical material. Therefore the first Methodist liturgical document produced by Wesley was for use in America rather than Britain. In addition, the growing rift developing between the two countries meant that those who thought of themselves as Americans would treat imported British material with suspicion.

The 1776 Declaration of Independence was a clear indication that Methodists in America could not be expected to use Church of England material. Wesley therefore published, in 1784, the first Methodist liturgical document, *The Sunday Service of the Methodists in North America, with Other Occasional Services*, a revision of the 1662 *BCP*.[1]

Wesley was a 'Prayer Book man' and *The Sunday Service* was a light revision and abbreviation of the *BCP*, including some amendments of Morning Prayer, and 'The Order for the Administration of the Lord's Supper'. None of the familiar collects within the service, such as the Collects for Purity, Peace and Grace, were omitted by Wesley, so they would have been known and used. However, he was more radical in trimming aspects of the church year and its associated collects. In particular, he justified what he had done in a Preface note, dated 9 September 1784: 'Most of the holy-days (so called) are omitted, as at present answering no valuable end.'

It is not entirely clear what Wesley meant here. One reading could suggest an approach redolent of the opinions of the more extreme reformers. A more generous interpretation, and one more likely in view of Wesley's High Anglicanism, suggests that Wesley was adapting material for use on Sundays (thus the title *The Sunday Service*) and very few such holy days fell on a Sunday. Almost all the holy days (apart from Christmas Day) included in the *BCP*, but not celebrated on a Sunday, were excised, including Maundy Thursday and Epiphany. Only Good Friday and Ascension Day remained, so Wesley excluded some twenty collects. Epiphany was thus no longer an 'anchor' for the following Sundays in the church calendar. Wesley ignored Lent, including Ash Wednesday, and in an unusually eccentric way continued a run of 'Sundays after Christmas' until he came to 'the Sunday next before Easter'.

His treatment of the remaining collects was very conservative (apart from the omissions mentioned above). For an American congregation, he altered the first Collect for the King to 'the supreme rulers of these United States'. Otherwise, as an ordained priest in the Church of England, in the High Church tradition, he followed the *BCP*, only displaying the most minor editorial changes. In the Christmas Day collect the words 'renewed by the Holy Spirit' become 'renewed by Thy Holy

---

1 David Chapman offers an excellent guide to the development of Methodist worship, in particular details of early Methodist worship books. See David Chapman, 2006, *Born in Song: Methodist Worship in Britain*, Warrington: Church in the Market Place Publications.

Spirit', an amendment now widely followed, and on the Twelfth Sunday after Trinity he added one word, 'pour *down* upon us the abundance of thy mercy'. One revision of note is that Wesley omitted the Declaration as to the Forgiveness of Sins, replacing it with the collect for the Twenty-fourth Sunday after Trinity, 'absolve thy people from their offences'.

An almost identical version of *The Sunday Service* for use in Britain was published by Wesley in 1786, but, as David Chapman comments, 'few Methodists were suited by temperament or education to appreciate their founder's intentions. Before long, Methodists on both sides of the Atlantic had abandoned Wesley's liturgical ideal.'[2]

The nineteenth century

After Wesley's death in 1791, Methodism and its worship were riven with disputes, as competing groups sought to follow their own patterns. These arguments are again well set out by Chapman. The Conference attempted to lay down a pattern for Methodist worship, but there were several different parties at play. As far as written liturgy was concerned, there was a difference of opinion between those who favoured the *BCP* and those who favoured Wesley's *Sunday Service*, known as 'our venerable Father's abridgement'. There was another division between those who wanted to use a book and the many Methodists, suspicious of written liturgy, who favoured different patterns of extempore prayer.[3]

The result of this was that there was no significant revision of Wesley's work until 1882, when the Wesleyan branch of the Methodist Church authorized a new volume, *The Book of Public Prayers and Services for the use of the People called Methodists*, which, interestingly, was based on the *BCP* rather than Wesley's 1784 book. The major change, as far as collects were concerned, was the reintroduction of Epiphany as a holy day in its own right, with its own traditional collect, 'O God, who by the leading of a star . . .'. This change also enabled the reintroduction into the church year of Sundays after Epiphany and Sundays in Lent. The Order for Morning Prayer and the Collects and the Calendar were based on the *BCP* and not on Wesley's *Sunday Service*, because

---

2 Chapman, *Born in Song*, p. 17.

3 In the early 1970s I was minister of a former Primitive Methodist church which refused to use any written congregational service book, only grudgingly allowing me to read from my own copy.

69

the Wesleyan chapels with a fixed Sunday morning liturgy tended to use the *BCP* and not Wesley's abridgement for Morning Prayer.

The *Book of Offices* 1936

When the three main branches of the Methodist Church (Wesleyan, Primitive and United) came together in 1932, the union gave the opportunity for a major revision of the service book that would meet the needs and requirements of the three branches. The *Book of Offices* 1936 was strongly influenced by earlier Wesleyan material. The Wesleyans alone had followed more formal liturgy and the sparse written liturgical material of the other branches of Methodism indicate no interest in the choice of collects. As far as the collects in the *Book of Offices* were concerned, revision was slight.

The *Methodist Service Book* 1975

By the 1960s, a further revision process was deemed necessary, as the result of the major changes that were taking place in all the Churches under the general influence of the Liturgical Movement. In 1963, a Joint Liturgical Group (JLG) had been established, drawing its membership from all the major Churches, except for the Roman Catholic Church, which provided an observer. Donald Gray has noted the significance of this for the Church of England in his chapter. Although the JLG carried no authority greater than that which its own members gave it, it proved highly influential, not least in the Methodist Church. Two leading figures on the JLG were the distinguished Methodist clergy, A. Raymond George and Gordon S. Wakefield, who together were primarily responsible for introducing the reforms of the Liturgical Movement into Methodism.

One of the JLG's three major aims, and a significant ecumenical contribution, was to produce a liturgical calendar and a lectionary that the members' Churches might be glad to have in common. This was published in 1968, together with collects for each Sunday.[4] The JLG produced a new pattern for the church year and a new style of lectionary, so there was a major rethink about collects. These were designed

---

4 R. C. D. Jasper (ed.), 1968, *The Calendar and Lectionary*, Oxford: Oxford University Press.

to fit in with the new liturgical patterns, and often to relate to the lectionary. The biggest innovation here was that each week of the two-year lectionary had a 'theme'. The JLG was at pains to say that the theme was only chosen after the lections had been agreed and that the titles were no more than *indications* of emphasis. As it was hoped that many of the collects would provide a unity with lesson and theme, it was obvious to the compilers that, in addition to many from the *BCP*, a number of new collects would be necessary. Several of these were selected from the 1963 *Book of Common Worship* of the Church of South India, often amended.

At that time the liturgy of the Church of South India was providing an innovative resource for practical liturgists, in a similar way to the influence that Taizé and Iona had on worship later in the century. South India gave its liturgists (drawn from Anglican, Methodist, Presbyterian and Congregationalist traditions) the opportunity to be more experimental and creative in a situation where innovation was easier because a new Church was being created, slightly less constrained by tradition and precedent. Of the 62 collects included in the JLG publication, 37 were sourced from the *BCP*, while the remainder were chosen from the Church of South India and ten other books of prayers, which were either officially or individually published.

In 1970 the Methodist Church approved a report substantially accepting the recommendations of JLG, and adding some additional lectionary material to meet particular Methodist liturgical requirements, such as Aldersgate Sunday (marking Wesley's conversion), Overseas Missions and Christian Citizenship. However, the only additional collects included were the traditional ones for Epiphany and All Saints. It is not clear why the 'new' Sundays and distinctively Methodist occasions were not accorded their own collects. Perhaps the creative juices of the revisers were not working sufficiently to produce new collects for these special Sundays. Alternatively, it is possible that the presence of George and Wakefield on the Methodist liturgical sub-group influenced a move to deviate from the JLG as little as possible (however, see below). All the collects in the report were, like the JLG recommendations, in the 'thou' form.

At some point between the publication of this report and the approval of the 1975 *Methodist Service Book* (*MSB*), a decision was made to move from the 'thou' form to the 'you' form, which resulted in further major amendments of the texts of the collects. In spite of a lone protest from Miss Pauline Webb at the Methodist Conference, a decision also to incorporate inclusive language in relation to humans ('men' and 'mankind' were prominent) was judged to be a step too far.[5] A number of the collects were further revised, a few were omitted and alternative ones added, thus making the *MSB* choice recognizable and distinctive from the JLG recommendations. Methodist liturgical scholars are just the same as their ecumenical partners in their desire to 'improve' what others have written. Thus, in the sequence of Advent collects, 'destroy the works of the devil' became 'break the power of evil', but 'at thy first coming didst send thy messenger to prepare ...' was improved by adding the name of John the Baptist. Some Methodist sensitivities were protected by omitting 'blessed' before Virgin Mary. Overall, my judgement is that the *MSB* collects are an improvement on the JLG recommendations, with the addition of better alternative collects than some of the original choices.

Finally, it is worth reflecting that this approach to the use of collects marked a perhaps unconscious shift in both the content and liturgical function of the collect. Traditionally in the Eucharist it had performed part of the Entrance Rite, and so 'collected' the intention of the gathered people in their coming together. The JLG approach to the collect was to link it to the Ministry of the Word (although often preceding it at the end of the Preparation). Many of the collects written in the 1970s by writers such as Janet Morley and Alan Gaunt can be seen to be based on a particular lection. Thus the JLG collects provide a transitional bridge between the traditional 'liturgical use', as can be seen in many of the seasonal collects, and the newer 'lection-based' use, which is particularly apparent in the Sundays after Pentecost.

Personal reflections

This might be an appropriate moment for a subjective reflection on Methodism's use of collects. Inevitably it is highly personal, but it does reflect over sixty years' involvement in both Methodist and Anglican worship. I grew up with the 1936 *Book of Offices*, which was used primarily for Holy Communion, but have no recollection of collects being read in church outside the Communion service, apart from the Collect for Peace. I have no recollection of Morning or Evening Prayer being used, although in my early school days I remember the headmaster, in the gathering gloom at the end of the day, dismissing us with a prayer that I thought began, 'Light and now darkness, we beseech thee O

---

5 Inclusive language in relation to God had not even begun to appear on the Methodist radar at that time.

Lord'. It should perhaps be added here that Morning Prayer remained part of the staple diet of Caribbean Methodists, and they 'imported' it back into Methodism in Britain in the 1950s and 1960s in some of the inner-city churches they joined.

My real introduction to collects came at the age of ten, when the boarding school I attended (not a Methodist one) required its pupils to learn each week the collect for the following Sunday. Before setting off to the parish church in a crocodile, we had individually to recite the collect of the day. I never remember attempting to start to learn it until after breakfast on the Sunday. Failure to recite the words accurately resulted in a rap on the knuckles with a ruler. Alas, most of the collects were learned for the day and disappeared from my memory along with much else I all too temporarily learned. Perhaps something unconsciously remained which was the seedbed of my later appreciation of them. Also, as a slow learner, I think I particularly appreciated the brevity of collects which, many years later, I discovered closely followed the tight Latin wording of the Sarum Missal collects.

I have no recollection of any mention of the collects or lectionary during my four years in theological college, but, when I emerged in the early 1970s into church ministry, drafts of what would become the 1975 *MSB* were in experimental use. I was initially attracted to the 'themes' (mentioned above) that often linked the lections, but they were more appropriate on some Sundays than others. Methodist ministers always start their ministry in a new church on 1 September when, all too often, the theme for that Sunday or the following one was somewhat unfortunately 'The Suffering Community'. As a new minister and a hard-pressed preacher I also appreciated the fact that the themes offered an interpretative 'key' to the Scripture readings. I think it was then that I started using the collects on a fairly regular basis, particularly when using the Sunday Service with Holy Communion.

Another reason I started doing this was that the *MSB* offered a more significant role for the weekly collect, moving it from the Order for Morning Prayer, which was very rarely used, to the Communion service or the Sunday Service. Those parts of the service that were judged to be the basic elements were marked with an obelus in the margin. It is surprising that in the Preparation part of the service only the collect of the day is thus marked, and not the confession or forgiveness. Although most Methodist congregations only celebrate Holy Communion once a month, they started using this service more often than they had used Morning Prayer, so both the use of collects and their place in people's spiritual awareness were likely to have increased.

The use of Methodist books of worship has never been obligatory and, until recently, only a tiny minority of services would have been 'from the book'. The various Methodist worship books are authorized for use by the Methodist Conference, but whether or not they are used regularly, occasionally or never is a matter for the liturgical taste of the minister, or local preacher, and to a lesser extent that of the congregation.

The *Methodist Worship Book* 1999

The *MSB* was one of the earlier new British liturgical books of the second half of the twentieth century and it was soon judged to be short of a number of liturgies and deficient in style. Less than fifteen years after it was published, pressure rose in the late 1980s for a new service book, and the Methodist Conference approved the setting up of an extended Liturgical Sub-Committee of the Faith and Order Committee to prepare it. The *MSB* had been published five years before the Church of England's *Alternative Service Book 1980* (*ASB*), but the *Methodist Worship Book* predated *Common Worship* by only one year when it was published in 1999.[6] While the *ASB* and the *MSB* were joined at the hip as far as collects were concerned, as the result of both Churches broadly accepting the collects of JLG, there was no equivalent acceptance of a JLG document to keep them on parallel courses in the two new service books.[7] Both Churches used versions of the *Revised Common Lectionary* (*RCL*), but this did not contain collects that were linked with weekly readings. So the Anglican Liturgical Commission and Methodist Liturgical Sub-Committee drew apart in their choice of collects, both influenced by the increasing number of collects available in the world Church and in the works of individual writers.

The *MSB* had followed a two-year lectionary cycle and had offered only one collect for each Sunday, apart from special holy days. When work started on the *MWB*, no decision had been taken on which of two lectionaries the Methodist Church should adopt. The Revd Raymond George had championed the new JLG four-year lectionary, but

---

6 *Methodist Worship Book*, 1999, Peterborough: Methodist Publishing House.

7 JLG did produce a four-year lectionary, which was adopted for a few years by the Methodist and United Reformed Churches, but its use succumbed to the more ecumenical *RCL*.

to adopt it would have been, paradoxically, a less ecumenical decision than to join the other major Churches in adopting the three-year *RCL*.

As the 1999 *MWB* was following the three-year *RCL*, it was judged appropriate to increase the number of collects to two per Sunday (but not three except on a few special days). This meant that the number of collects doubled. There is no doubt that this increased the appropriateness of the collects for particular Sundays, but if a congregation only heard a collect read when Communion was celebrated once a month, a wider variety meant that collects could become increasingly unfamiliar because of the wider choice.[8] The guiding principle used in the choice of collects was that one of them would relate to or be appropriate for the season, while the other might relate to one of the lections. This was only a guiding principle and not every selection for a particular Sunday follows this pattern. I suspect that I have been very much in a minority of preachers who have included one of the Sunday collects at every weekly service, thus familiarizing congregations with them.

One notable feature of the *MWB* collects is that they reflect a wide variety of addresses to God, trying consciously to avoid a dominance of masculine terms and power images. Instead, they reflect gentler, more inclusive terms. Wesley's theological writings were shot through with Arminianism, and this is consciously reflected in the number of times words such as 'grace', 'gracious' and 'all' are used in the *MWB* collects, which are either selected or edited or written by Methodists. The *MWB*'s Methodist pedigree even extended to quoting Wesleyan hymnody in the address to God in some collects.

It is also worth noting that the *MWB* includes a number of traditional collects which constitute a sort of 'primer' or basic vocabulary of collects such as the Sunday next before Advent ('Stir up'), the collects for Advent and Ash Wednesday, which may be used over a whole season, and some of the gems from Augustine, Gregory the Great and Cranmer. Though most of these may have been edited slightly, they are recognizably collects, reminding Methodists of the tradition in which they stand.

As the number of collects in use has increased, it has become increasingly difficult to trace and acknowledge sources. Amendment has been

---

8 I was a member of the group that prepared the choice of collects for the *MWB*, so the value of a weekly collect rose considerably in my liturgical awareness. My colleague the Revd Don Pickard has an immense knowledge of collects and did much of the detailed work. He contributed helpful material in this chapter on the process by which the collects were selected and amended.

added to amendment; collects have been 'split' in two and parts of two different ones then joined together.[9] Surprisingly, the 1975 *MSB* makes no mention of the work of the JLG in its Acknowledgements, or of any copyright issues in respect of the collects it reproduced. When the 1999 *MWB* was published, far greater care was taken in acknowledging sources, although it is admitted that in the processes of writing and revision it is inevitable that copyright material may be used unacknowledged.

As previously mentioned, the *MWB* doubles the number of collects used, compared with the *MSB*. While the *MSB* drew on 12 sources, the *MWB* lists no less than 27 sources in its Acknowledgements. These include many of the major Churches, as each has borrowed from each other, and individual writers such as Frank Colquhoun, Janet Morley and John V. Taylor. The Methodist Liturgical Sub-Committee has also altered the majority of them in varying degrees. The calendar is filled out further with provision for Mothering Sunday (as well as the Fourth Sunday in Lent), Holy Saturday, and Easter Day until Easter Dawn, generally with appropriate collects.

Apart from the provision of two collects for each Sunday, there is a wide provision of additional collects for special occasions. These include: Christian Unity, 'for we are strangers no longer but pilgrims'; Church Anniversary and Harvest; and the commemoration of John and Charles Wesley. Perhaps surprisingly, the 1975 *MSB* did not contain any collects for Special Days, except All Saints' Day, so there is no Aldersgate Sunday collect.[10] As a collect concerning John and Charles Wesley is the nearest Methodism gets to a *sanctorale*, more detailed mention should be made of such collects.[11]

---

9 The Revd Neil Dixon, who chaired the Liturgical Committee that prepared *MWB*, has done a remarkable job in giving a detailed analysis of the sources of almost all the collects in the book. See Neil Dixon, 2003, *Wonder Love and Praise: A Companion to the Methodist Worship Book*, Peterborough: Epworth Press, pp. 191–225. He also contributed helpful comments on a draft of this chapter.

10 Wesley's conversion occurred on 24 May, and is commemorated on Aldersgate Sunday, if it falls on 24 May, or on the preceding Sunday. Wesley's conversion took place in Aldersgate in the City of London.

11 I am very grateful to Norman Wallwork for his help and guidance in this section on the various Wesley collects and for his comments on an earlier draft of this chapter.

John and Charles Wesley

In 1935 K. Vaughan Jones and others composed the following collect as the prayer of the newly formed Methodist Sacramental Fellowship (MSF).[12] It was lightly revised by A. S. Gregory.[13]

> Almighty God,
> who raised up your servants John and Charles Wesley
> to proclaim anew the gift of redemption
> and the life of holiness,
> be with us their children
> and revive your work among us;
> that, inspired by the same faith
> and upheld by the same grace
> in Word and Sacrament,
> we and all your people may be made one
> in the unity of Christ's Church on earth,
> even as in heaven we are made one in him;
> who is alive and reigns with you and the Holy Spirit,
> one God, now and for ever. Amen.

This collect had already been altered and improved by the MSF by the time it reached the 1999 *MWB* by ending the first sentence after 'holiness'. It continues, 'Pour out your Spirit, and revive your work among us . . .'. 'All your children' is preferred to 'all your people' later in the collect, and 'Christ's Church' becomes 'your church'. This well-structured collect draws together a number of Wesleyan themes: John's preaching of redemption, and his call to a life of holiness; the work of the Spirit and the importance of the sacraments; and the call to revival which is an echo of a popular evangelical hymn – though written by Albert Midlane (1825–1909) and not by Charles – 'Revive thy work O Lord'.

In 2007, Norman Wallwork further amended the prayer for MSF use, omitting the invocations for revival and unity, but expanding it to:

> Pour out upon us the gift of your Holy Spirit
> that we may honour you in word and sacrament

---

12 The original version was in 'thou' language.

13 Gregory added the words 'and the life of holiness', and amended the original 'in our midst' to 'among us'.

and serve you in the needs of our neighbour;
through Jesus Christ our Lord.

Two other Wesley collects should be mentioned. In 1938, J. E. Rattenbury composed the original of a prayer for Wesley Day. The modern-language version reads:

O God,
who plucked, as a brand from the burning,
your servant John Wesley,
that he might kindle anew among the people
the flame of your love;
grant such a warming to our hearts
that we may spread its holy fire
to the uttermost parts of the earth;
through Jesus Christ etc.

This collect, which regrettably was not included in the *MWB*, contains some interesting allusions. At the age of five years John Wesley was, in the nick of time, rescued from a fire at his parents' rectory (his father, like John himself, was an Anglican clergyman) and the event influenced his self-understanding and subsequent ministry. He spoke of himself as 'a brand plucked from the burning'; at the moment of his conversion he described his heart as being 'strangely warmed'; the repeated use of 'fire' imagery reflects the sign of the Holy Spirit at Pentecost; and 'uttermost parts of the earth' reflects Wesley's maxim 'I look upon all the world as my parish'. The collect inevitably suffers from the fact that it can only refer to John and does not include Charles the hymn-writer of Methodism.

Instead of using this collect, or an amendment of it, the *MWB* includes a second collect, this one drawn from the Society of Saint Francis' *Celebrating Common Prayer*, which balances the brothers' preaching and hymn-writing ministries, but is otherwise rather bland:

God of mercy,
who inspired John and Charles Wesley
with zeal for your gospel:
grant that all your people may boldly proclaim your word
and evermore rejoice in singing your praises;
through Jesus Christ our Lord. Amen.
(*MWB*, p. 563)

Another distinctive Methodist service, marked by two further collects, is Watchnight, a service held over midnight at the beginning of the New Year. Although the practice of Watchnight has died out in many parts of the country, it is widely and popularly celebrated in the inner city where there are Methodists from the Caribbean and particularly West Africa, countries in which a night vigil tradition has remained strong. The Liturgical Sub-Committee created the following collect:

> Lord of history,
> to whom a thousand years are as a day:
> renew us by your Holy Spirit,
> that, while we have life and breath,
> we may serve with courage and hope;
> through the grace of your Son,
> our Saviour Jesus Christ. Amen.
> (*MWB*, p. 563)

The collect echoes the words of Psalm 90 and Isaac Watts's hymn 'O God, our help in ages past', which is frequently sung at Watchnight, and it also recalls Methodism's twin emphases of renewal and Christian service.

The most liturgically distinctive Methodist service is the annual Covenant Service, usually held on the first Sunday of the New Year. Wesley did not provide a collect in his version of the Covenant Service, but the *MWB* contains a beautifully drawn collect. It is an amendment of the Covenant collect in the 1963 Church of South India *Book of Common Worship*, which had already been amended and printed in the 1975 *MSB*. It reads:

> God of grace,
> through the mediation of your Son
> you call us into a new covenant.
> Help us to draw near with faith
> and join ourselves in a perpetual covenant with you;
> through Jesus Christ our Lord. Amen.
> (*MWB*, p. 283)

The words echo the invitation before Communion, words of Charles Wesley and a reminder of the one with whom we enter into the covenant, thus 'collecting' together the themes of the service.

Local Preachers (trained lay people) fulfil a vital role in the worshipping life of the Methodist Church, taking about 70 per cent of all Methodist acts of worship. The office is a permanent one. At the Admission and Commissioning Service this collect is prayed:

Lord our God,
as we rejoice in the ministry of preaching,
let the Gospel of your Son come to us,
not in words alone, but in power and love;
that through our life and witness
the world may believe;
through Jesus Christ our Lord. Amen.
(*MWB*, p. 331)

The collect reminds us that preaching is both word and action, and again echoes John Wesley's maxim about the world as his parish.

In addition to the provision of such a wide variety of collects, the *MWB* offers a number of services new to a Methodist service book, many of which provide a space for a collect, with the rubric (generally after confession and forgiveness) 'The collect of the day or another suitable prayer'. The 'Welcome Service for Ministers, Deacons and Probationers' contains a fine prayer in extended collect form, which was composed by the Liturgical Sub-Committee:[14]

God of truth,
you are worthy of higher praise than we can offer,
and of purer worship than we can imagine.
By your Holy Spirit,
assist us in our prayers
and draw us to yourself,
so that what is lacking
in our thoughts and actions
and in our words and music,
may be supplied by your overflowing love;
through Jesus Christ our Lord. Amen.
(*MWB*, p. 365)

In the 'Confirmation and Reception into Membership' service a specific collect is offered:

---

14 Purists might argue that this is not a collect, but it follows the collect form so precisely that it has been included here, and it is a very fine prayer.

Living God,
may all who are baptised into Christ
be sustained by the Holy Spirit,
that through lives of faith and love
your grace may be known
and your name honoured;
through Jesus Christ our Lord. Amen.
(*MWB*, p. 98)

Similarly, there are collects, apart from the collect of the day, in the variety of seasonal Holy Communion services, including Advent, when one of the collects for the day is printed as part of the text. In fact, in almost every service where a collect is called for, the actual text of one is provided under the rubric 'The collect of the day, or this or some other prayer'. This grants the collect a highly visible profile. Each of the Holy Communion Orders has its own post-communion collect, many of them reflecting the deep Methodist understanding of the Eucharist.

Whereas the 1975 *MSB* marked the collect by an obelus because of its significance, in the 1999 *MWB*, the collect is marked with an asterisk. But significantly, in the Preparation section of the *MWB* Communion services, there are also asterisks for an opening sentence of Scripture, and confession and forgiveness, which suggests a better balance.

The Methodist 'Prayer Handbook'

Early in this chapter, I said that many Methodists were not familiar with collects because service books are rarely used and preachers rarely read a collect. It is appropriate to end this chapter by modestly revising this judgement, based on the experience of corporate worship, by mentioning the 'Prayer Handbook'. For over a hundred years this booklet (with a number of different titles and guises) has been produced every year. It is now published and distributed by the Methodist Publishing House on behalf of the Methodist Council, which appoints its editorial committee.

What is significant about it is its wide popularity among lay people in the Church. It has a print run of about 35,000 copies, which means that about one in ten British Methodists purchases a copy mainly for personal use at home. The Prayer Handbook is also often used by the leaders of the opening devotions at mid-week meetings and in most

Methodist centres for theological training.[15] Every year the handbook contains material for each day of the month, including a number of traditional collects drawn from a wide variety of sources, so users will, over a 12-month period, become familiar with collects in a way they may never have become familiar with simply by attending church worship.

It may just be that in modern Methodism the spirituality of the home is now a better 'carrier' of the collect tradition than Sunday worship has been through the 250 years of the Church.

---

15 It is interesting to note that there was a similar print run when there were nearly 1 million Methodists in this country. I am grateful to Michaela Youngson for the information on the Prayer Handbook. The increased provision of collects in recent years has been the handiwork of Norman Wallwork, who has been one of the most influential Methodist liturgists over the last 30 years.

5

The Collect in the United Methodist Church and its Antecedents

KAREN B. WESTERFIELD TUCKER

The history and use of collects by the United Methodist Church and its direct ecclesiastical ancestors illustrates the trajectory of the broader liturgical history of those denominations. Born in 1968 with the merger of the Methodist Church and the Evangelical United Brethren, the United Methodist Church has roots in Anglicanism, in German Lutheran, Reformed, Mennonite and Pietistic traditions, and in the 'free' revival experience associated with the 'Awakenings' in early modern America. Although it is a relatively young union denomination, the United Methodist Church's history is also that of the United States, for its antecedent denominations on both sides trace their lines to eighteenth- and early nineteenth-century Churches created shortly after the emergence of the new nation. Yet the United Methodist Church is not solely an American denomination; today its churches can also be found in parts of Europe, Asia and Africa. United Methodist churches outside of the United States, as circumscribed by geographic region, are permitted to develop liturgical materials (in their own languages) theologically consistent with the views and practices of the denomination as a whole. Faced with this assortment of liturgical resources, this study will only examine historic and current English-language texts formulated for use in the United States.

The Methodist family line

The Methodist Episcopal Church was established as an independent denomination on American shores in 1784. In the course of the nineteenth century, internal disagreement within the Church on various issues, including the authority of the bishop, the holding of slaves, the race and economic status of members, and the proper approach for the pursuit of Christian holiness, culminated in the creation of several new Methodist/Wesleyan denominations. Two of these denominations, in addition to the Methodist Episcopal Church, are direct ancestors of the United Methodist Church: the Methodist Protestant Church (1830) and the Methodist Episcopal Church, South (1844). In 1939, these three bodies reunited to form the Methodist Church. The liturgical practices and books of these four denominations constitute the background of the United Methodist Church on the 'Methodist' side.

The Methodist Episcopal Church, 1784–1939

Methodism existed in the American colonies by the 1760s, at first informally transplanted by Irish and British immigrants sympathetic to the evangelical movement spearheaded by John and Charles Wesley, and then formally cultivated when John Wesley sent European-born lay preachers and approved American-born preachers to promote the Methodist cause. Methodism from the outset was conceived as a 'society' within the Church of England, and as such expected its adherents to attend the parish liturgies taken from *The Book of Common Prayer* as well as the peculiarly (and largely unscripted) Methodist services of preaching, prayer, love-feast and watchnight. Thus immigrant Methodists may have tucked Prayer Books among their belongings, and even many of those who did not would have been familiar with phrases from the Prayer Book's collects, either directly from the liturgies or indirectly from the poetry of Charles Wesley. That Charles found inspiration for his hymns from the collects is without doubt, though given the scriptural dependency of the collects it is sometimes unclear whether his source is Scripture itself or the collect or perhaps both. For example, one stanza from the hymn 'O all-atoning Lamb, O Saviour of mankind', included originally in *Hymns on God's Everlasting Love* (2nd series, 1742), strongly alludes to the collect for Ash Wednesday in the 1662 Prayer Book, but also in part echoes the Wisdom of Solomon 11.24:

> Almighty and everlasting God, who hatest nothing that thou hast made and dost forgive the sins of all them that are penitent; create and make in us new and contrite hearts, that we, worthily lamenting our sins, and acknowledging our wretchedness, may obtain of thee, the God of all mercy, perfect remission and forgiveness; through Jesus Christ our Lord.

O may I love like Thee,
And in Thy footsteps tread!
Thou hatest all iniquity,
But nothing Thou hast made.
O may I learn Thy art,
With meekness to reprove,
To hate the sin with all my heart,
But still the sinner love.[1]

Some native-born Americans who affiliated with the Methodists chose to attend the Anglican parish church, but many did not on account of the absence of nearby churches, theological differences, the preference for a more informal liturgical style, and/or political (especially anti-English) convictions. For these Methodists, the only likely exposure to the Prayer Book collects would have been through allusions in hymns by the Wesleys or other evangelical Anglican hymn-writers, and through borrowed phrases that slipped into the regularly used and widely preferred offerings of extempore and spontaneous prayer made during Methodist worship. Thus when John Wesley's abridgement of the 1662 Prayer Book entitled *The Sunday Service of the Methodists in North America, with Other Occasional Services*[2] was approved as the Methodist 'prayer book' at the founding conference of the Methodist Episcopal Church in December of 1784, it had a mixed reception. The liturgies for the baptism of infants, baptism of those of 'riper years', solemnization of matrimony, communion of the sick, burial of the dead, and ordinations of deacons, elders and 'superintendents' (bishops) proved to be less problematic than Morning and Evening Prayer and the ante-communion in the Order for the Administration of the Lord's Supper. The Methodist elder (presbyter) and historian Jesse Lee records that in 'large towns' and 'some country places' prayers were 'read' on Sunday, and that in a few places parts of Morning Prayer were 'read' on Wednesdays and Fridays. What was read is likely to have included the ordinary and proper collects. But Lee also notes that

---

1 George Osborn (ed.), 1868, *The Poetical Works of John and Charles Wesley*, vol. 3, London: Wesleyan Methodist Conference Office, p. 79.

2 Originally published in London by William Strahan in 1784; available in facsimile with introduction and commentary by James F. White, 1991, as *John Wesley's Prayer Book: The Sunday Service of the Methodists in North America*, Cleveland OH: OSL Publications. See John Lampard's essay above, for a description of Wesley's abridgement in regard to the Prayer Book's collects.

soon Wesley's 'prayer book' was laid aside, in part because Methodists preferred to pray with their eyes closed rather than open.[3]

Following John Wesley's death in 1791, the Methodist Episcopal Church opted to revise Wesley's *Sunday Service*, and in 1792 brought out its abridgement. The liturgies for Morning and Evening Prayer were deleted in their entirety, as were also the tables of lessons and the 'Collects, Epistles, and Gospels, to be used throughout the Year'. Only a few brief rubrics were specified to guide the Methodist preaching services held in the morning, afternoon and evening of the Lord's Day; no printed prayers were provided. The liturgies for the Lord's Supper, baptisms, weddings, funerals and ordinations each received revision; the order for the communion of the sick, with its collect, was deleted. Most of the collect-structured prayers in the revised rites were retained (for example, the last in the series of prayers prior to the baptism of an adult – 'Almighty, ever living God, whose most dearly beloved Son Jesus Christ'), though some were edited or relocated. For example, although the sentences to be read during the collection of alms now began the Lord's Supper rite (the ante-communion being deleted), the Collect for Purity ('Almighty God, unto whom all hearts be open, all desires known, and from whom no secrets are hid'), which had previously come after the Lord's Prayer at the opening of the rite, was placed to follow the confession and prayer for forgiveness. In this new position the Collect for Purity was still identified with its heading, 'The Collect'. Similarly, the heading 'The Collect' is kept for the prayer at the conclusion of the burial rite ('O Merciful God, the Father of our Lord Jesus Christ, who is the resurrection and the life') and for the initial prayers in the ordination rites for deacons, elders and bishops.[4] The prayers at the end of the ordination rites are identified as collects by rubric only in the diaconal and presbyteral liturgies.[5] Thus most of the clergy would only regularly encounter the term 'collect' in two occasional rites, assuming that those printed and denominationally authorized (but not mandated) orders were, in fact, used. Yet because the liturgies (at first termed 'Sacramental Services, etc.' and later called

---

3 Jesse Lee, 1810, *A Short History of the Methodists in the United States of America; beginning in 1766, and continued till 1809*, Baltimore MD: Magill & Clime, p. 107.

4 When the Methodist Episcopal Church in 1864 changed the language from the 'ordination' of a bishop to a 'consecration', the ritual text was largely preserved and with it 'The Collect'.

5 The rubric in the presbyteral rite survives to 1939; the rubric in diaconal rite was dropped in 1932.

'The Ritual') were not published in a separate book but rather included in a section of the *Doctrines and Discipline of the Methodist Episcopal Church* that was purchasable by clergy and laity alike, it is possible that awareness of the collect form of prayer was not entirely lost.

Even though further revisions were made to all the liturgical texts in 'The Ritual' during the nineteenth century, 'The Collect' headings and their related prayers in the burial and ordination services endured into the twentieth century, as did the Collect for Purity in the Lord's Supper liturgy. The rubrical identification of the final collects in the two ordination rites persisted as well. No new collects so identified were added to 'The Ritual' during this period, but in 1888 the rubrics for Sunday worship were replaced by a fuller *ordo* that, in response to a call from some of the membership to 'enrich' public worship, gradually became more complex in succeeding years. To assist in adding 'dignity' to Methodist Episcopal worship, Charles S. Harrower in 1891 published a version of Wesley's abbreviated psalter that had been included with his *Sunday Service*. At the back of the book as part of the 'Addenda' that contained 'valuable portions of the *Sunday Service* of 1784', Harrower designated a section for 'Prayers and Collects', and included therein the previously abandoned collects for Morning and Evening Prayer among others.[6] Harrower's book had no official standing in the Church, but it was endorsed by a Methodist Episcopal bishop and printed by the denomination's publishers, and represented a growing interest within the Church in studying and recovering the Wesleyan liturgical heritage. In this vein, nine years after Harrower's book appeared, a commentary on and history of the Methodist Episcopal liturgy was distributed that 'there may be preserved among us the loyalty of intelligence to the legacy of our Fathers, and a deep and abiding veneration for the Sacred Rites of the Church of God'.[7] Author R. J. Cooke comments at length on the collects in the Lord's Supper, funeral and episcopal ordination rites, and even defines the collect for those unfamiliar with the form: 'A brief prayer in a collection of people, or a number of such petitions collected into one. Collects are as ancient as Liturgies, and Liturgies carry us back to primitive Christianity.'[8]

---

6 Charles S. Harrower (ed.), 1891, *Select Psalms, Arranged for the Use of the Methodist Episcopal Church by John Wesley*, New York: Hunt & Eaton; Cincinnati OH: Cranston & Stowe, esp. pp. 266–75.

7 R. J. Cooke, 1900, *History of the Ritual of the Methodist Episcopal Church: With a Commentary on Its Offices*, Cincinnati OH: Jennings & Pye; New York: Eaton & Mains, pp. 8–9.

8 Cooke, *History of the Ritual*, p. 249.

With the turn into the twentieth century, collects were affirmed by the leadership of the denomination to be both a historic and a living form of prayer as attested in the publication of such unauthorized resources as Charles LeVerne Roberts's *Divine Service: A Compilation of Collects and Psalms for Use in the Public Worship of God in the Methodist Episcopal Church* (1903)[9] and (Bishop) Wilbur P. Thirkield's *Service and Prayers for Church and Home* (1918, 1928).[10]

Given the plethora of liturgical resources in circulation by the late 1920s compiled or composed by Methodist Episcopal authors, as well as those by others inside and outside the United States,[11] it is no surprise that in 1932 the Methodist Episcopal Church authorized greatly expanded orders of service for Sunday worship that included specific prayer texts. Three distinct orders were provided, two of which contain collects printed for possible use. The collect in Order of Worship II appears as the first prayer, and is taken (either directly or from an intermediary; the redactors do not identify sources) from one of William Bright's original prayers published in his *Ancient Collects*:[12]

---

9 Charles LeVerne Roberts, 1903, *Divine Service: A Compilation of Collects and Psalms for Use in the Public Worship in the Methodist Episcopal Church*, Cincinnati OH: Jennings & Pye. In the Editor's Note, Roberts explains that 'except in a few instances', the collects are 'taken from Mr. Wesley's "Sunday Service"' (p. 5). These exceptions include collects for Thanksgiving Day, Missionary Day, national occasions, Children's Day and Temperance Day.

10 Wilbur P. Thirkield, 1918 and 1928, *Service and Prayers for Church and Home*, New York and Cincinnati OH: Methodist Book Concern, 1918; New York: Methodist Book Concern, 1928.

11 In his book *The Pastoral Office*, Methodist Episcopal author and college president James Albert Beebe named as exemplary W. E. Orchard's *The Temple* (1914) and Mary W. Tileston's *Prayers Ancient and Modern* (1897), both of which went through multiple printings. See James Albert Beebe, 1923, *The Pastoral Office: An Introduction to the Work of a Pastor*, New York: Methodist Book Concern, pp. 58, 68.

12 William Bright, 1864, 3rd edn, *Ancient Collects and Other Prayers*, Oxford and London: J. H. and Jas. Parker, p. 233. Bright's original prayers, including this one 'For the Spirit of Prayer', are, in his words, constructed 'in imitation of the ancient model'. The 1928 *Book of Common Prayer* of the Protestant Episcopal Church in the United States of America included a version of Bright's prayer among the 'Additional Prayers' in the 'Forms of Prayer to be used in Families', but it was not likely to have been a direct source for the Methodist Episcopal text which is precisely as Bright includes it in *Ancient Collects*. Bright's collection went through multiple printings and editions in the nineteenth and twentieth centuries, and remains in print in the twenty-first century.

Almighty God, from whom every good prayer cometh, and who pourest out, on all who desire it, the spirit of grace and supplication: deliver us, when we draw nigh to thee, from coldness of heart and wanderings of mind; that with steadfast thoughts, and kindled affections, we may worship thee in spirit and in truth; through Jesus Christ our Lord. Amen.

The third order, entitled 'An Order for Morning or Evening Prayer', which is identified as adapted from Wesley's *Sunday Service*, contains the Collect for Grace from Wesley's (and the 1662 Prayer Book's) Morning Prayer (with the slight addition of 'which' in the final phrase). At the conclusion of the order is a rubric indicating that for the evening office two collects are to be substituted for the Collect for Grace. The first is the third collect from Evening Prayer 'For Aid against all Perils' in *Sunday Service*, slightly edited. The second is the fourth collect among the series of collects printed at the end of the communion office in the 1662 Prayer Book (which a rubric states may be used after the collects of Evening Prayer), but which is not found in Wesley's revision of the Lord's Supper – though the prayer is found in all three ordination rites in the *Sunday Service* (assuming that the sacrament would have been celebrated previously at the event) and continued in the Methodist Episcopal ordinal:

Direct us, O Lord, in all our doings, with thy most gracious favor, and further us with thy continual help; that in all our works, begun, continued, and ended in thee, we may glorify thy Holy Name, and finally, by thy mercy, obtain everlasting life; through Jesus Christ our Lord. Amen.

The variant wording at the beginning of the prayer – the 1662 Prayer Book has 'Prevent us, O Lord' as did the prayers in the ordination rites prior to the 1932 revision[13] – may show the influence of the 1892 *Book of Common Prayer* of the Protestant Episcopal Church in the United States of America (and the 1789 book before it) which has 'Direct us, O Lord'.[14] The rationale for the inclusion of this prayer – and the particular source(s) from which the revisers drew – is not known.

---

13 The first part of the prayer in Latin is 'Actiones nostras quaesumus Domine et aspirando praeveni, et adjuvando prosequere'. The prayer was taken from the Sarum Missal and the latter portion of the text reworked for the 1549 Prayer Book.

14 In the 1789 and 1892 Prayer Books, 'Direct us' is the third in the series

In 1932, several of the continuing rites of the Methodist Episcopal Church also saw major readjustments, principally the addition of new material (for example, responsive readings and specified Scripture sentences or readings; no true collects were inserted) to provide both enrichment and flexibility. The five collects that had been passed down from 1784 were kept, though the heading was maintained only in the diaconal and presbyteral ordination rites (the heading in the episcopal consecration rite was conflated into a rubric). Dropped from the burial collect was the phrase referencing the 'general resurrection on the last day', a noteworthy change that very likely reflected shifting views about death in the Church and in the society at large.[15] A variety of new occasional rites were introduced, and a few of them contain collect-style prayers, though they are not identified as such (for example, in the orders for dedicating hospitals and educational buildings). Oddly, the Collect for Purity is placed in The Order for the Dedication of an Organ following the saying/singing of the Gloria Patri and the presentation of the instrument for dedication. A few slight adjustments were made to 'The Ritual' in 1936, and it is these texts that the Methodist Episcopal Church brought to the merger in 1939.

The Methodist Protestant Church, 1830–1939

With the publication of its first *Constitution and Discipline* in 1830, the Methodist Protestant Church differentiated itself from the Methodist Episcopal Church both structurally – Methodist Protestants had no bishops and after 1874 no deacons – and liturgically – they engaged in an innovative reconstruction of their ritual inheritance from the Methodist Episcopal Church, conflating many of the prayers and Scripture sentences, and casting them in a written approximation of a 'free' style. Each of the four collects identified as such in the Methodist Episcopal liturgies had a different fate. No reference or allusion remains

---

of collects at the end of the communion rite; the 1789 book did not include the prayer in any of the ordination rites, placing it instead in an Office of Institution of Ministers into Parishes or Churches. The Protestant Episcopal Church's revised Prayer Book of 1928 removed the prayer from the communion text, but the prayer continued in the Office of Institution. In 1932, this prayer in the Methodist Episcopal ordination and episcopal consecration rites was changed from 'Prevent us' to 'Direct us'.

15 On changing views towards death, see the chapter on 'Methodist Funerals' in Karen B. Westerfield Tucker, 2001, *American Methodist Worship*, New York: Oxford University Press, pp. 199–223.

in the Lord's Supper liturgy to the Collect for Purity. Phrases from the collect in the burial rite were broken up and scattered throughout a much longer, single prayer. The collect at the diaconal ordination survived as a separate prayer, though it was significantly altered, while material from the collect in the rite for elders was split up and inserted into two separate prayers with the first remaining in the form of a collect:

> Almighty God, giver of every good and perfect gift, mercifully behold these thy servants now set apart for the office and work of elders in thy church. Grant so to replenish them with the truth of thy doctrine, and adorn them with innocency of life, that both by word and good example, they may faithfully serve the church in this office, to the glory of thy name, and the edification of thy people, through the merits of our Saviour Jesus Christ. Amen.[16]

Other than the prayers in the ordination rites, the collect as a prayer form disappeared from the authorized texts of the Methodist Protestant Church, though by the end of the century those clergy who opted to utilize the official marriage liturgy were praying the collect-style prayer from the Form of Solemnization of Matrimony in the *Sunday Service* ('O Eternal God, Creator and Preserver of all mankind'), but with the reference to 'Isaac and Rebecca' removed. These three collects were the only representatives of the form that the Methodist Protestant Church brought to the union in 1939.

The Methodist Episcopal Church, South, 1844–1939

Whereas the Methodist Episcopal Church was willing to engage in ongoing revisions of 'The Ritual' throughout its history, even radically so in the 1930s, and the Methodist Protestants abandoned or recast the liturgical texts that they had previously known, the Methodist Episcopal Church, South steered a more conserving course. Though they revised their received texts and approved the publication of new rites throughout their history, their version of 'The Ritual' in place in 1939 retained the majority of the collects that they inherited at their founding in 1844. The prayers with the designated heading 'The Collect' were preserved in the rites for the Lord's Supper, burial, ordinations

---

16 Methodist Protestant Church, 1830, *Constitution and Discipline of the Methodist Protestant Church*, Baltimore MD: John J. Harrod, p. 104.

and consecration of a bishop,[17] and the final prayers in the diaconal ordination rites were still specified as collects. Another – and familiar – collect was added with the inclusion of a new rite: the Form of Laying the Corner Stone of a Church, introduced in 1870, included 'Prevent us, O Lord, in all our doings', the initial wording of which was not altered either in this rite or in the ordination/consecration liturgies.

Given the efforts of Thomas O. Summers, who arrived in the United States from England in 1830 and contributed to the denomination's work as pastor, professional theologian, and editor for their publishing house, it is remarkable that more collects were not introduced into the official liturgy printed in the Church's book of *Doctrines and Discipline*.[18] In 1859, Summers produced *The Golden Censer: An Essay on Prayer, with a Selection of Forms of Prayer, Designed to Aid in the Devotions of the Sanctuary, Family, and Closet*,[19] which assembled a variety of prayer types, including collects from the 1662 Prayer Book: A Collect before the Lessons and Sermon; Collects after Sermon (four); collects for Advent, Christmas, Lent, Good Friday, Easter Day, Ascension Day, Pentecost and Trinity Sunday; Collects for Peace (two); 'Collect for Grace – Morning Prayer'; Collect for aid against all Perils – Evening Prayer; and Miscellaneous Collects (14).[20] Although Summers never gave a precise rationale for the collects selected, he provided a hint in part of his essay on prayer in which he justified the use of print prayer forms to his Methodist colleagues wary of such 'formality':

> Human compositions, prepared as aids to devotion, may be used with great advantage. The forms of the English liturgy stand foremost in this category. Many of those admirable prayers are expressed in the language of Scripture, and are exceedingly good to the use of edifying. Being provided with suitable words of prayer, the mind can

---

17 The Methodist Episcopal Church, South changed the episcopal rite from 'ordination' to 'consecration' in 1870, six years after the Methodist Episcopal Church.

18 For Summers's liturgical contributions, see L. Edward Phillips, 1989, 'Thomas Osmond Summers: Methodist Liturgist of the Nineteenth Century', *Methodist History* 27(4), pp. 241–53.

19 Nashville: Southern Methodist Publishing House, 1859.

20 The selection of collects for the church year were perhaps intended to fill in a liturgical gap since the Church's official rites contained no such references, and the denominationally sanctioned hymnal only made limited connections to the church year through a subject index. It is notable that Summers took these prayers from the Church of England's Prayer Book; elsewhere in the collection, he records the source of some family prayers as the 'Liturgy of [the] Protestant Episcopal Church'.

bring all its powers to bear upon the more strictly devotional work of stirring up the affections, in which principally consists the spirit of prayer. There has been too much stiffness in rejecting, as well as too much strictness in using, written or printed forms of prayer and praise. Some denounce extemporaneous devotion as unbecoming in an approach to the Majesty of the universe; for them every thing must be prepared beforehand, and if they have not their book they can neither sing nor pray. Others will tolerate nothing of the sort – not even the use of David's Psalter; or, if that, nothing beside the Psalter, and that in the most literal translation possible. The true course lies between the extremes. We may avail ourselves of prepared forms as aids to devotion. It will be all the better if they are lodged in our memories, so that we may with the greater readiness use them as the clothing of our ideas and emotions, in connection with words of our own, which will be spontaneously suggested to our minds. We humbly conceive that in this way, which recommended by many churches, – the Methodist churches in particular, – we may most effectually use this means of grace, praying with the Spirit and with the understanding also.[21]

As if to accentuate further the role of the collect in both public and private prayer, Summers brought out in 1867 an edition of Wesley's *Sunday Service* that contained the orders for Morning and Evening Prayer and the 'Collects, Epistles, and Gospels, to be used throughout the Year' lost in 1792. The previous year, in 1866, the denomination had approved the new version of the *Sunday Service* for optional use in 'any congregation that may choose to use it',[22] and there is evidence that some congregations took up the opportunity. Since the authorization of the 1867 *Sunday Service* was never rescinded, at the time of merger it was thus the Methodist Episcopal Church, South that brought to the table the largest 'official' collection of collects of any of the three denominations.

The Methodist Church, 1939–1968

Although the liturgical influences of the Methodist Protestant Church and the Methodist Episcopal Church, South are evident in the materials produced at the time of the creation of the Methodist Church in

---

21 Summers, *The Golden Censer*, pp. 31–2.
22 T. O. Summers (ed.), 1867, *The Sunday Service of the Methodist Episcopal Church, South*, Nashville TN: A. H. Redford, p. 5.

1939, it is the texts from the Methodist Episcopal Church that dominate the new Church's Orders of Worship and The Ritual found under the general heading Worship and Ritual in the *Discipline*.[23] To the collects that had been present in the Methodist Episcopal Church's liturgical resources from 1932 were added several more in a discrete section of Worship and Ritual entitled 'Aids to Individual and Congregational Devotion'. Therein the Collect for Purity and Bright's collect, 'Almighty God, from whom every good prayer cometh', show up in a subsection of Invocations – as well as in their 1932 locations. Of the ten collects in a subsection of Prayers and Collects, all but one can be traced to the 1662 Prayer Book,[24] though that book may not have been what was used as their direct source. The lone collect not from the Prayer Book was an original by William Bright in his *Ancient Collects*:[25]

> O God, by whom the meek are guided in judgment, and light riseth up in darkness for the godly, grant us, in all doubts and uncertainties, the grace to ask what Thou wouldst have us to do, that the spirit of wisdom may save us from all false choices, and that in Thy light we may see light and in Thy straight path may not stumble; through Jesus Christ our Lord. Amen.

In 1944, the Church authorized the publication of the *Book of Worship for Church and Home*, the first official and discrete worship book for Methodists since Wesley's *Sunday Service*,[26] and intended for public, family or small group, and private prayer. The *Book of Worship* is organized into six major units – Orders of Worship for General Use, Orders of Worship for Occasional Use, Aids in the Ordering of

---

23 Methodist Church, 1939, *Doctrines and Discipline of the Methodist Church 1939*, New York: The Methodist Publishing House, pp. 487–648.

24 The collects are, in the sequence found in the 1939 'Aids': the Collect for Grace from Morning Prayer; the Collect for the Second Sunday in Advent; the collect-style absolution in the Lord's Supper rite; the Collect for the Twenty-fourth Sunday after Trinity; the Collect 'Direct Us, O Lord' previously discussed; the Collect for the First Sunday after Epiphany; the Prayer of Saint Chrysostom; the Collect for Peace at Evening Prayer ('O God, from whom all holy desires'); and a prayer from the series of collects at the end of the communion office ('Grant, we beseech Thee, Almighty God') entitled in the 1939 materials 'For Use After the Sermon'.

25 Bright, *Ancient Collects*, p. 234.

26 The denomination continued through 1964 to publish in its *Discipline* general orders of worship, and the rites for Christian initiation and membership, the Lord's Supper, marriage, burial and ordination.

Worship, Aids to Personal and Family Devotion, The Ritual, and The Ministry to the Sick – and collects are abundant in every unit,[27] with numerous examples of them in sections of Prayers and Collects among the resources provided for days and seasons of the Christian year in the Aids in the Ordering of Worship. This inclusion of extensive liturgical material for the church calendar was an innovation, as no antecedent denomination had made such an offering in an authorized resource except for the Methodist Episcopal Church, South by its publication in 1867 of the *Sunday Service*. There was a peculiarity in the calendar, however: the season of 'Kingdomtide', which originated in the Federal Council of the Churches of Christ in America (in which Methodists played a key role), was intended thematically to emphasize the Kingdom of God on earth during the 13 or 14 Sundays at the end of the long season after Pentecost and Trinity.[28]

Some of the sources from which the collects and other prayers came are identified: the Acknowledgments at the end of the book cite 38 liturgical books or collections of prayers that were drawn upon; and the Index of First Lines in a few cases names the particular book from which a prayer was borrowed. For example, a collect for Easter Day taken from Walter Russell Bowie's *Lift Up Your Hearts*,[29] reflects the theological tenor of the time.

> Almighty and everlasting God, who didst turn the despair of the disciples into triumph by the resurrection of Christ; give us faith to believe that every good which hath seemed to be overcome by evil, and every love which hath seemed to be buried in darkness and death, shall rise again to life immortal; through the same Jesus Christ, who liveth with thee for evermore. Amen.[30]

---

27 The sudden popularity of the collect may have received some impetus from Methodist author Clarence Seidenspinner, who wrote, 'No form of prayer can express quite so nicely as the collect a single idea and petition'. See C. Seidenspinner, 1941, *Form and Freedom in Worship*, Chicago and New York: Willett, Clark & Co., p. 73. Seidenspinner was not a part of the commission designated to produce the *Book of Worship*.

28 On the origins of Kingdomtide, see Westerfield Tucker, *American Methodist Worship*, pp. 52–3.

29 Russell Bowie, 1939, *Lift Up Your Hearts*, New York: Macmillan Co.

30 The Methodist Church, 1944 and 1945, *The Book of Worship for Church and Home: With Orders for the Administration of the Sacraments and Other Rites and Ceremonies According to the Use of The Methodist Church*, Nashville TN: The Methodist Publishing House, p. 177.

The attentiveness of the commission that produced the *Book of Worship* to international liturgical developments is evident in the selection of a prayer from the *Book of Common Order of the Church of Scotland*[31] that was placed among Family Prayers:

> O Lord our God, who art in every place, and from whom no space or distance can ever part us; take into thy holy keeping those from whom we are now separated, and grant that both they and we, by drawing near to thee, may be drawn nearer to one another, in Jesus Christ our Lord. Amen.[32]

A prayer included in the section on Ministry to the Sick was borrowed from a resource produced by the Episcopal Church's recently founded Forward Movement:[33]

> O Lord, holy Father, by whose lovingkindness our souls and bodies are renewed; mercifully look upon this thy servant, that, every cause of sickness being removed, *he* may be restored to soundness of health; through Jesus Christ our Lord. Amen.[34]

The Methodist Church in 1956 determined to revise its successful *Book of Worship*, and in 1964 gave final approval to another *Book of Worship* 'to help further meet an awakened and growing need'.[35] Collects are plentiful throughout this book, and the single heading 'Collect' stands under most entries for the seasons and days of the liturgical year. As liturgical scholar James F. White observed, 'The BW [*Book of Worship*] may not make clear rubrically as to how the proper collects are to be used, but at least it supplies a magnificent collection of them. Some of them date from the sacramentaries of the sixth century.'[36]

---

31 Oxford: Oxford University Press, 1940.

32 *Book of Worship*, p. 327.

33 Forward Movement of the Episcopal Church, 1943, *Prayers Old and New*, 5th edn, Sharon PA: Forward Movement of the Episcopal Church. For a brief history of the Forward Movement, see their website: http://forwardmovement.org/forward-movement-story.html.

34 *Book of Worship*, p. 512.

35 The Methodist Church, 1964 and 1965, *The Book of Worship for Church and Home: With Orders of Worship, Services for the Administration of the Sacraments, and Aids to Worship According to the Usages of The Methodist Church*, Nashville TN: The Methodist Publishing House, Preface.

36 James F. White, 1970, 'The Order of Worship: The Proper Parts', in William F. Dunkle, Jr. and Joseph D. Quillian, Jr. (eds), *Companion to The Book of Worship*, Nashville TN and New York: Abingdon, p. 40.

Unfortunately, the specific source or origin for individual prayers is not provided within the book.

Many long-familiar collects remained in this, the final liturgical resource officially produced by the Methodist Church. Bright's collect 'Almighty God, from whom every good prayer cometh' appears as the Invocation in the Order of Worship: Complete Form; the Collect for Grace is the stipulated 'Collect' later in the same order. The Collect for Purity has kept its place at the beginning of the Lord's Supper liturgy. Although it is no longer named specifically as a collect, the prayer, 'O merciful God, the Father of our Lord Jesus Christ, who is the resurrection and the life', continues as an option among several prayers at the conclusion of the burial rite. The opening prayers in the diaconal and presbyteral ordination rites and in the episcopal consecration rite still are identified as collects and, with the exception of a slight change in word order in the deacon and elder rites, and the removal of a few words in the episcopal rite, remain as Wesley sent them in 1784.

The history of collects in the 'Methodist' line leading up to the United Methodist Church can thus be summarized as one of rejection and recovery as well as of continuity and expansion.

The Evangelical United Brethren family line

The roots of the Evangelical United Brethren Church, like those of the Methodist Church, go back to the 1760s in the American colonies and to the evangelical revivals of that period. German-speaking persons also experienced 'awakening', among them three from Pennsylvania: Philip William Otterbein, a German Reformed minister; Martin Boehm, a Mennonite; and Jacob Albright, a Lutheran. Otterbein and Boehm were founders of what in 1800 became the Church of the United Brethren in Christ. Albright organized a group in 1803 first known as 'Albrights' People' (*Die Albrechtsleute*), and, in 1816, officially named the Evangelical Association (*Evangelische Gemeinschaft*). Both of these Churches had friendly affiliations with the Methodists and with each other from their beginnings. Dissent within the Evangelical Association caused the emergence in 1892 of the United Evangelical Church; the two were reunited in 1922 as the Evangelical Church. Controversy among the United Brethren in 1889 split the denomination into two groups that became known as the Church of the United Brethren in Christ (New Constitution) and the Church of the United Brethren in Christ (Old Constitution); the latter body was led by Bishop Milton Wright, father of the aeronautical Wright brothers, and still exists as an independent denomination. In 1946, the Evangelical Church and the Church of the United Brethren in Christ (New Constitution) merged to form the Evangelical United Brethren Church. The liturgical practices and books of those denominations that figure as ancestors of the United Methodist Church will be examined as well as possible, given the limited availability of materials for the Evangelical Church and its antecedents. The actual pastoral usage of these formulations cannot be known, for, as was true with the liturgical resources in the Methodist line, these texts were considered to be optional.

The Church of the United Brethren in Christ, 1800–1946

The history of printed collects in the liturgical resources of the Church of the United Brethren in Christ and after 1889 in the 'New Constitution' Church is quite brief – for there were no collects. The denomination's *Origins, Doctrine, Constitution and Discipline* of 1861, for example, contained printed orders only for the ordination of an elder and for a marriage ceremony, and in neither of them are there formulated prayer texts, just rubrics inviting prayer. By the time of the printing of the last *Discipline* in 1941, some worded prayers were included in the rites contained in the section of 'Formulas and Forms', but the decided preference remained for extemporaneous or spontaneous prayer.

The Evangelical Association, the United Evangelical Church, and the Evangelical Church, 1803–1946

The history of the collect is less brief in this part of the family tree, but still not substantial. At least from 1868 onwards the Evangelical Association included within the marriage rite the collect 'O eternal God, Creator and Preserver of all mankind' found in the 1662 Prayer Book and in the rites of episcopal Methodism, though the reference to 'Rebecca and Isaac' apparently disappears from the United Evangelical Church's service[37] and is not found in the Evangelical Church's rite. For the Evangelical Association and the Evangelical Church, this prayer seems to be the only true collect contained in their entire Ritual. The United Evangelical Church, at least in 1916, also had collects in the ordination rites for deacons and elders that, except for a slight

---

37 Only a single copy of the *Doctrines and Discipline* of the United Evangelical Church, from 1916, was available to the author.

change in wording, were similar to ones in the ordinals of episcopal Methodism.

The indebtedness of this family to the liturgies of Anglicanism and/or episcopal Methodism is evident in other rites, though all three denominations chose to conflate individual prayers into longer constructions in imitation of a 'free' style similar to that used by the Methodist Protestants. Thus the wording of some collects survived in new prayers as the result of fragmentation, implantation or expansion. The prayer prior to the distribution of communion in the Evangelical Association's Lord's Supper rite of 1868 (which is identified by rubric as a confession) divides up the Collect for Purity throughout a longer text including part of the Prayer of Humble Access and Confession from the BCP Order for Holy Communion. The prayer reads in part:

> We are not worthy so much as to gather up the crumbs under thy table; for we have provoked thy just wrath and indignation against us, by our manifold sins and transgression, which we have committed by thought, word and deed, against thy holy Majesty; but thou art yet the same God, whose property it is, always to have mercy – who of thy great mercy hast promised forgiveness of sins to all them that, with hearty repentance and true faith, turn to thee – unto whom all our desires are known, and from whom no secrets are hid: Have mercy on us, have mercy on us, most merciful Father, for thy Son, our Lord Jesus Christ's sake, and let all our transgressions be cast behind thee into the sea of forgetfulness, and never more come into the light of thy countenance; and cleanse thou the thoughts of our hearts by the inspiration of thy Holy Spirit more and more, that we may perfectly love thee, and worthily magnify thy holy Name.[38]

The United Evangelical Church's rite of 1916 took a similar approach in overall style, but embedded the collect, thereby yielding a different result in part of its prayer:

> Forgive us all that is past, and grant, O merciful Father, for Christ's sake, that we may ever hereafter serve and please Thee in newness of life, to the honor and glory of Thy Holy Name. Almighty God, unto Whom all hearts are open, all desires known, and from Whom no

---

38 Evangelical Association, 1868, *The Doctrines and Discipline of the Evangelical Association*, Cleveland OH: W. W. Orwig for the Evangelical Association, pp. 97–8. Substantially the same prayer, with some word changes, was published in the Church's *Doctrines and Discipline* of 1913.

secrets are hid; cleanse the thoughts of our hearts by the inspiration of Thy Holy Spirit, that we may perfectly love Thee, and worthily magnify Thy Holy Name through Jesus Christ our Lord. Almighty God, our Heavenly Father, Thou, of Thy tender mercy, didst give Thine only Son, Jesus Christ, to suffer death upon the cross for our redemption, and He there, by the oblation of Himself, once offered, made a full, perfect, and sufficient sacrifice, and satisfaction for the sins of the world; and instituted, and in His gospel commanded us to continue, a memorial of His precious death until His coming again.[39]

A prayer in the Evangelical Church's burial rite expanded and reworked the original collect:

Merciful God, Father of our Lord Jesus Christ, who is the Resurrection and the Life; we humbly beseech thee, by thy blessed Son, Our Lord Jesus Christ, the Prince of life and glory, that thou wouldst raise us from the death of sin unto the life of righteousness, that when we are called upon to depart this life, we may rest in Him who is our hope, and that in the general resurrection at the last day we may be found in Him and receive from Him the gift of eternal life. Comfort and sustain those who mourn and grant that they too may at last inherit with those who have gone on before, the Kingdom of our Lord Jesus Christ, and that we, all together, may hear thee say to us, Come, ye blessed of the Lord, enter with joy, into the Kingdom prepared for you from the foundation of the world. Grant unto us these and all other mercies, O merciful Father, for the sake of Jesus Christ, our risen Lord and Redeemer. Amen.[40]

---

[39] United Evangelical Church, 1916, *The Doctrines and Discipline of the United Evangelical Church*, Harrisburg PA: Board of Publication of the United Evangelical Church, pp. 117–18. The Evangelical Church's prayer (still called a confession) continues in the same overall style – and with a partial quotation of the Collect for Purity – and although there are similarities with the prayers of its predecessors, is a differently formulated prayer.

[40] Evangelical Church, 1923, *Doctrines and Discipline of the Evangelical Church 1923*, Cleveland OH and Harrisburg PA: Evangelical Publishing House, p. 101. The prayer in this form seems to have persisted throughout the life of the denomination.

The Evangelical United Brethren Church, 1946–1968

Because of their shared theological and missional convictions, the Church of the United Brethren in Christ and the Evangelical Association (later Evangelical Church) for decades discussed the possibility of a merger. These conversations became more serious in the 1920s, and by 1942 a *Discipline* for the Evangelical United Brethren Church containing liturgical and other materials was produced by the Joint Commission on Church Federation and Union, even though formal union would not be consummated for four more years. The contents of the Ritual of 1942, which is essentially preserved in the Church's first official *Discipline* (1947), is markedly different from the formulations of the two predecessor Churches – there is an unmistakable indebtedness to the English Prayer Book tradition to a greater degree than already found in the 'Evangelical' line – though the influence of the former liturgical styles remains evident. Although the collects in this new Ritual are not numerous, they are nonetheless present distinctly as collects rather than as embedded material in longer prayers. A collect is said after an adult has been baptized, and two collects appear in the two different forms for Holy Communion: the Collect for Purity (Communion Collect) in the longer form, and the Prayer of Saint Chrysostom (Prayer of Invocation) in the shorter. The Collect for Purity also makes an appearance in the order for the Installation of a Conference Superintendent. Longer and shorter forms of the marriage rite contain the collect 'O Eternal God, Creator and Preserve of all mankind'. The collect at the beginning of the Ordination of Elders would be familiar to members of the Methodist Church, as would the first phrases of the Invocation at the Installation of a Bishop, though the petition is changed.

With the publication of the Church's *Discipline* of 1951, collects disappeared from adult baptism, the short form for Holy Communion, and the installation of the superintendent. To the remaining collects from 1947 were added several in the revised order for a Christian funeral, including a text of unknown origin:

> Almighty God, our eternal refuge and strength, grant unto us thy blessing in this hour. Lift our vision beyond the shadows of this world and help us to see the light of eternity that our spirits may grow calm and our hearts be comforted through Jesus Christ our Lord.[41]

---

41 Evangelical United Brethren Church, 1951, *The Discipline of the Evangelical United Brethren Church*, Dayton OH: The Otterbein Press; Harrisburg PA: The Evangelical Press, p. 480.

These were the collects in the Church's Ritual contained in the *Discipline* at the time of the merger with the Methodist Church. But the denomination had, in 1957, published another official liturgical resource containing collects: its hymnal. The Aids to Worship at the back of the book include three collects among the Invocations (the Collect for Purity, the Prayer of Saint Chrysostom, and Bright's 'Almighty God, from whom every good prayer cometh') and at least two among the general Prayers, one designated for use with the collection of monies and another ascribed to nineteenth-century British poet Christina G. Rossetti:

> Almighty God, whose loving hand hath given us all we possess, grant us grace that we may honor thee with our substance, and remembering the account we must one day give, may be faithful stewards of thy bounty, through Jesus Christ, Our Lord. Amen.
>
> O Lord, Shield of our help, who wilt not suffer us to be tempted above that we are able, help us, we entreat thee, in all our straits and wrestlings, to lift up our eyes unto thee, and stay our hearts on thee; through Jesus Christ, our Lord. Amen.[42]

If the history of collects in the Methodist line was one of rejection and recovery, continuity and expansion, then for the Evangelical United Brethren it was one of discovery.

The United Methodist Church, 1968–

Rather than rush to produce worship materials for the new United Methodist Church, especially given the liturgical ferment in the aftermath of the Second Vatican Council, the decision was taken to continue the official liturgical texts of both the Evangelical United Brethren Church and the Methodist Church while supplementary and experimental texts were produced in anticipation of larger collections of resources. In 1989 the authorized *United Methodist Hymnal* was published which, besides hymns, contains a limited number of rites, most of which bear little resemblance to their antecedents and instead carry stronger affinities with the liturgical – and ecumenical – consensus of the time. Among them is a paradigmatic order of Word and Table for

---

42 Evangelical United Brethren Church, 1957, *The Hymnal of the Evangelical United Brethren Church*, Dayton OH: The Board of Publication, The Evangelical United Brethren Church, nos. 521 and 524.

Sunday worship that includes as the opening prayer in Service I the Collect for Purity in a modernized version. Single prayers are interspersed throughout the hymns as convenient fillers of white space, but with a thematic linkage to the hymns nearby. Many of these prayers, particularly those related to the church year, are collects, some borrowed or adapted from sources such as *The Book of Common Prayer* and the *Lutheran Book of Worship* of the Evangelical Lutheran Church in America, and others composed for the book by United Methodist authors. One collect by the late Fred D. Gealy, New Testament scholar and hymnologist, picks up themes from the Wesleyan hymn tradition and from James 1.22:

> Glorious God, source of joy and righteousness,
> enable us as redeemed and forgiven children
>   evermore to rejoice in singing your praises.
> Grant that what we sing with our lips
>   we may believe in our hearts
> and what we believe in our hearts
>   we may practice in our lives;
> so that being doers of the Word and not hearers only,
>   we may receive everlasting life;
> through Jesus Christ our Lord. Amen.[43]

Several collects for the liturgical year were written by Laurence Hull Stookey, a former professor of homiletics and liturgics. The prayer for the Day of Pentecost alludes to the denomination's 'warmed heart' evangelical tradition:

> God of grace,
> you sent the promised gift of the Holy Spirit
>   upon the apostles and the women,
>   upon Mary the mother of Jesus and upon his brothers.
> Fill your church with power,
>   kindle flaming hearts within us,
>   and cause us to proclaim your mighty works in every tongue,
>   that all may call on you and be saved;
> through Jesus Christ our Lord. Amen.[44]

---

[43] United Methodist Church, 1989, *The United Methodist Hymnal: Book of United Methodist Worship*, Nashville TN: The United Methodist Publishing House, no. 69.

[44] United Methodist Church, *Hymnal*, no. 542.

With the publication in 1992 of *The United Methodist Book of Worship* – the current book – United Methodists possess ritual texts reworked in the light of recent liturgical scholarship and theological emphases, though, as was the case in the predecessor denominations, none of these texts is mandatory. Rites for new occasions (such as miscarriage), some containing collects, are bound with long-standing occasional services – though these now are framed in a new language that does not include the old collects. Hints of a bygone collect are all that remain in the first line of a prayer in the consecration rite for bishops:

> Almighty God, by your Son Jesus Christ and the Holy Spirit
>   you gave to your apostles many excellent gifts.
> Give your grace to all servants of your Church,
>   that we may with diligence and faithfulness
> fulfil our various ministries.
> Grant that we your people may follow where you lead
>   and live in joyful obedience to your will;
> through Jesus Christ our Lord. Amen.[45]

In this book the collect does not have the pride of place that it did in the two worship books of the Methodist Church. But it is still quite present. A page is devoted to teaching the history and structure of the collect form, using the Collect for Purity as an example.[46] The Methodist Church contributed its rediscovery of the riches of the church year to this volume, and in the resources for the year collects can be found. Collects are scattered among the prayers in the section of General Acts of Worship, and are drawn from an array of identified sources representing different times, places and ecclesiastical traditions. The Roman Catholic *Book of Blessings* has representative collects in this United Methodist book, as does the Presbyterian Church of South Africa.

Conversations are underway about a revision of this book, and although the final product has yet to be determined, it is likely that collects will be included. Undoubtedly the Collect for Purity will be among them, for it alone of all the collects connects the denomination's past to its present and unites the prayer of God's people on earth with that of the saints above.

---

45 United Methodist Church, 1992, *The United Methodist Book of Worship*, Nashville TN: The United Methodist Publishing House, p. 700.
46 United Methodist Church, *Book of Worship*, p. 447.

THE COLLECT IN THE UNITED METHODIST CHURCH

Almighty God,
to you all hearts are open, all desires known,
   and from you no secrets are hidden.
Cleanse the thoughts of our hearts
   by the inspiration of your Holy Spirit,
that we may perfectly love you,
   and worthily magnify your holy name,
through Christ our Lord. Amen.

6

The Collect in American Lutheran Liturgical Books: *Evangelical Lutheran Worship* (2006)

FRANK C. SENN

This chapter discusses the collects in American Lutheran Liturgy up to and including *Evangelical Lutheran Worship* 2006 (*ELW*), the new primary worship resource of the Evangelical Lutheran Church in America (ELCA) and the Evangelical Lutheran Church in Canada (ELCiC).[1] The liturgical material in *ELW* is largely based on the orders and texts in the *Lutheran Book of Worship* of 1978 (*LBW*),[2] which was in continuity with previous Lutheran worship books in America, but which also reflected ecumenical liturgical work in North America during the 1970s. As we examine the collects now in use in *ELW*, it is necessary first to establish the tradition of the collect in Lutheran liturgy in general, and in American Lutheran worship books in particular. Collects in early American Lutheran liturgies were taken from German hymnals, and these were largely translations of Latin originals.

The origin and form of the collect

The collect is a form of prayer unique to the Western Church. Collects found in the prayer books (sacramentaries) that bear the names of celebrated Roman popes (Leonine [Verona], Gelasian, and Gregorian) reflect the business-like conciseness and theological clarity that are

---

[1] ELCA and ELCiC, 2006, *Evangelical Lutheran Worship*, Minneapolis MN: Augsburg Fortress.

[2] Board of Publications, Lutheran Church in America, 1978, *Lutheran Book of Worship*, Minneapolis MN and Philadelphia PA: Augsburg Publishing House.

hallmarks of Roman cultural expression.³ They are characterized by a simple four- or five-part structure: (1) address to God (*Deus*), but sometimes to Christ in the old Gallican prayers; (2) an attribute or action of God or Christ introduced by a *qui*-clause (*Deus, qui* – O God, who . . .); (3) a petition that states the purpose of the collect; (4) a reason for or a consequence of the petition (*ut* – 'so that'); and (5) a termination. Parts (2) and/or (4) are missing in many collects.

Some collects may express thanksgiving, but they still offer a petition. Josef Jungmann points out that, unlike Eastern prayers, the Latin collects get to the point with not a word of praise and they end without a doxology.⁴ There is normally only one petition per prayer, or two at most, connected with the word *et*. The old Roman prayers usually terminate simply 'through Christ our Lord' (*per Christum Dominum nostrum*). The emphasis is always on the mediatorial role of Christ. One would assume, therefore, that the collects are being addressed to God the Father, as in the Roman Canon, but the Latin collects seldom use the term *Pater*. Perhaps in response to the Arianism of the Gothic peoples who moved into the territory of the Roman Empire, the termination of collects was later expanded to 'through Jesus Christ, your Son, our Lord, who lives and reigns with you and the Holy Spirit, one God, world without end'.

The sacramentaries provided three collects for each Mass: a collect for the day, a collect at the offertory (the *secreta*), and a post-communion collect. However, the form of the collect became ubiquitous in the Western rite and collects are used in the prayer offices as well as occasional offices such as baptism, confirmation, marriage and burial.

Luther and Early Lutheranism

The collect remained an important liturgical form in historic Lutheran liturgies. Lutheran liturgical reform in the sixteenth century was conservative in that it retained whatever could be retained from medieval Catholic liturgy. Nils-Henrik Nilsson makes this point too, in relation

---

3 The Gelasian and Gregorian Sacramentary manuscripts were found in France and represent an importation and emendation of Roman Mass traditions. See Eric Palazzo, 1998, *A History of Liturgical Books from the Beginning to the Thirteenth Century*, tr. Madeleine Beaumont, Collegeville MN: The Liturgical Press.

4 Joseph A. Jungmann SJ, 1986, *The Mass of the Roman Rite: Its Origins and Development*, tr. Francis A. Brunner CSSR, vol. 1, Westminster MD: Christian Classics.

to Swedish liturgical reform.[5] It was radical in that it simply deleted elements that were deemed contrary to the gospel of justification by faith alone or the all-sufficiency of the atoning sacrifice of Christ, such as the offertory prayers and the Canon of the Mass. Lutheran Reformers used historic texts and made evangelical 'corrections' where necessary.

In this, as in other areas of reform, the example of Martin Luther, the prophetic figure of the Reformation, was influential. The only prayers in Luther's Latin *Order of Mass and Communion for the Church at Wittenberg* (1523) are the Kyrie eleison, the collect of the day, the eucharistic Preface, the Lord's Prayer, and the post-communion collect. (Some psalms, canticles and hymns, of course, are also prayers addressed to God.) Concerning the collect of the day, Luther writes: 'the prayer or collect which follows, if it is evangelical (and those for Sunday usually are), should be retained in its accepted form; but there should be only one'.[6] (Because of the complications of calendar and votive masses, late medieval Mass orders sometimes provided for multiple collects, up to a maximum of seven.)

Luther's *German Mass and Order of Service* (1526) followed the same order as the 1523 *Formula Missae et Communionis*, except that the parts of the ordinary of the Mass were rendered in German verse and set to chorale tunes for congregational singing.[7] The only prayers in this Mass order were the Kyrie eleison (threefold instead of ninefold), the prayer of the day, and Luther's original post-communion prayer, which has had a long history of use in Lutheran liturgies.[8] Even the Lord's Prayer in the *German Mass* was given only as a piece of catechetical instruction.

The collects for the day had to be translated into German. It seems that this project was accomplished over a period of time and in conjunction with the publication of hymnals.[9] Most of the collects, with versicles and responses, were appended to individual hymns, although some stood alone. Most of the collects were loose translations of historic collects for certain days in the church year, although Luther wrote a few original ones. It is noteworthy that Luther preferred addressing

---

5 See Chapter 2.
6 Ulrich S. Leupold (ed.), 1965, *Luther's Works*, vol. 53, tr. Paul Zeller Strodach, Philadelphia PA: Fortress Press, p. 23.
7 Leupold, *Luther's Works* 53, pp. 61–90.
8 Luther's post-communion prayer has appeared in all of the English-language communion services since the Common Service of 1888.
9 Leupold, *Luther's Works* 53, pp. 129–46.

God as 'Dear Lord God' (*Lieber Herr Gott*), rather than using the traditional Latin address to 'almighty God' (*Omnipotens Deus*) or 'almighty everlasting God' *(Omnipotens sempiterne Deus)*. For example, Luther's version of the collect for the second Sunday of Advent, '*Excita, domine, quaesumus, corda nostra*', is:

> Dear Lord God, awaken us so that when Thy Son cometh we may be prepared to receive him with joy and serve thee with clean hearts; through the same thy Son Jesus Christ our Lord.[10]

'Dear Lord God' expresses the intimate relationship with our heavenly Father that the Reformer preferred to the more formal relationship indicated by abstract attributes of God in the Latin collects (though these are lacking in this particular example). We note that this collect was appended to Luther's version of the hymn attributed to Saint Ambrose of Milan, 'Saviour of the Nations, come', which Luther renders 'Come, the Heathen's Healing Light'.[11] In the Lutheran tradition proper hymns of the day developed along with proper prayers of the day.

The orders of the Mass in the various German Church Orders of the sixteenth century follow the models of Luther's *Formula Missae* and *Deutsche Messe*, sometimes blending Latin and vernacular elements.[12] The classical Lutheran Mass orders always included the collect for the day. Here the traditional collects were retained in Latin or in free German translation. Some new occasions in the Church's calendar, such as celebrations of the anniversary of the Reformation, required new prayers. Again, it took time to translate or write the collects needed for the days in the Church's year. Thus we find fewer collects provided in the early Church Orders (only 27 in Brandenburg–Nuremberg 1533, to take one example), and more in the later Church Orders (nearly two hundred in Austria 1570). Viet Dietrich, a friend of Luther and pastor of Saint Sebaldus Church in Nuremberg, composed prayers fuller than the traditional collect form, and related to the Epistles and Gospels of the church year. Though, in Luther D. Reed's opinion, they

---

10 Leupold, *Luther's Works* 53, p. 131. The Latin original is V, 1125, in Leo Cunibert Mohlberg OSB (ed.), 1968, *Liber Sacramentorum Romanae Aeclesiae Ordinis Anni Circuli* (Cod. Vat. Reg. Lat. 316/Paris Bib. Nat. 7193, 41/56 – *Sacramentarium Gelasianum*), Rome: Casa Editrice Herder, p. 170.

11 Leupold, *Luther's Works* 53, pp. 235–6.

12 See the outlines of Mass orders in Frank C. Senn, 1997, *Christian Liturgy – Catholic and Evangelical*, Minneapolis MN: Fortress Press, pp. 332–8.

were 'limited in content and stereotyped in form',[13] they attained great popularity in Germany and Sweden and were used as 'text collects' in the pulpit before or after the sermon.

Collects were also needed for the morning and evening prayer offices for congregational use, which were styled Matins and Vespers. In the offices, the collects came after the Gospel canticle.[14] Sometimes there was just one collect for morning or evening, which might be taken from Luther's morning and evening prayers in the *Small Catechism*. Another morning prayer was the collect for grace ('O Lord . . . who has safely brought us to the beginning of this day: defend us this day with your mighty power . . .'), which was derived from the monastic office of Prime. A standard evening prayer was the collect for peace ('O God, from whom all holy desires, all good counsels, and all just works do proceed: give to your servants that peace which the world cannot give . . .'), found in the Gelasian Sacramentary. These collects for grace and for peace would later achieve a place in American Lutheran orders of Matins and Vespers, beginning with the Common Service of 1888.

Early American Lutheran liturgy

Lutheran settlers and pastors in the British North American colonies brought their hymnals and agendas with them. Since they came from different German territories, as well as from other countries, for example Sweden and the Netherlands, there was no common book or language used for worship. Henry Melchior Muhlenberg, sent from Halle to be a pastor in Pennsylvania, established the first Lutheran Church organization in the New World, the Ministerium of Pennsylvania, in 1748. One of the first acts of the Ministerium, meeting in Philadelphia, was to adopt a common liturgy that Muhlenberg had prepared, following the order of Saint Mary's German Lutheran Church in the Savoy district of London. This was a typical Lutheran Mass order that included a collect for the day and a closing collect, as well as a general prayer of thanksgiving and intercession or the Litany after the sermon (the position of intercessions in the late medieval pulpit office of Prone). The handwritten Muhlenberg liturgy lacked propers, such as collect, Epistle and Gospel. Pastors were advised to use the

---

13 Luther D. Reed, 1959, *The Lutheran Liturgy*, 2nd edn, Philadelphia PA: Fortress Press, p. 285.

14 Senn, *Christian Liturgy*, pp. 338–42, offers outlines of the orders of Matins and Vespers.

appropriate ones in the Marburg hymnal, which was widely used by Germans throughout the British colonies. Here we see the advantage of including collects in the hymnals. The hymnals were used for home devotions as well as for public liturgies and therefore the collects were also available for devotional use. Christopher Sauer of Germantown, Pennsylvania, printed an American edition of the Marburg hymnal in 1762, which, according to Reed, 'contained the historic Epistles and Gospels of the Church year and the series of collects by Viet Dietrich in his Nuremberg *Agenda-büchlein* (1543)'.[15]

The 1748 Liturgy remained in use for nearly forty years. At a meeting in 1782, after the American Revolution, the Ministerium resolved to print a new agenda and hymnal, which was adopted in 1786. The liturgy was drastically revised in a way that reflected the rationalism of the times. The historic collects for the day were omitted, as were the Gloria in excelsis and the Creed. The collect was replaced by a series of prayers prepared by a Dr Helmut. Permission was also given to the minister to pray *aus dem Herzen* (*ex corde* or spontaneously). However, the collects, Epistles and Gospels were missed by many and were consequently printed in an appendix in 1790, and reintroduced into the main body of the 1795 edition of the *Kirchen-Agenda*.

Rationalism and revivalism were in the ascendancy in early nineteenth-century America, and both movements are reflected in early nineteenth-century American Lutheran hymnals. The 1818 *Liturgie und Kirchen-Agenda* marked a further decline in the liturgical order. An English-language service was developed which could be used in congregations desiring to worship in English, but it represented a greater decline in the historic liturgical orders than the German orders. Songs of a revivalist character were introduced into English-speaking congregations, who lacked translations of the German hymns. Spontaneous prayers 'from the heart' were preferred to the historic collects or Litany. Realizing the inadequacy of liturgical material in English for Lutheran congregations, the General Synod appointed a committee in 1843 to translate the German liturgy into English. This was but a slight improvement.

The first signs of real improvement came in 1855, when the Ministerium of Pennsylvania resolved to translate into English a German liturgy based on the work being done in Germany. But there were serious dislocations from the historic order: the Introit was read by the minister after the Gloria in excelsis and before the collect for the day, and the introits and collects were not historical texts. Moreover,

---

15 Reed, *The Lutheran Liturgy*, p. 167.

the Epistle could be read after the Gospel, and the minister 'might' read the Creed. But this still represented an advance over the previous English-language liturgies.

Actually, work on English-language liturgy for Lutherans in America was becoming the cutting edge of Lutheran liturgical work. Ironically, classical Lutheran liturgical orders would be recovered in the English language more than in their languages of origin. This is evident in the *Church Book* of the General Council of the Lutheran Church, published in 1868, which was largely the work of Charles Porterfield Krauth and Beale Melanchthon Schmucker. The *Church Book* marked a return to the Muhlenberg-type liturgy of 1748. It included a series of collects for the Sundays and festivals of the church year and an anthology of collects for 'particular necessities and circumstances'.[16]

The Common Service (1888 and beyond)

The work of liturgical restoration evident in the *Church Book* was carried further in the preparation of the Common Service of 1888. This collaborative work of the three Lutheran Church organizations that were most established in America – the General Council, the General Synod and the United Synod of the South – was based on the principle of 'the common consent of the pure Lutheran liturgies of the sixteenth century, and when there is not an entire agreement among them the consent of the largest number of greatest weight'.[17] The 'three honored names' of the principal drafters of the Common Service were Beale Melanchthon Schmucker (1827–88), George Unangst Wenner (1844–1934), and Edward Traille Horn (1850–1915). The Common Service included the Sunday Morning Service (Ante-Communion) and the Service of Holy Communion, as well as Matins and Vespers, with all their propers, including collects.

Because the Common Service was officially adopted by each Church body for inclusion in its hymnal, there were variations in its texts and rubrics. A standard form of the Common Service was put into the *Common Service Book* (1917)[18] in anticipation of the merger of the

---

16 General Council of the Lutheran Church, 1868, repr. 1872, 1873, 1882, *Church Book for Use of Evangelical Lutheran Congregations*, Philadelphia PA: Lutheran Book Store.

17 Reed, *The Lutheran Liturgy*, p. 183.

18 United Lutheran Church in America, 1917, *Common Service Book of the Lutheran Church*, Philadelphia PA: The Board of Publication of the United

three sponsoring groups into the United Lutheran Church in America in 1918. But the Common Service was also adopted and used by the English Synod of Missouri in 1911, which merged with the Missouri Synod and thus brought the Common Service into that tradition. *The Lutheran Hymnal* of 1941 (*TLH*),[19] authorized by the Synodical Conference and used in the Lutheran Church-Missouri Synod (LCMS), was a variant of the Common Service with all its propers. Also, English-speaking congregations of the Iowa Synod, the Joint Synod of Ohio, the Norwegian Synods, the Augustana (Swedish) Synod, and the Icelandic Synod were given the option of using the Common Service or English translations of the synods' Swedish or Norwegian or Danish or Finnish or Icelandic liturgies. Translations of the Common Service into different languages by missionaries carried it into parts of Latin America, Africa, India and Japan.

Service Book and Hymnal (1958)

The ideal of 'one Church, one liturgy' for Lutherans in America, first articulated by Muhlenberg, was becoming a reality. A great stride forward was the formation of a Joint Committee on the Common Liturgy representing eight Lutheran Church bodies in North America. This Committee produced the *Service Book and Hymnal* (*SBH*) in 1958.[20] The eight bodies merged to form the American Lutheran Church in 1960 and the Lutheran Church in America in 1962, and the *SBH* marked the high-water mark of liturgical restoration.

In his classic commentary, *The Lutheran Liturgy*, published in 1947 and revised in 1959, Luther D. Reed provided the original texts and sources of all the collects and prayers in the *Common Service Book* and subsequently in the *SBH*.[21] A perusal of the sources of the collects for the day in The Holy Communion (the Mass) shows that the majority of them are taken from the so-called Leonine (Verona), Gelasian and Gregorian sacramentary traditions. Many of the collects in the *SBH* were the same as the series in the Roman Missal, as were many

---

Lutheran Church in America. A second edition, with music, appeared in 1918, and a text edition in 1919.

19 Lutheran Church-Missouri Synod, 1941, *The Lutheran Hymnal*, St Louis MO: Concordia Publishing House.

20 *Service Book and Hymnal of the Lutheran Church in America*, 1958, Minneapolis MN: Augsburg Publishing House; Philadelphia PA: United Lutheran Publication House.

21 Reed, *The Lutheran Liturgy*, pp. 465–622.

of the Introits, Epistles, Graduals and Gospels. Perhaps the second-largest source of English texts of collects for the day was *The Book of Common Prayer*, especially where the Prayer Book provided original texts. This is especially true for feast days of apostles and evangelists and All Saints' Day.

The prayers for special use do not all follow a strict collect form and come from diverse sources, including the Latin sacramentaries, German Church Orders, *The Book of Common Prayer*, *The Book of Common Order* of the Church of Scotland. In addition, they include original compositions from a variety of authors both historical and contemporary. A source of many prayers was William Bright's *Ancient Collects*.[22] The American Lutheran scholars Henry Eyster Jacobs, Paul Zeller Strodach, George Rise Seltzer and Luther Dotterer Reed also contributed original prayers to the collection.[23]

The *Lutheran Book of Worship*

In 1968 the LCMS invited the other major Lutheran church bodies in North America to join together in preparing a new hymnal. While the other Lutheran bodies had adopted the *SBH* just ten years previously, *SBH* was in Elizabethan/Jacobean English and there was a desire for more contemporary speech in worship. Also, much new liturgical work was being done in a number of Church bodies during the 1960s, especially in the Roman Catholic Church after the Second Vatican Council. An Inter-Lutheran Commission on Worship (ILCW) was formed by the four participating church bodies. The ILCW participated in the International Commission on English Texts (ICET) and maintained communication with the Standing Liturgical Commission of The Episcopal Church in the United States, which was preparing its own revised *Book of Common Prayer*. This book appeared in a provisional form in 1976, and was authorized in 1979. The ILCW issued a series of paperback liturgical resources for trial use similar to the Prayer Book Studies of the Standing Liturgical Commission.

A major decision of the ILCW was to render all texts in current English rather than in archaic English. While *The Book of Common Prayer* of the Episcopal Church included collects and prayers in 'traditional' language, this practice was not followed in *LBW*, except for

---

22 William Bright, 1887, *Ancient Collects*, London: Oxford University Press.
23 Reed, *The Lutheran Liturgy*, pp. 284–6.

retention of the traditional Lord's Prayer along with the ICET text. Collects were rendered in the indicative rather than the subjunctive mood, with less use of relative clauses than the typical Cranmerian prayers. Thus, the Christmas Day collect, 'O God, who hast made this most holy night to shine with the brightness of the true Light' (*SBH*), became 'Almighty God, you have made this holy night shine with the brightness of the true Light' (*LBW*). The petition was also amended from 'Grant, we beseech thee, that as we have known on earth the mysteries of that Light, we may also come to the fulness of his joys in heaven' to 'Grant that here on earth we may walk in the light of Jesus' presence and in the last day wake to the brightness of his glory'. 'Mysteries of that Light' was deemed opaque to modern believers and 'in the last day wake to the brightness of his glory' expresses the specific hope of the resurrection, rather than the nebulous 'joys of heaven'. A thorough examination of changes in the historic collects from the *SBH* to the *LBW* (and from *LBW* to *ELW*) would demonstrate significant theological shifts that accompany a change in worship books.

Another major decision made by the ILCW that affected the collects was to develop a Lutheran version of the Roman Catholic three-year *Lectionary of the Mass*. It must have occurred to the Liturgical Texts Committee of ILCW that an expanded lectionary strained the use of the historic collects, because in some instances alternative 'prayers of the day' and 'additional prayers' for the seasons were provided in *Contemporary Worship 6*.[24] The additional seasonal prayers were not continued into *LBW*, but alternate prayers of the day were provided in 19 sets of propers.[25]

Another decision made by the ILCW was to follow the new Roman Sacramentary in using the brief termination of collects on the 'ordinary' Sundays after the Epiphany and after Pentecost, 'through Jesus Christ our Lord', rather than the full trinitarian termination which continues 'who lives and reigns with you and the Holy Spirit, one God, now and forever'.

A new practice in the *LBW* Ministers' Edition was to provide psalter collects for use with the psalms in the daily prayer offices of Morn-

---

24 Inter-Lutheran Commission on Worship, 1973, *Contemporary Worship 6: The Church Year: Calendar and Lectionary*, Minneapolis MN: Augsburg Publishing House; Philadelphia PA: Board of Publications Lutheran Church in America; St Louis MO: Concordia Publishing House.

25 Philip H. Pfatteicher, 1990, *Commentary on the Lutheran Book of Worship: Lutheran Liturgy in its Ecumenical Context*, Minneapolis MN: Augsburg Fortress, pp. 129–30.

ing Prayer (Matins), Evening Prayer (Vespers) and Prayer at the Close of the Day (Compline). This was a practice being retrieved in Roman Catholic circles, in particular under the leadership of William G. Storey in the Graduate Program in Liturgical Studies at the University of Notre Dame.[26] The aim was to foster a christological interpretation of the psalms. Most of the psalm collects in *LBW* are adapted from the Roman Catholic Liturgy of the Hours. Others were composed by Philip Pfatteicher, myself and some of my students at Christ Seminary–Seminex.[27]

As with previous Lutheran worship books in America, a selection of 'Petitions, Intercessions, and Thanksgivings' was provided in *LBW* for use in the prayer offices and for other particular needs and occasions, both corporate and personal. Most of these are in collect form. Pfatteicher provides the source of each prayer.[28] A perusal of the sources indicates that the great majority of these prayers are shared with the Episcopal Church's *Book of Common Prayer*.[29] This is because Eugene L. Brand, the Project Director of the ILCW, and Philip Pfatteicher, who selected the prayers, had in hand the draft *Proposed Book of Common Prayer*.[30]

Evangelical Lutheran Worship (2006)

By the 1990s, Churches that had published primary liturgical books in the 1970s were publishing supplementary sources. The ELCA and its publishing house produced the authorized *With One Voice* (1995), the African American worship book *This Far by Faith* (1999), and the Spanish-language worship book *Libro de Liturgia y Cántico* (1998). These publications indicate an increasing desire for more gender-inclusive language and multicultural liturgical resources.

---

26 William G. Storey, Frank C. Quinn and David F. Wright OP, 1973, *Morning Praise and Evensong*, Notre Dame IN: Fides Publishers.

27 Pfatteicher, *Commentary*, pp. 517–18.

28 Pfatteicher, *Commentary*, pp. 392–411.

29 The Episcopal Church of the USA, 1979, *The Book of Common Prayer*, New York: Church Hymnal Corporation. See pp. 814–41, 'Prayers and Thanksgivings'.

30 In detailing the sources of prayers that *LBW* shared with *The Book of Common Prayer*, Pfatteicher was able to draw upon Marion Hatchett, 1981, *Commentary on the American Prayer Book*, New York: Seabury Press, pp. 556–71.

AMERICAN LUTHERAN LITURGICAL BOOKS

The *LBW* had taken steps in these directions, but they were deemed minimal by the standards of the end of the century. By 2000 the ELCA, along with the ELCiC, decided that the time had come to work towards 'the next generation' of worship resources. A 'Renewing Worship' project was launched, the first phase of which was a consultative process to develop principles for language, music, preaching and worship space. As regards language used in collects, the following principle would especially apply: 'The church continually builds upon the vocabulary of the scriptures, expanding the treasury of language and images in order to proclaim the fulness of the triune God.'[31] Each principle employed statements on background and application. Background information on this principle noted that the address 'Father' 'has become more prevalent in the last two centuries, sometimes overshadowing other ways of addressing God', and that '[c]urrently, churches and individuals are exploring other words and images to complement the word "Lord"'. Among the applications of this principle is this: 'Careful crafting of texts to minimize the use of gender-specific pronouns for God helps to avoid conveying the impression that God is either male or female.'

Drafting liturgical material was the second phase of 'Renewing Worship'. Editorial teams collected, developed and revised liturgical materials for provisional use. Gail Ramshaw and I, who served on the Language Consultation, also served on the team that worked on the church year calendar and propers. Gail Ramshaw drafted the collects for use with the *Revised Common Lectionary* and the 12 readings in the Easter Vigil. I drafted the collects for lesser festivals, commemorations and occasions, as well as the special orders for Ash Wednesday, Palm Sunday, Maundy Thursday, Good Friday and the Easter Vigil. All of these texts and orders were reviewed and amended by the full editorial committee, which included Barbara Berry-Bailey, Craig Mueller, Michael Burk, Cheryl Dieter, Frank Stoldt and Martin Seltz. The results of our work were published in a trial-use resource.[32] The trial-use resources, evaluated by pastors, congregations, bishops and the churchwide council, provided the basis for the final *ELW*. On account of the review process, not everything in the trial use resources made it into the final *ELW*. At this point it is not possible to determine who was responsible for the final decisions on texts. In what follows,

---

31 ELCA and ELCiC, 2002, *Principles for Worship*, Minneapolis MN: Augsburg Fortress, p. 12.

32 ELCA and ELCiC, 2004, *The Church's Year: Propers and Seasonal Rites*, Minneapolis MN: Augsburg Fortress.

I will describe what the drafting committee decided and indicate what did and did not survive into the *ELW*.

The drafting committee made a number of decisions with regard to the prayer of the day. First, we decided that a prayer was needed for each set of propers over the span of the three-year *Revised Common Lectionary*. Second, as far as possible we would use historic collects and prayers. Only where no prayers could be found that correlated with readings in the *Revised Common Lectionary* would we compose new prayers. Third, we would follow the historic collect principle of offering one petition per prayer, or two at most. Other denominational prayer collections we looked at that had been prepared for use with the Roman Lectionary or *Revised Common Lectionary* (for example, the ICEL *Opening Prayers* and the Presbyterian *Book of Common Worship*) tried to include a reference to each of the readings in the prayer text.[33] We would not do that. Fourth, therefore, we decided that our prayers of the day should point to the readings but not assume that the assembly had already heard them. Fifth, we returned to the use of full trinitarian terminations for the prayers of the day on Sundays and festivals, thus abandoning the Roman/*LBW* custom of terminating prayers on 'ordinary' (green) Sundays 'through Jesus Christ our Lord'. As an alternative to 'who lives and reigns with you and the Holy Spirit' we proposed, in a nod to Eastern prayers, which are more doxological than Western prayers (and also to diminish the language of kingship), 'whom with you and the Holy Spirit we worship and praise, one God, now and forever'. We also expanded 'through Jesus Christ' with 'our *Savior* and Lord' to parallel 'worship and praise'.

The expansion 'Savior and Lord' was retained in *ELW*, but, for reasons unknown to me, neither the full trinitarian termination on Sundays after the Epiphany and after Pentecost nor the phrase 'whom we worship and praise' was retained. So the *ELW* collects follow the Roman/*LBW* pattern on Sundays after the Epiphany and after Pentecost of ending 'through Jesus Christ, our Savior and Lord' and the full trinitarian termination includes the phrase 'who lives and reigns with you and the Holy Spirit, one God, now and forever'.

The *LBW* prayers had not followed the lead of the 1969 English language Roman Sacramentary in preferring 'Father' as the addressee, even when the Latin had *Deus*. This preference for Father-language

---

33 International Commission on English in the Liturgy, 1997, *Opening Prayers: Scripture-related collects for Years A, B & C of the Sacramentary*, Norwich: Canterbury Press; Presbyterian Church (USA), 1993, *Book of Common Worship*, Louisville KY: Westminster John Knox Press.

undoubtedly reflected an effort, relating to the sensibilities of the 1960s, to give a greater sense of intimate relationship with God. Sometimes the ideology of one generation runs foul of the ideology of the next generation. In any event, there was no need to eliminate 'Father' from many of the *LBW* collects. But a practice has developed in recent years of modifying 'God' with adjectives such as 'gracious', 'compassionate', 'holy', in addition to 'almighty', 'eternal', 'most merciful', and similar expressions. This way of addressing God by using an appropriate attribute of God based on the main petition of the collect is found in many *ELW* prayers. Thus, one finds such formulations as 'God of grace', 'God of glory', 'God of compassion', 'God of majesty', 'God of peace and unity', 'God of wisdom'.

Another decision of the drafting committee that was carried over into *ELW* was to specify more clearly when a prayer is addressed to Christ. Thus, historic Advent collects of Gallican provenance began 'Stir up your power, O Lord, and come'. Here we specified 'Stir up your power, Lord *Christ*'. The Advent prayers carried this introduction throughout all three years on all four Sundays: 'Stir up your power, Lord Christ, and come. By your merciful protection . . .' (Advent 1, ABC); 'Stir up our hearts, Lord God, to prepare the way of your only Son. By his coming . . .' (Advent 2, ABC); 'Stir up the wills of your faithful people, Lord God, and open our ears . . .' (Advent 3, ABC); 'Stir up your power, Lord Christ, and come. With your abundant grace and mercy, free us from the sin that . . .' (Advent 4, ABC). The petition in each of these 12 prayers relates to the readings of that day.

With regard to the lesser festivals, Joseph, Guardian of Jesus (19 March), was added to the calendar and given an original collect. Collects were provided for a Day of Mourning among the propers for special occasions (what, in the Roman Catholic tradition, would be votive Masses).

According to our task force count of all these proper collects, 'Renewing Worship'/*ELW* retained approximately fifty *LBW* collects, mostly altered. Eighteen collects were adapted from Latin collects not in *LBW*. Thirty-three collects in *ELW* are based on prayers in the *Book of Common Worship*. Twenty-five are adapted from the collection of the Consultation on Common Texts. Three are taken from the Episcopal *Book of Alternative Services*. Seven more are from Thomas Cranmer, altered. Twenty-one are adapted from other historic figures and sources (three from Martin Luther). Thirty-two collects are entirely new compositions. Not surprisingly, twenty-one of these are for propers in the time after the Epiphany and after Pentecost, which have readings not found in the historic one-year lectionary to which the historic collects are more or less related.

The issue of whether proper collects ought to be provided also for the offertory and post-communion prayers, as in the classical Latin sacramentaries, was raised in the drafting committee. The committee decided that not every one of the classical collects is a gem just because they are old, and agreed that it would be better to provide a selection of good seasonal offertory and post-communion prayers to augment the ones set in place in the order for the Holy Communion. These are provided in *ELW*.[34]

Other collects in *ELW* were the work of other 'Renewing Worship' drafting committees, such as the collects for the daily prayer offices and the psalm prayers. The collects for the prayer offices are all based on *LBW* prayers. Surprisingly, Luther's morning and evening prayers were emended from 'Let your holy angels have charge of us, so that the wicked one may have no power over us' to 'Let your holy angels be with us, so that . . .'. Luther undoubtedly expected the angels to take a more active role.

One of the most controversial features of *ELW* is the psalter, which eliminates all third-person pronouns referring to God. Perhaps to avoid repeating 'God', some of the verses are given a change of direction from proclaiming what God has done to praying to God, and therefore using 'you'. If all of the psalms had been turned into prayer, the argument in favour of praying the psalms might have been more compelling. But there is no consistency. The language of kingship has also been stripped from the psalms and the psalm prayers are emended accordingly. Thus, Psalm 97 begins 'The Lord reigns', rather than 'The Lord is king'. The *LBW* prayer for Psalm 97 begins 'God our king'. In *ELW* 'Our king' is omitted. *LBW*'s 'Among the peoples you work wonders, and rain terror upon your enemies' becomes simply 'You work your mighty wonders among us'. Every one of the psalm prayers was emended, usually with an eye towards removing anything that might cause offence to contemporary sensibilities.

Finally, as in the previous worship books, there is a section of 'Additional Prayers' for various needs and occasions.[35] The number of prayers greatly expands the provisions of *LBW*, reflecting in part an appreciation of new situations for which prayer may be needed, and which were not current concerns in 1978. The prayers are arranged in categories that might make finding a suitable one somewhat easier than

---

34 *ELW* Leaders Edition, pp. 138–9.
35 *ELW* Leaders Edition, pp. 140–60.

was the case in *LBW*. Reflecting contemporary needs and sensibilities, this collection offers more prayers for times of disaster (the aftermath of Hurricane Katrina and the Tsunami), civic mourning (the aftermath of the 11 September 2001 terrorist attacks), and for the creation (concerns over global warming).

The *Lutheran Service Book* (2006)

It seems unfair not to include in this chapter reference to the other major Lutheran liturgical resource published in the same year as *ELW*: *Lutheran Service Book* (*LSB*) of LCMS.[36] *ELW* and *LSB* represent the first English-language Lutheran liturgical resources that have not been inter-Lutheran projects since the Common Service. We noted that LCMS initiated and participated in the work of the ILCW in the 1970s. While the LCMS did not finally approve the *LBW*, its own *Lutheran Worship* of 1982 (*LW*) was a variant of *LBW* and an updating of *TLH*.[37] The collects in *LW* had to serve both the three-year *LBW* lectionary and the one-year 'historic lectionary'. In some cases, where *LBW* departed from the collects for particular Sundays that are shared with the *BCP*, *LW* used the *BCP* collects (for example on the Third Sunday in Lent). A more traditional style, with subordinate clauses, was retained in the *LW* collects. After 1978, the ELCA and LCMS pursued their own liturgical work with minimal consultation and co-operation.

The collects in the *LSB* are an updating of those in *LW*. The *LSB* does not provide the collects of the day in the Pew Edition; they are in the Altar Book. This is a significant departure from the American Lutheran tradition of making the collects available to the people of the Church.[38]

Muhlenberg's vision of 'one Church, one Liturgy' still eludes North American Lutherans. Nevertheless, our liturgical resources continue

---

36 Lutheran Church-Missouri Synod, 2006, *Lutheran Service Book*, St Louis MO: Concordia Publishing House.

37 Lutheran Church-Missouri Synod, 1982, *Lutheran Worship*, St Louis MO: Concordia Publishing House.

38 The LCMS Commission on Worship and Concordia Publishing House are rectifying this by publishing a separate booklet entitled *LSB: Collects of the Day*. The publisher's blurb says, 'This little booklet contains all of the Prayers of the Day for the Sundays and Seasons, Feasts, Festivals and Occasions in the Lutheran Service Book, including both the three-year and one-year lectionaries. Great for use at home, church meetings, and other settings.'

to draw upon a common repertoire of liturgical texts. Among these are the collects that have survived in Western Christian use for some fifteen hundred years. Lutherans are still praying the same prayers with each other and with Christians in other traditions, even if we sometimes stumble over the words as we use each other's worship books. Our work on the collects may be of use to other Western traditions as they revise their worship books.

7

Between Form and Freedom: The History of the Collect in the Reformed Tradition

PAUL GALBREATH

A deliberate tension between form and freedom lies at the centre of liturgical practice in the Reformed tradition. The Directory for Worship that is a part of the Constitution of the Presbyterian Church (USA) states it as a basic principle of worship:

> The Church has always experienced a tension between form and freedom in worship. In the history of the Church, some have offered established forms for ordering worship in accordance with God's Word. Others, in the effort to be faithful to the Word, have resisted imposing any fixed forms upon the worshipping community. The Presbyterian Church (USA) acknowledges that all forms of worship are provisional and subject to reformation. In ordering worship the Church is to seek openness to the creativity of the Holy Spirit, who guides the Church toward worship which is orderly yet spontaneous, consistent with God's Word and open to the newness of God's future. (W-3, 1002)[1]

Since the dramatic reform of worship practices in Strasbourg and Geneva during the sixteenth century, Reformed ecclesial bodies have drawn on the historic shape and pattern of liturgical forms, while at the same time creating space for these forms to be articulated and embodied in distinctive ways. The history of the collect in the Reformed tradition includes a narrative of use, neglect and transformation that

---

[1] Presbyterian Church (USA), 1991–92, *The Constitution of the Presbyterian Church (USA), Part I: Book of Order, Directory for Worship*, Louisville KY: General Assembly of the Presbyterian Church (USA).

enlightens not only the Reformed approach to this particular form of prayer, but in some ways points to the broader liturgical practices within the Reformed tradition.

Before beginning this historical survey, the reader should be aware of a few disclaimers. By its nature, the Reformed tradition is a highly diverse and sometimes eclectic collection of congregations whose shared liturgical identity is grounded in particular readings and interpretations of Scripture and who set out broad parameters for liturgical interpretation and adaptation to take place. It is impossible to provide a full picture of the Reformed approach to any particular liturgical practice in a tradition as broad as that represented by Reformed congregations. In the light of these limitations, this chapter looks briefly at historical snapshots of the use and adaptation of the collect at particular times and places in Reformed Churches. This survey will pay particular attention to the use and adaptation of the collect in Reformed bodies in the United States, concentrating especially on the practices of the Presbyterian Church (USA).[2] This is not to overlook the significance of Reformed bodies around the world, but to illustrate the adaptive liturgical principles found in the use of collects in Reformed history.

The historical roots of the collect

In his essay 'The Collect in Context', Patrick Regan defines the teleological aim of the collect as providing a 'culminating point of all that comes before the service of the word'.[3] Regan describes the place of the collect in the oldest extant account of a papal Mass, the *Ordo Romanus Primus*, which comes from eighth-century Rome. Here, the collect clearly fulfils the role of bringing the opening movement of the Mass to completion. The entrance rite includes the procession of the liturgical leaders of the assembly, a sung psalm and the Gloria Patri, Kyrie eleison and Gloria in excelsis Deo. Then, the presider offers the collect as prayer that brings this opening act of the liturgy to completion.

---

2 In particular, the essay concludes with an examination of the place of the collect in the Presbyterian Church (USA) and in the denominations that led up to the historic reunion of Presbyterian Churches in the North and South.

3 Patrick Regan, 2008, 'The Collect in Context', in James Leachman and Daniel McCarthy (eds), *Appreciating the Collect: An Irenic Methodology*, Farnborough, Hampshire: St Michael's Abbey Press, 2008, pp. 105–39, p. 96.

Similarly, James White describes the development of the liturgy at an even earlier time of liturgical transition. White notes that the rapid expansion of Christianity in the fourth-century Roman Empire brought change to liturgical practice as a matter of necessity. With the move to larger spaces for Christian assembly came a need to adapt practices for the gathering of worshippers. Thus, White describes the expansion of the opening of the rite as providing travelling music to allow the procession of clergy to move to the front of the assembly and take their places in the liturgical assembly. Once the assembly has gathered in this manner, the collect brings this opening act to a conclusion.[4]

Regan helpfully describes the collect's summative nature in both the High Mass and the Low Mass of the Roman Rite as that which brings the entrance rite to full fruition. The collect offers the first occasion for the presider's voice to be heard by the assembly and the completion leads to a change in the posture of the assembly, who are seated following the 'Amen'.[5] This descriptive analysis leads Regan to conclude that 'the collect shines forth in all its pristine splendour as both the culmination and conclusion of the entrance procession'.[6]

Reformation transformations

I have underscored this analysis of the role and place of the collect in its historical development in order to contrast it with the liturgical development of the sixteenth-century Protestant Reformation. Martin Luther's approach to liturgical reform in Germany has been characterized as conservative and evangelical.[7] Luther described the place of the collect at the end of the opening rite in his works *Formula Missae* and *Deutsche Messe*: 'In the third place, the *Oratio* (prayer), or Collect which follows, if it is pious (and those appointed for the Lord's Days usually are), should be preserved in its accustomed use; but there should be but one.'[8] Thus, for Luther, the primary change in the use

---

4 James White, 2000, *Introduction to Christian Worship*, 3rd edn, Nashville TN: Abingdon Press, p. 156. White's own description of the role of the collect as that which 'concludes the introductory rite' and 'introduces the lessons for the day' offers a distinct parallel to the developments of the collect in the Reformed tradition.

5 Regan, 'Collect in Context', p. 98.

6 Regan, 'Collect in Context', p. 99.

7 See Bard Thompson, 1961, *Liturgies of the Western Church*, New York: Meridian Books, p. 100.

8 Thompson, *Liturgies*, p. 109.

of the collect was to limit the number of collects to one, in a conscious move away from the practice that had developed of introducing multiple prayers at this point in the service.[9]

By contrast, the liturgical reformation of the congregations where John Calvin served in Strasbourg and Geneva involved clearer distinctions from earlier practice and at times the transformation of received practices, since they were grounded in a distinctive theological framework. The precursor to these changes is generally identified as the set of revisions to the Mass in Strasbourg made by Diebold Schwarz. On 16 February 1524, Schwarz celebrated Mass in German in Saint John's Chapel in the Cathedral in Strasbourg. Significant changes included the congregation's participation in the *Confiteor* (confession), which had previously been said by the priest alone.[10] Schwarz's service became the model for the service outlined by Martin Bucer for use in Strasbourg and other Reformed congregations.

The order of the opening rite included confession of sin, scriptural words of pardon, absolution, a psalm or hymn, Kyrie eleison, Gloria in excelsis, a collect for illumination, a metrical psalm, Gospel reading, and a sermon.[11] This outline provided a liturgical pattern and theological approach for Calvin's work in Strasbourg and in Geneva.

Reformed worship is grounded in a distinctive reading of Scripture. Thus, following Bucer's lead, Calvin's liturgy begins with a biblical citation: 'Our help is the name of the Lord, who made heaven and earth. Amen.' This use of Scripture serves as a biblical warrant for the assembly's gathering and leads to a prayer of confession and absolution or pardon to all who repent of their sin. In Strasbourg, these actions were followed by the congregational singing of the Ten Commandments, a way of allowing a biblical text to inform the practices of the covenant community's shared way of life.

In Geneva, the prayer of confession was followed by the singing of a psalm by the congregation. Bard Thompson describes how the absolution came to be omitted:

---

9 Regan notes that there could be up to seven prayers offered during medieval times. Regan, 'Collect in Context', p. 98.

10 John Barkley, 1976, *Worship of the Reformed Church*, Richmond: John Knox Press, p. 14.

11 Barkley, pp. 14–15. One can argue that the singing of two psalms allows the collect for illumination to continue to function as the culmination of the opening rite as much as an opening to the reading of the Word. This prayer provides a kind of transitional bridge in the service. As we will see, Calvin's alterations to the order in Geneva cause a more dramatic shift to this prayer.

In Strasbourg Calvin supplied an Absolution no less forthright than that of Bucer; but when he returned to Geneva, the people objected to this 'novelty', illustrating their hostility by jumping up before the end of the Confession to forestall an Absolution. Thus he yielded to their scruples.[12]

In both cases, the congregation's song serves as the culminating act of the gathering of the assembly for worship. A 'collect for illumination' follows this opening rite.[13] Thus, while Calvin maintained the place of the collect in the liturgy, he dramatically altered its function. The prayer no longer serves primarily to sum up what has preceded it. Instead, it points to that which is to follow, namely the reading of Scripture and the sermon. It is also important to note that in the Genevan liturgy, Calvin described the purpose of this prayer and noted that 'the form is left to the discretion of the Minister'.[14]

Several features of this adaptive liturgical practice deserve special notice. First, Calvin's foundational requirement of the role of the collect for illumination is that the prayer should be distinctively pneumatological. The primary purpose of the prayer is to request the Spirit's presence to bring insight to the assembly as Scripture is read, in order that the Church may hear, understand, and receive the Word read and proclaimed. This distinctive theological approach to Scripture stands over against those who argued for the transparency of Scripture. Calvin's own commitment to careful exegetical work (a characteristic shared by many others in both Roman Catholic and Protestant communities of the time) remained subservient to the conviction that it is the Holy Spirit who brings to life the interpretation of Scripture. His particular approach to the collect is based firmly on a theological understanding of the role of the Holy Spirit.

While this chapter will examine other aspects and approaches in the development of the collect in the history of Reformed congregations, this insight remains fundamental and basic to Reformed Churches. It is an approach that stands in marked contrast to the classic Roman approach to the collect, which, as Gerard Moore notes, typically has an 'implicit, rather than explicit pneumatology'.[15] Moore's analysis

---

12 Thompson, *Liturgies*, p. 191.

13 These orders of worship and an example of this collect may be found in Thompson, *Liturgies*, pp. 197–9.

14 Calvin, in Thompson, *Liturgies*, p. 199.

15 Gerard Moore, 2008, 'The Vocabulary of the Collects', in Leachman and McCarthy, *Appreciating the Collect*, pp. 175–95, p. 189.

of the Roman collects emphasizes instead the central christological framework of the collect in the Roman tradition.

Second, Calvin's approach to the collect has a particular aim in mind: illumination. Calvin's theological approach to Scripture was reinforced in this aspect of his liturgical practice. The prayer seeks guidance from the Spirit in order that the Church may understand the reading of Scripture. In contrast to the distinctive supplicatory aim of the Roman collects, Calvin's approach to the collect takes on a particular exhortatory characteristic. The minister beseeches God for grace and guidance from the Holy Spirit in order that God's Word may be faithfully read and heard by the gathering. The ultimate goal for Calvin is the edification of the Church.[16] Thus, a particular ecclesiological understanding is implicit in the use of this prayer. The Church, the covenant community of the faithful, seeks guidance from Scripture through the presence of the Holy Spirit in order to cultivate lives marked by humility and obedience.

Third, for Calvin the collect clearly points towards the basic role of Scripture as foundational for the gathering of the assembly. The collect is an act of preparation in order for the congregation to hear and understand Scripture as it is read and proclaimed. Hence, there is an overtly biblical framework for this prayer. Moore notes that Roman collects may often employ biblical vocabulary in both implicit and explicit ways throughout the prayers, but that at least some liturgical scholars have argued that the Roman collect is 'non-biblical in nature'.[17] By contrast, the biblical nature of Reformed collects takes a different turn. Calvin's collect for illumination is a preparatory act for the hearing of particular biblical texts on a particular day by a particular congregation. This approach is grounded in a high reverence for Scripture as fundamental to the life of the assembly, and allows the possibility that the language of the prayer may be shaped and influenced by texts read on this occasion.

Fourth, Calvin's approach to the collect is based on the practice of this prayer as an offering by the minister. In place of an established text, the minister is given licence to offer a prayer for illumination that is guided by the primary aims of this form of prayer. Calvin did provide examples, such as this one, adapted from a prayer by Bucer:

---

16 This language of beseeching and edification comes from Calvin's liturgy, in Thompson, *Liturgies*, pp. 198–9.

17 Moore's brief outline of the debate about the biblical nature of collects is insightful on this point. Moore, 'Vocabulary', pp. 176–7. See n. 5 in particular.

Almighty and gracious Father, since our whole salvation standeth in our knowledge of thy Holy Word, strengthen us now by thy Holy Spirit that our hearts may be set free from all worldly thoughts and attachments of the flesh, so that we may hear and receive that same Word, and recognizing thy gracious will for us, may love and serve thee with earnest delight, praising and glorifying thee in Jesus Christ our Lord. Amen.[18]

It is not clear whether Calvin's practice – and that of those who followed him – was to rely on a written (prepared) collect for illumination or to offer an extemporaneous prayer guided by the primary purpose for this prayer. In either case, it is important to understand that this new approach to prayer usurped the place of a shared, historical text.[19]

Fifth, there is a surprising quality to this prayer. Compared to other prayers from Calvin's liturgy, this prayer is generally terse in style and focused in its aim. Perhaps certain patterns from the historic, textual approach to collects which Calvin had certainly experienced in French Roman Catholic churches continued to underlie the construction of the collect for illumination and guide the language into lean and focused compositions.

Finally, there is an implicit pedagogy in Calvin's approach to the collect. The desire to nurture piety in the home and in daily life is a hallmark of Calvin's work in the church in Geneva, and continues to be a primary constitutive practice of Reformed Christians. Thus, the transformation of the collect, with its link to reading Scripture and interpreting Scripture in the light of the Spirit's presence in our lives, suggests a practice that can be readily transported from the Sunday assembly to private household devotions. Calvin's approach to the collect models a distinctive understanding of prayer which finds its roots

---

18 Thompson, *Liturgies*, p. 209.

19 Significant transitions in posture are outlined in Calvin's Strasbourg liturgy. The rubrics direct that the congregation should begin the service kneeling and stand for the singing of the law. The first table of the law is followed by a prayer to receive the law and then the congregation stands to sing the second table of the law. Afterwards, the congregation kneels, for the prayer for illumination. These movements underline the transformed role of the collect in the Reformed liturgy in contrast to the Roman use of the collect, as well as exemplifying the distinctive role of posture that is associated with the collect. Rubrics are taken from The United Presbyterian Church in the USA, Board of Christian Education, 1959, *The Calvin Strasbourg Service*, Philadelphia: Board of Christian Education.

in the service for the Lord's Day but is easily transferable to the devotional life of the faithful.

A heritage in transition

We have seen how Calvin's characteristically theological approach to the collect brought about a dramatic transformation. While the prayer remained in the same location in the Sunday assembly, it took on new features which served the primary aim of pointing the assembly forward to the reading of Scripture. This marked a departure from the collect's previous function as a prayer summing up the opening rite. The new liturgical use of the collect was further developed by John Knox, who helped bring Calvin and the practices and theological convictions of the Reformation to the Church of Scotland.

Calvin's Strasbourg liturgy was translated into German and provided a basis for Knox's work in compiling the *Forme of Prayer* for the Church of Scotland in 1556. Following Calvin, Knox's liturgy noted that, after the singing of a psalm by the congregation, the minister 'prayeth for th' assistance of God's Holy Spirite, as the same move his harte, and so procedeth to the Sermon'.[20] Thus, the practice established by Calvin in Geneva became normative for the Church of Scotland. Whereas the Church of England translated ancient Latin prayers for use in the liturgy and crafted new prayers in the light of these patterns, the Church of Scotland generally adopted the practice established by Bucer and Calvin in Strasbourg and Geneva. However, a contrasting vision for the role of the collect developed alongside this practice in the Church of Scotland.

In 1595, a Scottish metrical psalter was published that included a set of prayers in the Scottish dialect for each psalm. This collection of prayers was a translation of the French prayers written by Clement Marot and Theodore de Bèze in 1567. The prayers had previously appeared in the French psalter published in 1561. They are characterized by their reliance on 'pre-Reformation liturgies' and have been described as '*nouvellement adjoustées* rather than in the strict sense new'.[21] These prayers build on the classic Roman form of the col-

---

20 *The Liturgy of John Knox*, 1886, Glasgow: University Press, 1886, p. 99.
21 D. D. Bannerman, 1933, *The Scottish Collects from the Scottish Metrical Psalter of 1595*, Edinburgh: The Church of Scotland Committee on Public Worship & Aids to Devotion, Occasional Paper 5, p. 6.

lect, which at the time was uncommon in Scottish use. In outline, the Roman form has five distinct parts:

1 the invocation;
2 the recital of some doctrine or fact of the Faith which is made the basis of the petition;
3 the petition itself;
4 the aspiration expressive of what the consequence of the petition is expected to be;
5 and the pleading of the Name of our Lord as the ground of confidence that the prayer will be accepted.[22]

This Scottish edition of psalter prayers followed the earlier form of the Roman collect while expressing the prayer in a distinctly Scottish style. Even here, though, the collection shows a significant shift in the final ten prayers, which 'abandoned the collect form' and no longer relied on the earlier French prayers.[23]

The importance of this for our study shows that, while the function of the collect in the Lord's Day service radically shifted in the light of Calvin's practice in Geneva, an alternative vision of the historic understanding of the collect remained. To cite but one example from this important collection, here is the prayer following Psalm 23:

> Eternal and Everlasting Father, Fountain of all felicity; we render Thee praises and thanks for that Thou hast made known to us our Shepherd and Defender Who shall deliver us from the power of our adversaries. Grant unto us that we, casting away all fear and terror of death, may embrace and confess Thy truth, which it hath pleased Thee to reveal to us by Thy Son, our Lord and sovereign Master, Christ Jesus.[24]

While the transformation of the Roman collect into a prayer for illumination reoriented the practice and understanding of this particular prayer in the Reformed tradition, the older approach to the collect was maintained. It is important to note that these collections of collects

---

22 These five parts are listed in Bannerman, *The Scottish Collects*, p. 6.
23 Bannerman, *The Scottish Collects*, p. 7.
24 Bannerman, *The Scottish Collects*, p. 16. Some of these prayers have been included in the psalm prayers that are provided in *Book of Common Worship*, Louisville KY: Westminster John Knox Press, 1993.

(both the original French prayers and their largely derivative Scottish prayers) are woven into the fabric of the psalter, a place of distinct importance in Reformed worship. Since the opening rite in the liturgies of Calvin and Knox concluded with the singing of a psalm by the congregation, the development of a body of collects attached to the psalter provided a form of collective memory of prayers that serve to sum up the movement at a particular place in the service. While Sunday practice in Reformed congregations caused the collect for illumination to point in a different direction, the use of collects in daily prayer was preserved in this important collection. Harold Daniels notes that as early as the fifth century,

> psalm prayers were replaced by the *Gloria Patri* to defend against Arianism. It is something of an irony that, following the Second Vatican Council, the psalm prayer was restored to the Roman Catholic Church, replacing the singing or saying the *Gloria Patri* at the conclusion of a psalm.[25]

The gift of the collect that was part of the Roman Mass was thus preserved in an approach to the psalter in the practices of daily prayer in the Reformed tradition.

The shift towards freedom

While forms or at least orders for the liturgy provided a collective pattern for Reformed Churches, ongoing disputes between the Church of England and the Church of Scotland created a rift that led to a re-examination of the role of worship books. This issue came to a head in the meeting of the Assembly of Divines at Westminster and led to the adoption of *The Directory for the Publick Worship of God* which was approved for use in the Church of Scotland in 1645. In the preface to the Directory, the Assembly noted the important contributions of prayers and forms that had been provided for the use of the Church, but explained that, 'after earnest and frequent calling upon the name of God, and after much consultation, not with flesh and blood, but with his holy word,' they had 'resolved to lay aside the former Liturgy, with the many Rites and Ceremonies formerly used in the Worship

---

25 Harold Daniels, 2003, *To God Alone Be Glory: The Story and Sources of the Book of Common Worship*, Louisville KY: Geneva Press, p. 165.

of God; and [had] agreed upon this following Directory for all the Parts of publick Worship, at ordinary and extraordinary Times'.[26] This called the Church to the work of further Reformation.

The Directory included a brief section on prayer before the sermon. Noteworthy is the fact that, after the reading of Scripture and the singing of the psalms, 'all the prayers for the Lord's Day are drawn up into one body without any dividing of them'.[27] In this dramatic move, the distinctive theological and liturgical pattern of the opening rite of the early Reformed Churches is obliterated. In the place of distinct forms of prayer, a general and extended prayer is offered that is marked largely by confessional and penitential language. The Directory offered a suggested shape to this lengthy prayer (the minister is 'to call upon the name of the Lord to this Effect') that ultimately concluded with a petition for the preacher and the congregation. This implied request for illumination is transferred from the reading and hearing of Scripture to the proclamation of the Word. Calvin's collect for illumination on behalf of all those who will hear Scripture in the context of an act of worship becomes a solitary act of the minister, who is encouraged in his work to seek by prayer the illumination of the Spirit as he studies Scripture 'in his private Preparations, before he deliver in Publick what he hath provided'.[28] This dramatic change prompted one commentator to conclude:

> When one today looks back over this long prayer with its many subheadings and painfully accurate exposition of every possible occasion, it is no wonder that the verbal portions of the Directory were almost wholly disregarded, and its very prolixity was no doubt the chief reason for its non-use.[29]

---

26 *The Directory for the Publick Worship of God* in The Church of Scotland, 1745, *The Confession of Faith: the longer and shorter catechisms ... directories, form of church-government, &c. of publick-authority in the Church of Scotland*, Philadelphia: Ben Franklin, p. 9.

27 Thomas Leishman (ed.), 1901, *The Westminster Directory*, Edinburgh: William Blackwood and Sons, p. 89.

28 *The Directory for the Publick Worship of God*, p. 17.

29 Stephen Hurlburt (ed.), 1944, *The Liturgy of the Church of Scotland Since the Reformation*, Washington DC: The St Albans Press, p. 80. Story comments on the worship practice of the Scottish church at this time that, 'The prayers were reduced in number to two at the most, and were drearily long and uninteresting.' In Barkley, *Worship of the Reformed Church*, pp. 30–1.

In many liturgical matters the Directory for Worship remained silent, and as a result its influence on Scottish practice is open to debate.[30] However, the Westminster Directory remained normative for the Scottish church and was adopted by the first General Assembly of the Presbyterian Church in the United States in 1788.

Restoring order

Liturgical renewal came to the Church of Scotland from one of its original sources. In 1840, the republication of Knox's Liturgy, *The Book of Common Order*, began a prolonged period of re-examination and recovery. In Scotland, the publication of Knox's liturgy restored the role of the prayer for illumination. During the same period, the appearance of the *Liturgy and other Divine Offices of the Church* in the Catholic Apostolic Church created a flurry of interest in liturgical reform. In contrast to Knox, the Catholic Apostolic Liturgy placed the collect before the reading of Scripture.[31]

In the United States, the Mercersburg movement in the German Reformed Church was led by Phillip Schaff and John Nevin, who published a *Book of Worship* in 1858 which was revised and adopted in 1866. Alongside these efforts at liturgical renewal, the Church Service Society played a decisive role in providing new liturgical resources for the Church of Scotland. These movements sought in various ways to restore liturgical forms to the worshipping life of Reformed congregations. In this process, the place of the prayer for illumination was reasserted and at times held in tension with a recovery of the use of collects.

Collect or prayer for illumination?

Further liturgical developments within the Reformed tradition demonstrate a primary commitment to Calvin's vision of the prayer for illumination. However, there remained a historic interest in the traditional Roman understanding of the collect. During the twentieth century,

---

30 On this point in particular, see Barkley, *Worship of the Reformed Church*, p. 31.

31 The placement of the collect in the *Euchologion* suggests that the collect functions as a preface to the reading of Scripture rather than in its summative role in the Roman Mass.

worship books for Reformed Churches adopted various approaches to the question of the place of the collect and/or the prayer for illumination in the liturgy. Barkley comments on the different approaches to the prayer for illumination between the Scottish, English, Welsh and Irish rites. The Irish rite maintained a place for the collect as well as a prayer for illumination before the reading of Scripture. Other Reformed Churches in England, Scotland and Wales adopted a different strategy:

> In the Scottish, English, and Welsh rites the prayer for illumination is placed before the sermon, but surely illumination is also necessary in the lections. The readings as well as the sermon, as Calvin maintained, are proclamation of the Gospel. That is why the prayer for illumination, as with Bucer and Calvin, ought to come not simply before the sermon, but before the readings and the sermon as a unity, and so within the preparation.[32]

The liturgical order had been complicated since the time of the Westminster Directory by the tendency for the sermon to move to a later position in the service. This movement, however, did create the possibility for a recovered use of prayers in the opening rite in the *Book of Common Order* in 1940 in the Church of Scotland. In this order, a call to prayer (according to the seasons of the church year) is followed by a collect for purity which precedes the confession and pardon.[33] In these services, the prayer for illumination maintains a place before the sermon, much later in the service.

The development of new worship resources for Presbyterian Churches in the United States has recognized the historical and theological distinction between the Roman collect and the prayer for illumination. The provisional rites in the Service for the Lord's Day included the option of a prayer for illumination or a collect for the day following the Gloria in excelsis and preceding the reading of Scripture. The commentary on this proposed order of worship noted:

> Though a prayer for illumination is in keeping with our Presbyterian tradition, some congregations may prefer to use the collect for

---

32 Barkley, *Worship of the Reformed Church*, p. 33.

33 Hurlburt, *The Liturgy of the Church of Scotland*, p. 109. Note that this order resembles none of the previous ones since it inserts the form(s) of collect(s) before the confession and pardon. The possibility of the collect thus returns, but not as a conclusion of the opening rite.

the day prior to the reading of Scripture. The collect for the day is customary in many churches. *The Book of Common Worship* provides such collects for each Lord's Day and for the special days and seasons of the Christian year.[34]

The publication of the *Worshipbook* in 1970 included a full set of collects for Sundays and feast days throughout the church year. The outline of the service, though, shows a continued Reformed preference for the prayer for illumination.[35]

Recent developments

With the publication of the *Book of Common Worship* (*BCW*) in 1993, the Presbyterian Church (USA) moved further to make room for both a collect and a prayer for illumination as part of the Service for the Lord's Day. The provisional rites followed the direction of the *Worshipbook* by listing a prayer for illumination *or* the 'prayer for the day' immediately preceding the reading of Scripture. However, an option is also included for the use of the prayer for the day as part of the praise and adoration in the opening movement of the rite, immediately following a call to worship.[36] By the time of the publication of the *BCW*, the liturgical landscape for the collect had once again shifted. The prayer for illumination is firmly returned to its original place before the reading of Scripture, after the completion of the Gathering/Opening Rite. However, the 'Prayer of the Day' or an Opening Prayer is included immediately following a call to worship. The description of the service also notes that 'the prayer of the day may be used later in the service, for example, as the concluding collect to the prayers of the people' which occur after the sermon.[37]

---

34 *Service for the Lord's Day and Lectionary for the Christian Year*, 1964, Philadelphia: The Westminster Press, pp. 27–8.

35 The listing of the service includes the Prayer for Illumination as part of 'The Basic Structure' and the Collect for the Day as an 'Addition or Variant Form'. Presbyterian Church in the USA, 1970, *The Worshipbook: Services*, Philadelphia: The Westminster Press, p. 21.

36 Presbyterian Church (USA), 1984, *The Service for the Lord's Day, Supplemental Liturgical Resource 1*, Philadelphia: The Westminster Press, p. 26. Note once again, though, that while a collect returns to the opening part of the rite, it is placed in a new location in the order of service.

37 *Book of Common Worship*, p. 35.

Similar tendencies and tensions between the use of a collect (prayer of the day) and a prayer for illumination can be found in Reformed bodies in other parts of the world. *The Book of Divine Services* for the Presbyterian Church in Cameroon maintains the place of the prayer of the day in its historic location in the Roman Mass (at the close of the opening rite) while adding a prayer for illumination immediately preceding the sermon.[38]

In Germany, a new worship book for Reformed congregations provides three options for the Lord's Day Service:

Form One – Prayer for illumination as optional at the close of the gathering rite and before the reading of Scripture.
Form Two – Prayer for illumination at the close of the gathering rite.
Form Three – Prayer of the day at the close of the gathering rite.[39]

The Book of Common Worship for the Presbyterian Church in the Republic of Korea very briefly describes the prayer for illumination, suggesting that it be placed before the sermon.[40] Collects, mostly based on the lectionary and some occasions of historical importance in the Korean church, may be used at other points in the service for the call to worship and in litanies of thanksgiving and confession.[41]

These variations in structure underscore the continued tension within various Reformed constituencies, as they seek to honour historical and liturgical distinctions, while at the same time remaining open to ecumenical influences.[42]

---

38 *Book of Divine Services, Vol. 1, The Services on Sundays, Holy Days, and Special Days*, 1984, Karlsruhe: Verlagsdruckerei Gebr. Tron KG, pp. 4–5. It is worth noting that the book includes a prayer of the day and a prayer for illumination for each Sunday and feast day.

39 *Reformierte Liturgie: Gebete und Ordnungen für die unter dem Wort versammelte Gemeinde*, 1999, Wuppertal: Neukirchener Verlag, pp. 34–5. The rubrics following the prayer of the day are helpful to note: 'Das *Kollektengebet* faßt den Eröffnungs- und Anrufungsteil zusammen und führt – mit der Bitte um das rechte Hören – zum Verkündigungsteil hin. Es schließt mit einer erkenbarren Formel, damit die Gemeinde mit "Amen" einstimmen kann' (p. 46).

40 General Assembly of PCRK, 2003, *The Book of Common Worship for the Presbyterian Church in the Republic of Korea*, Seoul: PCRK Press, p. 51.

41 *The Book of Common Worship PCRK*, Part I: Sunday Worship, pp. 95–201.

42 A similar tension between the use of collects and prayers for illumination can be found in the resources of the Presbyterian Church in Korea. *The Book of Common Worship PCRK*, p. 51, describes the prayer for illumination very briefly with a suggested placement before the sermon. Collects, mostly based

Concluding observations

In some ways, many within the Reformed Church would argue that it has gone full circle in its treatment of the collect. Yet in other ways, the Reformed Churches have continually redefined its place and use. What began in Strasbourg and Geneva in the sixteenth century continues to hold sway. As we have seen, the transformation of the collect into a prayer for illumination was a liturgically bold and theologically decisive act. It reoriented the liturgy while still maintaining the traditional space for this prayer, and in so doing allowed it to point in a completely new direction. Here again the primary theological watchword of the Reformed Church was influential, *Ecclesia reformata, semper reformanda*, the Church reformed, always being reformed according to the Word of God and the call of the Spirit.[43] The movement between form and freedom, central to the life and practices of Reformed congregations, brought ongoing liturgical change, as Reformed Churches worked to establish their theological and liturgical identity. In this regard, the study of the history of the collect in the Reformed Church provides insight into far more than one brief prayer; it foreshadows the broader liturgical history of Reformed congregations.

---

on the lectionary and some Korean church historical occasions, may be used in other parts of the service for the call to worship, litanies of thanksgiving, and litanies of confession (Part I, Sunday worship, pp. 95–201).

43 See *The Constitution of the Presbyterian Church (USA), Part II, Book of Order*, G-2.0200.

8

Written Prayers in an Oral Context: Transitions in British Baptist Worship

CHRIS ELLIS

The study of Free Church worship is far from straightforward. The researcher has virtually no published prayer books which might facilitate the tracing of liturgical developments, certainly from the late sixteenth century to the mid-nineteenth century. Free Church worship has been, for most of its life, an oral medium in which representative persons have prayed on behalf of the congregation. Not only has there been little expectation of a vocal contribution by the congregation, but the prayers of that leader have almost invariably been extempore. Indeed written prayers, whether for minister or congregation, were regarded with grave suspicion until relatively recently. While there are some changes to this generalization, which we can examine below, a reflection on this antipathy to written prayers will not only be of ecumenical and historical interest, but may offer the opportunity to explore aspects of Christian spirituality that underpin these denominational attitudes and worship practices.

Baptists number some 37,000,000 baptized church members worldwide, with an adherents' community estimated at something around 105,000,000.[1] They are predominantly evangelical in theology and mostly trace their origins to the Radical Reformation, through the separatists of the English Reformation in the late sixteenth and early seventeenth centuries. There are two main strands which converged into the British Baptist tradition. First, there were the General Baptists who were Arminian in theology and who had some contact with the Dutch Mennonites in the early decades of the seventeenth century. Second, there were the Particular Baptists who were Calvinistic in theology

---

1 See 'About the BWA' on the Baptist World Alliance website: http://www.bwanet.org/. There are a number of Baptist groups in addition to those in membership of the BWA.

and numerically larger. This group was in close fellowship with fellow Calvinists, especially the Independents, later to be the Congregationalists, and, after the ejections of 1662, the Presbyterians.

These groups saw themselves as the heirs to the Puritans, or rather, to those groups who separated from the Elizabethan Church of England because they did not consider it sufficiently reformed. In search of a pure Church which was free of state control, they established congregations that displayed a gathered ecclesiology, what became known as 'believer churches'.[2] Baptists eventually distinguished themselves from other separatists by taking the theology of a believer Church to its logical conclusion and reserving baptism only for those who were believers.

The foundations of free prayer

The worship of these groups was an important expression of their restorationist search for a pure Church which ordered its life according to biblical principles. Thus we might see them as the left wing of the Reformation reaction against the liturgical practices of the Catholic Church,[3] both in its medieval forms and in its Tridentine developments. In our ecumenical age we may be embarrassed by the invectives and suspicion of previous generations, but if we are to understand their spiritualities and learn from their wisdom, then we need to read their invectives in context.

The Baptist story begins with a group of émigré Separatists who gathered in Amsterdam under the leadership of John Smyth and Thomas Helwys in 1609. Their worship was spontaneous, and no books were allowed to be used in this proto-Baptist congregation. John Smyth had established the principles underlying this practice in his *Differences of the Churches of the Separation*, where he claimed that, because

> wordes and syntaxe are signes of thinges, and of the relations and reasons of things . . . it followeth that bookes or writinges are in the

---

2 See G. H. Williams, 1962, *The Radical Reformation*, London: Weidenfeld and Nicolson, and D. F. Durnbaugh, 1968, repr. 1985, *The Believers' Church: The History and Character of Radical Protestantism*, Scottdale PA: Herald Press.

3 See J. F. White, 1989, *Protestant Worship: Traditions in Transition*, Louisville KY: Westminster John Knox Press, for a taxonomy of Protestant denominations and their worship as degrees of reaction against the Church of Rome, especially pp. 21–4.

nature of pictures or Images & therefore in the nature of ceremonies: & and so by consequent reading a booke is ceremoniall.[4]

Thus inspiration is seen as a vital and necessary part of true worship. Two members of the Amsterdam congregation, Anne and Hughe Bromhead, in a letter of 1609, explained why written prayers were unacceptable:

> no Apocrypha must be brought into the public assemblies for there only God's word and the lively voice of his own graces must be heard in the public assemblies. But men's writings and the reading them over for prayer are apocrypha, therefore may not be brought into the public assemblies.

The immediacy of encounter with God is valued, so that the human words that are uttered are seen as the promptings of the Spirit – 'the lively voice of his own graces'. Having rehearsed what was to become a familiar argument, that nothing may be done in worship that does not have scriptural warrant, and that the *reading* of prayers does not have such warrant, the Bromheads continue, 'we may not in the worship of God receive any tradition which brought our liberty into bondage: therefore read prayers, etc.'[5]

Here there may be a double reference. Negatively, the English émigré congregation was in Amsterdam because of persecution and a refusal to participate in the Prayer Book worship of the Established Church. Later in the century *The Book of Common Prayer* would be seen as an instrument of repression whereby local worship was constrained and believers made subject to ecclesiastical authority.[6]

Positively, there is reference to that view of prayer which sees it as inspired at the moment of utterance by the work of the Holy Spirit. In such an understanding, books will only get in the way, 'because true

---

4 John Smyth, 1608, 'The Differences of the Churches of the Separation: containing a description of the Leitovrgie and Ministries of the visible Church', in W. T. Whitley (ed.), 1915, *The Works of John Smyth fellow of Christ's College 1594–8*, Cambridge: Cambridge University Press, pp. 269–320, pp. 278–9.

5 C. Burrage, 1912, *The Early Dissenters in the Light of Recent Research (1550–1641)*, vol. 2, Cambridge: Cambridge University Press, p. 74.

6 John Owen was later to accuse those who imposed liturgies of bringing 'fire and faggot into the Christian religion', and even those Independents and Presbyterians like Richard Baxter, who were prepared to use written prayers on occasion, were galvanized against such prayers by the events that followed 1660.

prayer must be of faith uttered with heart and lively voice'. If God wants to inspire our worship here and now, then 'it is presumptuous ignorance to bring a book to speak for us unto God'. Sinful human beings are unable to pray aright and they need the activity of the Spirit to prompt them – Romans 8.26 is a classic text which undergirds much of the writing about free prayer.[7]

In the middle of the eighteenth century, the High Calvinistic Baptist John Gill, commenting on 1 Corinthians 14.15, saw the Spirit as not only 'the author of prayer', but the one who informs our inadequate native intelligence about the matters for which we should pray. Even to pray 'with understanding' is to be dependent upon the Spirit, for 'to "pray with the understanding" is to pray with the understanding illuminated by the Spirit of God, or to pray with an experimental spiritual understanding of things'.[8]

This immediacy is not only an experiential openness to the Spirit, but an honest and urgent petitioning of God which flows from the deepest needs and hopes of the one praying. Members of that early Amsterdam congregation had claimed that using written prayers is to offer God a human invention, rather than the Spirit-inspired pleadings of spontaneous worship:

> to worship the true God after another manner than he hath taught us is idolatry but God commanded us to come unto him heavy laden with contrite heart to cry unto him for our wants, etc. Therefore we may not stand reading a dead letter instead of pouring forth our petitions . . .[9]

Written prayers were also believed to encourage hypocrisy by requiring worshippers to mouth words that may not truly express their sentiments or beliefs. Isaac Watts, while advocating the preparation of public prayer in advance of worship, argued that liturgical forms inevitably led to a lack of sincerity and the offering of inappropriate prayers:

> It leads us into the danger of hypocrisy and mere lip-service. Sometimes we shall be tempted to express those things which are not the

---

7 In fact, Horton Davies points out that John Owen's *Discourse of the Work of the Holy Spirit in Prayer* is an extended sermon upon that text. H. Davies, 1948, *The Worship of the English Puritans*, London: Dacre Press, p. 103.

8 J. Gill, 1751, *Two Discourses; the One on Prayer, the Other on Singing of Psalms*, London: G. Keith & J. Robinson, pp. 30–1.

9 Burrage, *The Early English Dissenters*, vol. 2, p. 74.

very thoughts of our own souls, and so use words that are not suited to our present wants, or sorrows, or requests; because those words are put together, and made ready beforehand.[10]

This argument is a negative form of that positive argument that claims that free prayer can be truly contextual and sensitively pastoral in ways that are not open to pre-written liturgies.[11] Indeed, Watts claims that such openness to the needs of a particular congregation is not possible with prescribed prayers, for they will either be general or inaccurate:

> a form . . . renders our converse with God very imperfect: For it is not possible that forms of prayer should be composed, that are perfectly suited to all our frames of spirit, and fitted to all our occasions in the things of this life, and the life to come . . . It is much sweeter to our own souls, and to our fellow worshippers, to have our fears, and our doubts, and complaints, and temptations, and sorrows represented in most exact and particular expressions, in such language as the soul itself feels when the words are spoken.[12]

Not only is a sense of dependence upon the Spirit intrinsic to free prayer, and therefore an expression of the fellowship of *believers*, but the ad hoc nature of this prayer enables it to be the prayer of *this* local church – the concerns of *this* congregation, the needs and aspirations of *this* group of people on *this* particular day.[13]

John Bunyan and the spirituality of spontaneous prayer

John Bunyan offers a good case study for examining many of these themes. The classic text is his book *I will Pray with the Spirit and with Understanding Also*, written in Bedford jail where he spent a good

---

10 I. Watts, 1715, 'A Guide to Prayer; or a Free and Rational Account of the Grace and Spirit of Prayer with Plain Directions how Every Christian may Attain Them', in J. Doddridge, 1753, *The Works of the Reverend and Learned Isaac Watts, D.D*, London: J. Barfield, pp. 105–96, p. 127.

11 The American Baptist John Skoglund in the mid-twentieth century spoke of 'localized' prayer being made easier by free prayer. J. Skoglund, 1974, 'Free Prayer', *Studia Liturgica* 4, pp. 151–66, p. 162.

12 Watts, *Guide to Prayer*, pp. 127–8.

13 The rubrics of late twentieth-century service books in the Anglican and Roman Catholic traditions now provide an opportunity for free intercessions and petitions for the same pastoral reason.

many years following the restoration of Charles II. The book is a blend of invective against the imposition and use of the *BCP* and, at the same time, a series of expositions on the nature of prayer in the Free Church tradition, which I believe stands comparison with many better known devotional classics.

While the polemical sections of Bunyan's book may deter some readers from accessing the rich and inspirational sections on prayer, it remains a work of considerable significance. The very unevenness of the writing, with its negative diatribes against liturgical, Prayer Book worship and its positive descriptions of personal prayer, provide us with an extended expression of Free Church spirituality and a classic account of how that spirituality was theologically undergirded and located within post-Reformation liturgical developments.

It is perhaps simplest to list some of the objections which Bunyan placed against Prayer Book worship, and it is not surprising that his tone is the opposite of eirenic given his imprisoned circumstances. It is likely that the polemics are a reiteration of the arguments Bunyan would have used at his trial and they may be found in other writings of the period.[14] This force of law that accompanied the revised *BCP* of 1662 is evident in Bunyan's criticism:

> Only let me say, it is a sad sign, that that, which is one of the most eminent parts of the pretended Worship of God, is AntiChristian; when it hath nothing but Tradition of men, and the strength of Persecution to uphold, or plead for it. (Use 3)

This concern for freedom is a crucial aspect of Free Church spirituality. It is the freedom from state, or centralized control, as well as the freedom to offer prayer as led by the sovereign Holy Spirit:

> It must be a praying with the Spirit, that is the effectual praying; because, without that, as men are senceless, so hypocritical, cold, and unseemly in their prayers; and so, they with their prayers, are both rendered abominable to God.

In addition, it is a freedom to pray according to the needs of those praying or of those for whom they offer prayer. Consequently, the assigning

---

14 See H. Davies, 1970, repr. 1996, *Worship and Theology in England: From Cranmer to Baxter and Fox, 1534–1690*, Grand Rapids MI and Cambridge: Eerdmans, esp. p. xx.

of fixed prayers through the Christian year is sarcastically derided as replacing authentic prayer with a pre-packaged form:

> But here now, the wise men of our dayes are so well skill'd, as that they have both the *Manner* and *Matter* of their Prayers at their finger ends; setting such a Prayer for such a day, and that twenty years before it comes. One for *Christmass, another for* Easter, and six dayes after that. They have also bounded how many syllables must be said in every one of them at their publick Exercises. For each Saints day also, they have them ready for the generations yet unborn to say.

To understand these powerful invectives we not only need to recognize that their author was imprisoned, but also to take note of the theological convictions that led to such immoderate language. At the beginning of the book, Bunyan states clearly his definition of prayer, and the rest of the work provides an exposition of this:

> Prayer is a sincere, sensible, affectionate pouring out of the heart or soul to God through Christ, in the strength and assistance of the holy Spirit, for such things as God hath promised, or, according to the Word, for the good of the Church, with submission, in Faith, to the Will of God. It is the opener of the heart of God, and a means by which the soul, though empty, is filled. By Prayer the Christian can open his heart to God as to a Friend, and obtain fresh testimony of God's Friendship to him.[15]

The core vision is that prayer flows from a heart which is touched by the Spirit of God, and the core convictions are that such prayer be sincere, intelligible and born of a love of God. Such spirituality is more concerned with strength and integrity of intent than beauty or clarity of language:

> O how great a task is it, for a poor soul that becomes sensible of sin, and the wrath of God, to say in Faith, but this one word, *Father!* I tell you, how ever hypocrites think, yet the Christian, that is so indeed, finds all the difficulty in this very thing, it cannot say, God

---

15 John Bunyan, 1663, 'I will Pray with the Spirit and with Understanding also', in Robert L. Greaves (ed.), 1976, *The Doctrine of the Law and Grace unfolded and I will pray with the Spirit*, Oxford: Clarendon Press, p. 235.

is its *Father* ... That one word spoken in Faith, is better than a thousand prayers, as men call them, written and read, in a formal, cold, luke-warm way.

The best Prayers have often more groans than words; and those words that it hath, are but a lean and shallow representation of the heart, life, and spirit of that Prayer.

There are suggestions here of a phenomenology or a spirituality of prayer. Prayer is not identified with the words, but with an inner reality whereby the Spirit operates on or in the heart of a human being and lifts that person to God. Because words may well fail in true prayer, we must conclude that prayer itself is almost independent of words – an activity of the mind and affections. In so far as words are relevant, they *express* that reality (or else are incapable of doing so), but the words of others cannot provoke or serve that inner reality. Thus, the placing of prayer beyond words in an inner realm inevitably has implications for pastoral practice. If external words cannot serve prayer, then prayer books will be of little use.

There is, of course, a serious flaw in Bunyan's argument. Whenever he or anyone else was leading the Bedford congregation in prayer their extempore words would be an external shaping of the prayers of the congregation. Bunyan defined prayer as a pouring out of the heart and we may describe this view as 'expressive prayer' – prayer that expresses that which is sincerely felt by the one praying. However, when a leader of worship leads a congregation in prayer, whether spontaneously or through the use of pre-composed words, we may describe such prayer as 'impressive prayer' in which the words of the leader, external to the congregation, lead and shape the communal prayer. Both expressive and impressive prayers were functioning in Bunyan's meeting house whenever one person led the community in prayer. Once this distinction has been acknowledged, it is difficult not to recognize the validity of written prayers as one way of leading a congregation in worship, just as the oral words of a leader have been accepted.

This personal spirituality is central to Free Church worship and has led to the tendency of not making a sharp distinction between public and personal prayer. Bunyan's concern for sincerity expresses a view of the Church as a covenant community formed freely by its members, rather than the civil religion of an assembled parish. Of course, all forms of Christianity are likely to claim a high regard for personal sincerity, and the *BCP* is no exception, yet worship enforced by law is likely to militate against a concern with inward intentions by many of the worshippers who are assembled because the law or social convention dictates it.

At the very beginning of his book, Bunyan states 'Prayer is an Ordinance of God, and that to be used both in Publick and Private', with no distinction seemingly made between the types of discourse.[16] Prayer is indivisible, whether offered in the closet or a cathedral.

Commentators on the Reformation have suggested that the medieval laity became increasingly alienated from church worship because the words of the priest were indistinct and in a language that many could not understand. Alister McGrath suggests that much of the Reformation was a lay movement, stimulated in part by the increased education of the newly emerging professional classes.[17] A view of the world that saw God concerned with the details of everyday life was likely to contribute to a spirituality where the separation between the sacred and everyday life was eroded. This shift in how the world was viewed was particularly noticeable in the worship styles of the Separatists. Dignity in worship did not require formal ceremonial undertaken by an elite class, but could involve the participation of members of the congregation in leading parts of worship as well as in extempore prayer.[18] Devotional practices developed which enabled members of the congregation to engage in their own private devotions during the service while other things were happening.

The developing practice of prayer in Baptist worship

As we have already noted, tracing the development of Free Church worship is not straightforward, as there were few liturgical texts – other than sermons and, eventually, hymn books. However, there are a few contemporary descriptions in sources such as letters and minute books

---

16 Bunyan, *I will Pray with the Spirit*, p. 235.

17 A. E. McGrath, 1987, *The Intellectual Origins of the European Reformation*, Oxford: Blackwell, pp. 10–12; A. E. McGrath, 1991, *Roots that Refresh: A Celebration of Reformation Spirituality*, London: Hodder and Stoughton, pp. 44–5.

18 Murray Tolmie's account of Thomas Lambe's General Baptist congregation in Thomas Edwards's *Gangaena* (1646) describes a lively participation in discussing, and even interrupting, the sermon. Murray Tolmie, 1977, *The Triumph of the Saints: The Separate Churches of London 1616–1649*, Cambridge and New York: Cambridge University Press, pp. 76–7.

that enable us to piece together a broad picture of liturgical developments, including the practice of public prayer.[19]

From the early seventeenth to the late nineteenth century, two emphases are clear. First, virtually all prayer in worship is extempore, reflecting the kind of Free Church spirituality we have been examining. The concern is both for freedom from external constraint and an openness to the direction and inspiration of the Holy Spirit. Second, public prayer will be univocal, with one representative person speaking on behalf of the gathered congregation. I am not aware of any examples of a Baptist congregation praying together by uttering the same words at the same time – whether read or memorized – with two possible exceptions. On the other hand, the development of hymnody provided a means whereby congregations might pray in unison, and we shall return to this important trajectory below.

Baptist worship has primarily comprised the offering of sung praise and extempore prayers, together with the reading of Scripture and preaching. By the end of the seventeenth century there is evidence of short prayer, possibly of an invocatory nature, being offered at the beginning of the service, and a more extended period of prayer being offered later which would include praise, confession and thanksgiving, as well as intercessions and petitions.[20]

The morning service at the Independent Bury Street Church, where Isaac Watts was the minister, began with a metrical psalm sung by the congregation. All we can say with certainty is that, after the congregational psalm, a short prayer of invocation was offered, asking 'for the Divine presence in all the following parts of worship', and this was followed by an exposition of Scripture. After a hymn, the minister entered the pulpit, and

> prays more at large, for all the variety of blessings, spiritual and temporal, for the whole congregation, with confession of sins, and thanksgiving for mercies; petitions also are offered up for the whole world, for the churches of Christ, for the nation in which we dwell, for all our rulers and governors, together with any particular cases which are represented.[21]

---

19 For an account of the developing pattern of worship among British Baptists, see C. J. Ellis, 2004, *Gathering: A Theology and Spirituality of Worship in Free Church Tradition*, London: SCM Press, pp. 39–70.

20 So the Paul Alley Church in London in its foundation document of 1696. See Ellis, *Gathering*, p. 105.

21 T. G. Crippen, 1913, 'From the Bury Street Church Records', *Transactions of the Congregational Historical Society* 6, p. 334.

Here we have a full description of what came to be known as the 'Long Prayer' and which was the main form of free prayer in Nonconformist worship into the early part of the twentieth century. Of particular note here is the allusion to 'particular cases which are represented', which refers to the practice of individual members of the congregation writing particular requests on pieces of paper which were taken to the minister in the pulpit for inclusion in the prayer. Here is an example of the pastoral localization of free prayer, though in a congregation large enough to require such an arrangement instead of it being assumed that the minister will already know the needs of the congregation. After the sermon there was a short prayer and a benediction. As there had already been ample opportunity for petitionary prayer, it is more likely that this latter prayer followed on from the themes of the sermon.

By the early twentieth century, little had changed except an increase in the number of hymns, alternating with parts of the service. There was normally one long prayer, the opening of worship would sometimes include Scripture sentences and a prayer of invocation, and there would sometimes have been a brief prayer at the conclusion of the sermon. Some of the praying was now done in the hymnody, though the chief prayer was still a long collection of miscellaneous concerns. By the beginning of the twentieth century, there were some voices calling for the breaking up of this prayer into shorter prayers and this trend continued as the century progressed.[22]

In 1996 I conducted, in conjunction with the Baptist Union of Great Britain, a national survey of Baptist worship practices and attitudes which provided evidence of considerable diversification in Baptist worship in recent years.[23] Some worship remained 'traditional', while other worship showed the influence of charismatic renewal or liturgical reform, with some evidence of interaction and blending between these two movements.[24] As to the form of prayer in contemporary

---

22 See, for example, Hugh Martin's suggestions for reform in the 1950s: 'My second reform is the breaking up of the "long" prayer, which it is hard to defend. It is both too long and too miscellaneous, putting together as it does thanksgiving, petition, penitence and intercession.' H. Martin, 1957, 'The Conduct of Baptist Worship', *Baptist Quarterly* 17 (4), pp. 148–58, p. 155.

23 C. J. Ellis, 1999, *Baptist Worship Today*, Didcot: Baptist Union of Great Britain.

24 It is possible that some liturgical reform has come into Baptist life as a result of charismatic Baptists experiencing a positive encounter with charismatic worship within liturgical traditions. See, for example, D. McBain, 1997, *Fire over the Waters: Renewal among Baptists and Others from the 1960s to the 1990s*, London: Darton, Longman and Todd, pp. 177–82.

Baptist worship, while only a tenth of churches offered prayer in the 'traditional' pattern of one main prayer, over 60 per cent of churches claimed to have a prayer of praise and confession early in the service, followed by separate intercessions later. A further 21 per cent intersperse prayers through the service in relation to other components. Here is a pattern that *appears* to diverge from the supposedly traditional pattern of a long prayer, though, as we have seen, prayer was rarely confined to the 'long' prayer alone.

The present separation of praise and confession from intercessions may well reflect the influence of the Liturgical Movement, with its encouragement for rational development through the service and for clear functions for the several parts. Alternatively, it could reflect an increased concern that praise should be a major component in worship, though this in turn may reflect charismatic influence.[25]

From no text to some text

Though there was a small amount of correspondence concerning read prayers in the Baptist newspaper *The Freeman* in the middle of the nineteenth century,[26] we are safe to generalize that, into the twentieth century, virtually all prayer in Baptist churches was free prayer. However, that is not to say that all prayer was spontaneous. For example, Isaac Watts's *Guide to Prayer* was widely respected and read in Particular Baptist circles in the eighteenth century.[27] In that book, he recommended that we avoid what he saw as two extremes in prayer. On the one hand, we should avoid 'a confining ourselves entirely to pre-composed forms of prayer' and, on the other, 'an entire dependence on sudden motions and suggestions of thought'.[28] He identifies 'extempore prayer' as being 'when we, without any reflection or meditation beforehand, address ourselves to God, and speak the thoughts of our hearts, as fast as we conceive them'. Distinct from this is 'conceived' or 'free prayer', 'when we have not the words of our prayer formed beforehand, to direct our thoughts, but we conceive the matter or substance

---

25 Ellis, *Baptist Worship Today*, p. 32.
26 See, for example, the correspondence 'On Public Prayer' of 10 and 17 June 1857.
27 Watts's works were recommended reading for those preparing for ministry at the (Baptist) Bristol Academy. See J. Rippon, 1790, *The Baptist Annual Register*, vol. I, London, p. 255.
28 Watts, *Guide to Prayer*, p. 125.

of our address to God, first in our minds, and then put those conceptions in such words and expressions as we think most proper'.[29] This conceived prayer may not involve a detailed working out of what will be uttered in public, but should include what he describes as 'premeditation' involving the preparation of the heart as well as a reflection on the subjects for prayer.[30] In 1996 churches were asked about those prayers which were not read from a book. Replies suggested that 68 per cent were offered extempore, with 30 per cent being sketched out beforehand and 18 per cent being prepared in detail.[31] About a third of free prayer currently offered in Baptist churches may be viewed as 'conceived prayer' as articulated by Isaac Watts, while over two-thirds is still offered spontaneously.

Yet, whether free prayer is conceived or spontaneous, it is still quite different from either the use of service books or the reading of pre-composed prayers by the leader of worship. We not only need to distinguish between extempore or conceived free prayer, but between different forms of pre-composed prayer. First, there are those prayers and responsive sequences that are put in the hands of the congregation so that all might pray aloud certain words. Second, there are those written prayers, published in worship manuals or collections of prayers, that the leader of worship may read as though their own. In turn, this use of material written by others needs to be distinguished from written prayers that have been prepared and written for the occasion by the person leading worship.

In our survey of worship practices, only 1 per cent of respondents said that prayers were *usually* read from a book, while 52 per cent replied that prayers were *sometimes* read. Only 42 per cent said that prayers were *never* read. Again, we probably need to see this change as a reflection of more than one influence.

Worship manuals and books of worship resource material have been increasingly available. Indeed, manuals to assist the leader of worship in performing certain offices have been available since early in the twentieth century. As well as the wider publishing of local experiment, such as that of Henry Bonner and F. C. Spurr of Hampstead Road

---

29 Watts, *Guide to Prayer*, pp. 125–6.

30 Watts, *Guide to Prayer*, p. 129.

31 We must remember that these responses relate to free prayer, not all prayers. We also need to register a measure of caution as many of the responses will have been returned by people other than those leading the prayers and so may not always represent what is actually happening.

Church Birmingham,[32] there were national attempts to offer assistance to those leading worship. Books were produced at first which simply, and very tentatively, offered an order of service for communion, with baptismal, marriage and funeral services. Prefaces tried to make clear that what was offered was not mandatory or an infringement of the freedom of local worship, but a resource to aid the worship leader. Later examples developed beyond this simple provision to include other sequences for use in worship, such as the commissioning of deacons, as well as material to be used through the Christian year and prayers for various occasions.

This development can be seen clearly in the line of publications available to those who lead Baptist worship. F. B. Meyer compiled a *Free Church Service Manual*, which was published by the National Free Church Council.[33] Around 1927, M. E. Aubrey, the General Secretary of the Baptist Union, compiled a similar, but rather fuller, volume entitled *A Minister's Manual*, which was specifically intended for Baptists.[34] In 1960, E. A. Payne and Stephen Winward produced *Orders and Prayers for Church Worship*, which was to be reprinted several times and which included liturgical resources from the wider Church as well as a substantial number of sequences and prayers entitled 'Ordinances of the Church'.[35] The book also included an influential introduction which was regarded as a classic statement on worship by those Baptists who were increasingly identifying with the issues of the Liturgical Movement.

---

32 See F. C. Spurr and H. Bonner, 1930, *Come Let Us Worship: A Book of Common Worship for Use in Free Churches*, London: Kingsgate Press. This was the fruit of local liturgical experiment by successive ministers and the congregation of Hampstead Road Church, Birmingham, and was revised and published nationally by the Baptist Union publishing house. Spurr claimed in the introduction (p. vii) that the material, in the form of complete services of worship with responsive prayers, had been in use in the Birmingham church for forty years. This places local use of liturgical services at the end of the nineteenth century. While we must see this as an exceptional situation, its wider publication in 1930 probably indicates a changing mood.

33 F. B. Meyer (ed.) 1911, *Free Church Service Manual*, London: National Council of Evangelical Free Churches.

34 M. E. Aubrey, 1927, *A Minister's Manual*, London: Kingsgate Press, 'containing orders of service for marriage, dedication of infants, baptism of believers, communion of the Lord's Supper, burial of the dead and other occasions'.

35 E. A. Payne and S. F. Winward, 1960, *Orders and Prayers for Church Worship: A Manual for Ministers*, London: Carey Kingsgate Press.

In 1980, the replacement, *Praise God*, was published by the Baptist Union, though this did not seem to gain wide support, with many continuing to use copies of Payne and Winward's *Orders and Prayers*.[36] *Patterns and Prayers for Christian Worship*, which attempted to offer material for particular offices and occasions while also offering wider prayer material, was published in 1991.[37] The preparation of *Patterns and Prayers for Christian Worship* benefited from an awareness of the cool reception that its predecessor had received.[38] As well as the increased need for a new book following the changes in worship language and culture since 1960, charismatic Baptists were now expressing a need for some written material to help with certain parts of worship and these views were canvassed and incorporated in the developing of the book.[39]

In 2005, *Gathering for Worship: Patterns and Prayers for the Community of Disciples* was published.[40] It is the largest collection of services and prayers to date and is the first official Baptist worship resource to have been informed intentionally by the insights of liturgical theology.[41] The patterns of worship that it offers attempt to express what Baptists believe about baptism, the Lord's Supper, ministry and other matters. In so doing it both offers Baptists a range of opportunities for Christian formation, and provides their ecumenical friends with a means of understanding Baptist convictions.

So what are the factors that have led to an increased use in written prayer material among Baptist congregations? More recently, I would suggest it is the fruit of increased ecumenical contact and a more eclectic approach to the culture, or cultures, of worship. Encountering liturgical prayer in united services and a deepening search for meaningful expressions of spirituality encourage an exploration of and reception

---

36 A. Gilmore, E. Smalley and M. Walker, 1980, *Praise God: A Collection of Resource Material for Christian Worship*, London: The Baptist Union of Great Britain and Ireland.

37 The Baptist Union of Great Britain, 1991, *Patterns and Prayers for Christian Worship*, Oxford: Oxford University Press.

38 While there is no statistical evidence available for the perception that *Praise God* was not widely accepted, the perception influenced the brief given to the group that was commissioned to compile *Patterns and Prayers for Christian Worship*.

39 See, for example, the introduction (pp. 1–17), especially the third pattern for an 'Open Service' on p. 17 and the third pattern for the Lord's Supper, pp. 74–5.

40 C. J. Ellis and M. Blyth, 2005, *Gathering for Worship: Patterns and Prayers for the Community of Disciples*, Norwich: Canterbury Press.

41 See, for example, the Preface, pp. xiv–xix.

of resources beyond narrow denominational boundaries. For many Baptists, as for evangelicals more generally, the influence of charismatic renewal has loosened some of the previous restraints and has enabled the acceptance of liturgical forms found in charismatic worship practised in other traditions.

But what of the earlier moves towards the use of written material, albeit by the leader of worship rather than as responses to be uttered by the whole congregation? The introduction of hymnody must be seen as particularly important in drawing the Free Churches from an antipathy to read prayers under any circumstances towards a position where such written material might be welcomed within a mixed economy of extempore, pre-composed and published prayers. The introduction of hymnody was neither easy nor rapid. The General Baptists never took to congregational singing, as their conservative approach to worship practices judged it to be unbiblical.[42] The Particular Baptists sang psalms from the beginning, but through the course of the eighteenth century the singing of composed hymns began to supplement these.[43]

When Thomas Grantham, a leading General Baptist, opposed the singing of words that were of a human composition, a category that included metrical psalms along with hymns, he cautioned that such singing 'opens a gap for forms of prayer'.[44] Grantham was quite correct, and when the possible use of written prayers was debated in the Baptist press during the nineteenth century, the precedent of hymns was cited. For in hymns congregations often address God in words that have obviously been pre-composed:

> There is, in fact, no objection, *on principle*, against our using forms of devotion, provided we do not hinder those whom the Divine Spirit prompts to utter the wants and feelings of the hour or of the times, from doing so freely. The use of a *certain proportion* of pre-composed prayers would no more do this than the use of pre-composed hymns . . .

---

42 The exceptions were the General Baptists of the New Connexion who, as a group born of the Evangelical Revival, broke from the older General Baptists partly because they considered them to be theologically heterodox and partly because they believed singing to be a gospel ordinance.

43 For a summary description of the development of hymn-singing among Baptists, see Ellis, *Gathering*, pp. 153–64.

44 T. Grantham, 1678, *Christianismus Primitivus: or, The Ancient Christian Religion, in its nature, certainty, excellency, and beauty, (internal and external) particularly considered, asserted, and vindicated &c*, London: Francis Smith.

I will only say that both prayers and praises *with responses* should form a part large enough to give variety to the service, and relief to the occupant of the pew; and that in my opinion, we should have a number of prayers, as great, perhaps, as we have of hymns, from which those who conduct the service should select for each occasion, announcing them as we now do hymns. The collection should include all the best prayers in the Prayer-book.[45]

This fascinating letter to *The Freeman* in 1868 is way ahead of its time and it is difficult to know whether it represents some isolated local practices or simply the musings of a prophetic imagination! But the argument is clear: the singing of hymns provides a clear precedent for the congregational use of written prayers in a denomination that did not then accept such prayers.

We have seen how the early books of prayer resources for ministers were primarily for pastoral offices and communion. Since the publication of *Orders and Prayers for Church Worship: A Manual for Ministers* in 1960,[46] the range of material offered has increased to include provision for all kinds of special occasions in the worship of a local church, as well as more general material, some of which has offered the possibility of simple responses by the congregation. In each case there has been extensive use of material from the service books of other denominations. In *Orders and Prayers* much was drawn from the *BCP*, but the revolution in worship language that was hastened by the introduction of modern translations of Scripture meant that subsequent books looked to the new liturgical provisions that were appearing in many denominations as the fruit of liturgical renewal.

The collect as a promising form

Amidst this ecumenical borrowing collects had their place, though they did not dominate. I suspect the doxological flourish at the close of each was too rhetorically exotic for some Baptist tastes, as even the use of written prayers needed to be delivered in a way that appeared natural, if not spontaneous, in a culture that had for so long prized sincerity expressed as spontaneity. Nonetheless, I believe a case can be made for Baptists to develop the collect as a form of prayer that would fit well within their worship.

---

45 Letter from 'A Sexagenarian', *The Freeman*, 2 October 1868.
46 Payne and Winward, *Orders and Prayers*.

From a theological perspective we may observe that the collect is grounded in the nature of God. The petition that is customarily offered as the second clause of the prayer usually grows out of some divine attribute or activity that has been named in the first clause. This has much to commend it as a way of prayer, for the focus on God has both confessional and formational characteristics. The linking of a petition to a statement of faith about God has two particular merits to commend it. First, the focusing of prayer in the nature of God enables the congregation to confess its faith and at the same time be shaped by that faith. Second, the linking of that attribute to the subsequent petition earths the theological confession in the needs of the world and the congregation, thus providing a holistic perspective on faith in God and concern for God's world.

Furthermore, from a liturgical perspective, the function of the collect as a way of gathering preceding prayers could be particularly apposite in a denomination that might use open prayer, periods of silence or extempore petitions. The variety of prayer material, or a diversity of people praying, might be helpfully summed up through an appropriate collect. Baptists are very unlikely to disavow the freedom of local leaders and congregations to order their worship, and variety is likely to be an increasing characteristic of culturally blended worship,[47] so the use of a collect has great potential to gather and focus variegated periods of prayer.

Whether this potential is tapped we shall have to wait and see, but in the meantime Baptist worship continues to be a mixed economy of extempore and written prayer. In this it offers material that has been developed by local worship leaders, provided by denominational editors and borrowed from ecumenical partners. At the same time, those ecumenical friends have begun to discover the possibilities of free prayer while continuing to prize litanies, responses and, of course, collects.

---

47 See R. E. Webber, 1994, *Blended Worship: Achieving Substance and Relevance in Worship*, Peabody MA: Hendrickson.

9

Collects and Lectionaries

DAVID KENNEDY

Introduction

In the Western liturgy historically, the relationship between the collect of the day and the eucharistic readings has been understated and somewhat ambiguous. While the seasons of the Christian year naturally set the broad framework for the variable parts of the Mass, including the prayer 'of the day', there was no 'thematic' approach as such, and the collect often was a 'stand alone' prayer related to aspects of Christian revelation on certain Sundays in seasonal time, but on the vast majority of Sundays to more general Christian virtues and themes such as protection, deliverance and peace. Marion Hatchett admirably summarizes the historical position:

> On special occasions the collect of the Roman rite was related to the lections or to the theme of the day. On other occasions, however, it was of more general nature and consisted of a petition related to the special needs of the time. The fact that the collect was inserted in the rite at the time of the barbarian invasions and the decline of the Roman empire surely explains why so many of the collects from earlier sacramentaries are petitions for peace and protection. Attempts to link collects with the lections of the day are a waste of time and artificial. The earlier sacramentaries simply provided a number of formularies for use on ordinary Sundays. A comparison of the printed Sarum missals with the first printed Roman missal reveals that, for the period after Pentecost, though the series of collects and of lections was basically the same, the collects were frequently not related to the same lections and not said on the same Sunday. Essentially the collect of the day is the conclusion to the entrance rite.[1]

---

1 Marion J. Hatchett, 1980, *Commentary on the American Prayer Book*, San Francisco: Harper & Row, pp. 323–4.

In successive editions of *The Book of Common Prayer* in England, the collects have been placed with the Epistles and Gospels set for the Holy Communion. This is where in the *BCP* the shape of the Christian year is given expression, beginning with Advent Sunday. The earlier Table and Kalender is concerned solely with the appointment of psalmody and lessons for daily Morning and Evening Prayer on the basis of the civil calendar. Use of the collects is not confined to Holy Communion; they are also to be said at the daily offices. The Prayer Book communion lections are a conservative revision of those in the Sarum Missal; the collects are a mixture of translations and adaptations from Sarum and new compositions. In the Sarum rite, in conformity to what has been stated above, while some collects related to the themes of the Christian year, others were general in scope, bearing no relation to the appointed lections at Mass. That continued to be the case in collects translated and adapted from the Latin for the Reformed rites. In newly composed collects in the *BCP*, however, it is noticeable that there is a stronger connection between collect and lections. So, the collect for Advent Sunday (from the Prayer Book of 1549) effectively quotes the Epistle from Romans 13: '. . . that we may cast awaye the workes of darkness, and put upon us the armour of light . . .'. Similarly, the newly composed collect for Advent 2 (1549),

> Blessed lord, which hast caused all holy Scriptures to bee written for our learning; graunte us that we maye in suche wise heare them, read, marke, learne, and inwardly digeste them; that by pacience, and coumfort of thy holy woorde, we may embrace and euer hold fast the blessed hope of euerlasting life, which thou hast geuen us in our saviour Jesus Christe[2]

paraphrases the sentiment of the Epistle from Romans 15:

> Whatsoever things are writte aforetime, they are written for our learning, that we through pacience, and comfort of the scriptures, might haue hope.

Other examples are Advent 3 (1662), Epiphany 6 (1662), Quinquagesima (1549), Lent 1 (1549), Easter 2 (1549) and the Sunday after Ascension (1549). Many of the collects for holy days were extensively

---

2 *The First and Second Prayer Books of Edward VI*, 1949, London: J. M. Dent & Sons Ltd, pp. 32 and 34.

rewritten, not least to expunge the invocation of saints. This illustrates the didactic concerns of the Protestant Reformation to make Scripture accessible, and to apply it to Christian living and discipleship.

Twentieth-century liturgical renewal arising from the Liturgical Movement and the growing ecumenical consensus about the shape of eucharistic worship, with a conscious balance between 'the table of the word' and the 'table of the sacrament', has led to a new evaluation in both the Roman Catholic Church and the Churches of the Reformation about the place of the reading of Scripture within the liturgy. Most contemporary eucharistic liturgies have the basic structure of

- gathering rites
- ministry of the word
- ministry of the sacrament
- dismissal.

The collect or prayer of the day usually concludes the gathering rites, but can also act as a 'hinge', introducing the lections of the day. This chapter will explore how different Churches have come to different conclusions about the relationship of collect and lectionary, revealing that some of the historical ambiguity is still very much with us today.

New approaches to the lectionary

Since the mid-1960s, there have been three main lectionaries in use in the Churches, the Joint Liturgical Group two-year lectionary of 1967, the Roman Catholic three-year lectionary for Mass of 1969 (2nd edn, 1981), and the ecumenical revision of the Roman Lectionary, the Common Lectionary of 1983, which became the *Revised Common Lectionary* in 1992.

The Joint Liturgical Group 2-year lectionary

In 1967, the British Joint Liturgical Group, an ecumenical body with representatives from the main denominations, published a two-year, thematically based lectionary, with provision for Old Testament lesson, Epistle and Gospel. This was in conjunction with the reordering of the calendar, relating each Sunday of the year to one of the three major festivals:

Christmas: 9 Sundays before Christmas (incorporating Advent)
6 Sundays after Christmas
Easter: 9 Sundays before Easter (incorporating the 'gesimas' and Lent)
6 Sundays after Easter
Pentecost: The Day of Pentecost
21 Sundays after Pentecost.[3]

In the JLG scheme, a 'controlling lection' was designated for each period, namely, the Old Testament lection for the Sundays before Christmas, the Gospel reading for Christmas to the Day of Pentecost, and the Epistle lection for the period after Pentecost.

The 'thematic' approach can be illustrated by the stated themes of the nine Sundays before Christmas, based on salvation history: the Creation, the Fall, the Covenant of Preservation (Noah), the Election of God's People (Abraham), the Promise of Redemption (Moses), the Advent Hope, the Word of God in the Old Testament, the Forerunner, the Annunciation.[4] The compilers were insistent that the themes themselves were 'no more than *indications* of emphasis' and that they must not 'give false rigidity to the hearing of Scripture or the preaching of the Word of God'.[5]

This lectionary (with adapted calendar and some minor revision) was adopted by the Church of England in its liturgical revision in the late 1960s and early 1970s, culminating in *The Alternative Service Book 1980*, and by other Anglican and Protestant Churches, both in Britain and Ireland and in other parts of the world. A subsequent four-year lectionary, based on the Roman principles but giving John's Gospel its own year, did not gain wide acceptance, as attention had shifted to the *[Revised] Common Lectionary*.

The Roman Catholic three-year lectionary

For Roman Catholics, the ground-breaking Order of Readings for Mass of 1969 gave expression to section 51 of the Constitution on the Sacred Liturgy (1963):

---

3 Ronald C. D. Jasper (ed.), 1967, *The Calendar and Lectionary: A Reconsideration by the Joint Liturgical Group*, London: Oxford University Press, pp. 36–41.

4 Jasper, *The Calendar*, pp. 20 and 21. Most Churches adopting this scheme deleted the lections for Noah, inserting a new set of lections on the Remnant of Israel for the Fifth Sunday before Christmas.

5 Jasper, *The Calendar*, p. 20.

The treasures of the Bible are to be opened up more lavishly, so that richer fare may be provided for the faithful from the table of God's word. In this way a more representative portion of the holy scriptures will be read to the people in the course of a prescribed number of years.[6]

The old annual Tridentine lectionary with provision for an Epistle, gradual psalmody and Gospel gave way to a three-year cycle, embracing Old Testament, New Testament and Gospel lections as well as psalmody. The Gospel reading was determinative, as one would expect in a Catholic eucharistic lectionary, focusing on Matthew in Year A, Mark (supplemented by John) in Year B, and Luke in Year C, although Johannine readings also appear in Years B and C. The Gospel was complemented by the Old Testament lesson on the basis of typology, prophecy fulfilment or thematic link. The psalm was a response to the Old Testament lection. The New Testament lessons were selected for seasonal propriety, with semi-continuous readings from particular Epistles in 'ordinary time'. In Eastertide, lections from the Acts of the Apostles replaced the Old Testament lection. This lectionary was adopted by some Anglican Churches, notably in the USA, Australia and Southern Africa, and some Protestant Churches such as the United Church of Canada.

The *Revised Common Lectionary*

Meanwhile, in North America, the adoption of the new Roman Lectionary by a number of Anglican and Protestant Churches around the world led to a further ecumenical initiative in the setting up of the Consultation on Common Texts in 1978. This body adapted the Roman Lectionary in the light of criticisms such as the omission of verses and pericopes relating to women, and the desire to include more narrative, especially relating to cultural and ethnic diversity. This revision was published as the *Common Lectionary* in 1983. After a period of experimental use, further refinements led to the publication of the *Revised Common Lectionary* in 1992. The *RCL* follows the basic principles of the Roman Lectionary with one important addition: two tracks are provided for the Old Testament Lesson in 'Ordinary Time',

---

6 Holy See, 1963, 'The Constitution on the Sacred Liturgy (*Sacrosanctum Concilium*)', in Austin Flannery OP (ed.), 1996, *The Basic Sixteen Documents: Vatican Council II: Constitutions, Decrees, Declarations*, Northport NY: Costello Publishing Co., Dublin: Dominican Publications, pp. 117–61, p. 136.

one following the Roman linked model and another providing for continuous or selected readings through particular Old Testament books. While the New Testament lesson had always been free-floating, adoption of the continuous track means that in the 'green season', all three lessons are unrelated.

Collects and the new lectionaries

Lutheran Book of Worship (USA), 1978

The Inter-Lutheran Commission on Worship, representing some four Lutheran traditions in the USA and Canada, published the *Lutheran Book of Worship* in 1978.[7] It adapted the new Roman Lectionary, abandoning 'Sundays of the Year' and designating the 'Ordinary Time' lections to specific Sundays after Epiphany (culminating with the Transfiguration of our Lord), and Sundays after Pentecost. For each Sunday, a 'Prayer of the Day' (sometimes alternatives are offered) was designated for use in all three lectionary years. So while the prayers are set out along with the lections, they relate more to the themes of the seasons in the 'active part' of the Christian year and are generalist in non-seasonal time. The prayers are concise and include new compositions along with traditional texts rendered in contemporary English. An example from seasonal time is Advent 1, which, along with other prayers for the Advent season, draws on the verb *excita* ('stir up') from the medieval collects:

> Stir up your power, O Lord, and come. Protect us by your strength and save us from the threatening dangers of our sins, for you live and reign with the Father and the Holy Spirit, one God, now and forever.[8]

An example from Ordinary Time is Pentecost 14; the Gospel readings are Matthew 16.21–26 (A, 'let them take up their cross'), John 6.60–69 (B, the end of the 'Bread of Life' discourse) and Luke 13.2–30 (C, '... people will come from east and west'). The collect appears to have the Year C Gospel in mind:

---

7 See Frank Senn's chapter in this volume.
8 Lutheran Church in America, Board of Publications, 1978, *Lutheran Book of Worship*, Minneapolis MN and Philadelphia PA: Augsburg Publishing House, p. 13.

God of all creation, you reach out to call people of all nations to your kingdom. As you gather disciples from near and far, count us also among those who boldly confess your Son, Jesus Christ our Lord. (*LBW*, p. 27)

The Book of Common Prayer of the Episcopal Church (USA), 1979

Unlike the English Prayer Book, the *BCP* 1979 of the Episcopal Church separates the collects and the lectionary provision. This is because the lectionary is to be used at the principal morning service, whether that be a Eucharist or the daily office. The new Roman Lectionary was adopted. Lections were designated for up to nine Sundays after the Epiphany, but for the 'Season after Pentecost' the lections as a series of 'propers' are determined by date (Proper 1 as the Sunday closest to 11 May, etc.). The collects are provided in traditional and contemporary form. Like *LBW*, they relate to the broad themes of the seasons, and so are generalist in non-seasonal time. In the eucharistic liturgy, the collect serves as the opening prayer. Within the synaxis, which is given the main heading 'The Word of God', there are seven sub-headings:

- The Collect of the Day
- The Lessons
- The Sermon
- The Nicene Creed
- The Prayers of the People
- Confession of Sin
- The Peace.

The Alternative Service Book 1980

Here, the two-year JLG thematic lectionary was adopted. For each Sunday and major festival, an introductory and post-communion sentence, collect, portion of psalmody, and two sets of readings for Years 1 and 2 were provided. The catechetical nature of the approach is illustrated by the provision for Pentecost 15 with the theme 'Those in authority'. The controlling lesson (New Testament) for each year was

Year 1: Romans 13.1–7   You must all obey the governing authorities.

Year 2: 1 Timothy 2.1–7   I urge that petitions, prayers, intercessions, and thanksgivings be offered for all ... for sovereigns and all in high office.

This was complemented by the other lections: in Year 1, Isaiah 45.1–7, the election of Cyrus, and Matthew 22.15–22, the question of paying taxes to Caesar; in Year 2, 1 Kings 3.4–15, King Solomon's prayer for wisdom, and Matthew 14.1–12, King Herod's execution of John the Baptist. To complement these lections, the two sentences were 1 Peter 2.13, 'Be subject for the Lord's sake to every human institution', and Revelation 11.15, 'The kingdom of the world is to become the kingdom of our Lord, and of his Christ, and he shall reign for ever.' The Psalms appointed were 82 and 20, and the collect:

> Almighty Father,
> whose will is to restore all things
> in your beloved Son, the king of all:
> govern the hearts and minds of those in authority,
> and bring the families of the nations,
> divided and torn apart by the ravages of sin,
> to be subject to his just and gentle rule;
> who is alive ... (*ASB*, p. 709)

This collect, adapted from the pre-Vatican II Roman Missal's provision for the Feast of Christ the King,[9] illustrates just how thematic this approach to collect and lectionary is.

The United Methodist Book of Worship (1992)

The United Methodist Church (USA) adopted with minor adaptation the *Revised Common Lectionary* for its 1992 *Book of Worship*.[10] The Entrance rites (whether or not the service includes Holy Communion) make provision for 'opening prayer', including a prayer of the day, the Collect for Purity and a penitential prayer. Here a permissive note offers a wide range of possibilities for the prayer relating to the day:

---

9 Martin R. Dudley, 1994, *The Collect in Anglican Liturgy: Texts and Sources 1549–1989*, Alcuin Club Collection 72, Collegeville MN: The Liturgical Press, pp. 230 and 231. The same collect and lections appear in *Methodist Service Book* (1975), p. 159, and *The Book of Common Order* of the Church of Scotland (1979) (appointed for Pentecost 16), p. 173.

10 See Chapter 5 in this volume.

A prayer of the day may be a printed prayer such as one of the classic collects, or it may be an extemporaneous prayer. It may be prayed in unison or led by one person. It may be preceded or followed by silence. It may be a prayer suited to any occasion or any Lord's Day; or it may address God in the light of the theme of the day or season of the Christian year.[11]

Banks of model prayers, drawn from a wide range of resources, are provided in the seasonal resources section, and a further bank in the 'General Acts of Worship' section, where the structure of the collect is set out, and where it is noted that 'opening Prayers are frequently collects'.[12] While the approach here is generalist with regard to the *RCL*, the convention within Methodist piety of using crafted or extemporaneous prayers relating, if desired, to the lectionary reading should be noted.

Book of Common Worship (1993)

A new approach can be seen in the publication of the 1993 *Book of Common Worship* of the Presbyterian Church (USA) and the Cumberland Presbyterian Church.[13] Adopting the *RCL*, the compilers also provided complementary liturgical material in the section Resources for the Christian Year. This includes a 'Sentence of Scripture' and a 'Prayer for the Day' for Sundays and festivals in each of Years A, B and C of the lectionary. Usually, three different prayers of the day are provided for each occasion, and each prayer is designated either to one particular year, or to two or all three lectionary years, thus providing an element of choice for the presiding minister. For example, for the Second Sunday in Lent, the lectionary readings are:

Year A   Gen. 12.1–4a; Ps. 121; Rom. 4.1–5, 13–17; John 3.1–17
Year B   Gen. 17.1–7, 15–16; Ps. 22.23–31; Rom. 4.13–25; Mark 8.31–38
Year C   Gen. 15.1–12, 17–18; Ps. 27; Phil. 3.17—4:1; Luke. 13.31–35

The prayer for the day is set out thus:

---

11 *The United Methodist Book of Worship*, 1992, Nashville TN: The United Methodist Publishing House, p. 20.
12 See p. 447 for the structure and pp. 456–68 for the selection of opening prayers.
13 See Chapter 7 in this volume.

1.   Years A B C

   God of mercy,
   you are full of tenderness and compassion,
   slow to anger, rich in mercy,
   and always ready to forgive.
   Grant us grace to renounce all evil
   and to cling to Christ,
   that in every way we may prove to be your loving children;
   through Jesus Christ our Lord . . .

2.   Years A B C

   God of all times and places,
   in Jesus Christ, lifted up on the cross,
   you opened for us the path to eternal life.
   Grant that we, being born again of water and the Spirit,
   may joyfully serve you in newness of life
   and faithfully walk in your holy ways;
   through Jesus Christ our Lord . . .

3.   Year A

   God of our forebears,
   as your chosen servant Abraham
   was given faith to obey your call
   and go out into the unknown,
   so may your church be granted such faith
   that we may follow you with courage
   for the sake of Jesus Christ our Lord . . . (*BCW*, pp. 224–5)

Prayers 1 and 2 have clear baptismal allusions, arising from the setting in Lent as a primary time of preparation for Christian initiation at Easter, and prayer 2 alludes to the Gospel reading in Year A ('water and the Spirit'). Prayer 3 directly relates to the Year A Old Testament lesson, the call of Abraham to leave his father's house, and to the New Testament lesson from Romans 4, which speaks of Abraham's faith.

This approach can also be illustrated from the Ordinary Time provision. *BCW* did not include the *RCL* provision of alternative tracks for the Old Testament lesson, preserving the typological approach of the Roman Lectionary. The Twentieth Sunday in Ordinary Time (Sunday between 14 and 20 August inclusive), therefore, has the following lections:

Year A   Gen. 45.1–15; Ps. 133; Rom. 11.1–2a, 29–32; Matt. 15.10–20, 21–28
Year B   1 Kings 2.10–12; 3.3–14; Ps. 111, Eph. 5.15–20, John 6.51–58
Year C   Isa. 5.1–7; Ps. 80.1–2, 8–19; Heb. 11.29—12.2; Luke 12.49–56.

The prayer for the day provision is set out as follows:

1.   Years A B C

   Almighty God,
   you have broken the tyranny of sin
   and sent the Spirit of your Son into our hearts.
   Give us grace to dedicate our freedom to your service,
   that all people may know the glorious liberty
   of the children of God;
   through Jesus Christ our Lord . . .

2.   Year B

   Ever-loving God,
   your Son, Jesus Christ, gave himself as the living bread
   for the life of the world.
   Give us such knowledge of his presence
   that we may be strengthened
   and sustained by his risen life
   and serve you continually;
   through Jesus Christ . . .

3.   Year C

   Almighty and ever-living God,
   increase in us your gift of faith,
   that, forsaking what lies behind
   and reaching out to what is before,
   we may run the way of your commandments
   and win the crown of everlasting joy;
   through Jesus Christ our Lord . . . (*BCW*, pp. 368–9)

Prayer 1 is not related to any of the lections appointed for Years A, B or C. It is taken from the *Book of Alternative Services* of the Anglican Church of Canada for the same Sunday (Proper 20), but ultimately derives from England (*ASB*, Pentecost 4). The changes were for the sake of inclusive language and imagery:

> Almighty God,
> you have broken the tyranny of sin
> and sent the Spirit of your Son into our hearts,
> *whereby we call you Father.*
> Give us grace to dedicate our freedom to your service,
> *that all mankind may be brought*
> to the glorious liberty of the children of God;
> through Jesus Christ our Lord . . . (*ASB*, p. 653)

The opening clause of prayer 2 relates directly to the Gospel reading from John 6; the rest of the prayer is adapted from England (*ASB*, Easter 1):

> *Almighty God,*
> *who in your great mercy made glad the disciples*
> *with the sight of the risen Lord*:
> give us such knowledge of his presence
> that we may be strengthened
> and sustained by his risen life
> and serve you continually *in righteousness and truth*;
> through Jesus Christ . . . (*ASB*, p. 602)

Prayer 3 relates specifically to the New Testament reading, the conclusion of the long exposition on people of faith in the Old Testament, with the 'cloud of witnesses' opening to Hebrews 12 which includes the image of 'running the race'. This prayer is also drawn from Canada (Proper 29), slightly adapted from England (*ASB*, Pentecost 19).

A Prayer Book for Australia (1995)

The approach of the Presbyterian *BCW* was taken and developed by the Anglican Church of Australia in *A Prayer Book for Australia* (*APBA*), which appeared in 1995.[14]

---

14 The Anglican Church of Australia, 1995, *A Prayer Book for Australia*, Alexandria, NSW: Broughton Books.

COLLECTS AND LECTIONARIES

The Anglican Church of Australia adopted the Roman three-year lectionary in *An Australian Prayer Book* of 1978. This book made provision for either a one-year series of collects and readings based on the collects, Epistles and Gospels of the *BCP*, or the Roman three-year pattern of readings with a choice of collects drawn from either 1662 (re-cast in more contemporary idiom) or the Roman Missal.

APBA adopts the *Revised Common Lectionary* in full. So, unlike the American book, the *RCL* provision of alternative tracks for the Old Testament readings in Ordinary Time was followed, the first, placed in square brackets, relating to the Gospel reading, and the second, allowing for preaching through Old Testament books in a more systematic manner.

APBA uses many of the opening prayers from the *BCW* of the Presbyterian Church (USA), but with some important changes. Most significantly, the provision of collects was expanded. For each Sunday there is a 'Prayer of the week', and three prayers 'of the day'.

The 'Prayer of the week' is a mixed collection of traditional collects from the *BCP* (in contemporary idiom) and other collects from the 1985 collection *Alternative Collects*.

They are intended for both Sunday and weekday services when the three-year lectionary was not in use. However, a note allows use of the weekly prayers with the three-year cycle at the discretion of the presiding minister. These prayers are more general in content, reflecting the broad themes of seasonal time and the lack of specific themes in Ordinary Time. In addition, in Advent the prayer 'Almighty God, give us grace that we may cast away the works of darkness', and in Lent, the prayer 'Almighty and everlasting God, you hate nothing that you have made', may be used as the 'Prayer of the *season*', reflecting the rubric in the *BCP* that both prayers were to be read daily at the Eucharist and offices during their respective seasons.

The prayers 'of the day' relate specifically to the three-year cycle and a particular prayer is designated to each of the three years so there is not the same scope for choice as in *BCW*. Where the *BCW* prayers have been continued, attention has been given to the question of how God is named. Some American texts using 'Almighty God' are changed, for example to 'Saving God', 'Life-giving God' or 'Gracious God'. This complements the more traditional approach of the 'Prayer of the week'. Sometimes, the American texts are adapted. An example arising from theological issues is Advent 4, where the *BCW* prayer begins

> God of grace,
> you chose the Virgin Mary, full of grace,
> to be the mother of our Lord and Savior . . . (*BCW*, p. 176)

and the Australian text reads

> Gracious God,
> you chose the virgin Mary, by your grace,
> to be the mother of our Lord and Saviour . . . (*APBA*, p. 472)

Or the issue may be about style, language or propriety of expression. One of the *BCW* prayers for Easter 2, a text by Janet Morley, begins

> Risen Christ,
> whose absence leaves us *paralysed*
> but whose presence is overwhelming . . . (*BCW*, p. 326)

This is re-cast in *APBA*:

> Risen Christ,
> whose absence leaves us *in despair*
> but whose presence is overwhelming . . . (*APBA*, p. 506)

Another good example is the *BCW* prayer for Year C of Advent 4 which includes a rhetorical question, a most unusual literary device in this genre:

> Who are we, Lord God,
> that you should come to us?
> Yet you have visited your people
> and redeemed us in your Son.
> As we prepare to celebrate his birth,
> make our hearts leap for joy at the sound of your word,
> and move us by your Spirit to bless your wonderful works.
> We ask this through him whose coming is certain, whose day draws near,
> your Son, our Lord Jesus Christ . . . (*BCW*, p. 177)

APBA re-casts this, while still retaining the allusions to the canticle Benedictus (appointed as an alternative to Ps. 80.1–7) and the Gospel reading, Luke 1.39–55, the meeting of Mary with Elizabeth:

Gracious God,
you have visited your people and redeemed us in your Son:
as we prepare to celebrate his birth,
make our hearts leap for joy at the sound of your word,
and move us by your Spirit to bless your wonderful works.
We ask this through him whose coming is certain,
whose Day draws near,
your Son, our Lord Jesus Christ . . . (*APBA*, p. 473)

A final example reveals how a text is expanded to make a deliberate echo of one of the lections. For Advent Sunday, the *BCW* text prays:

Keep us awake and alert, watching for your kingdom,
and make us strong in faith,
so that when Christ comes in glory to judge the earth,
we may joyfully give him praise . . . (*BCW*, p. 173)

The Australian form incorporates a reference to the saints from the New Testament reading (1 Thess. 3.13):

And may he so strengthen your hearts in holiness that you may be blameless before our God and Father at the coming of our Lord Jesus Christ with all his saints . . .

thus:

. . . keep us awake and alert, watching for your kingdom,
and make us strong in faith,
so that when Christ comes in glory to judge the earth,
we may go out joyfully to greet him;
and, with all your saints, may worship you for ever;
through Jesus Christ our Lord . . . (*APBA*, pp. 465–6)

APBA provides some forty new texts for Sundays. Almost invariably, the new texts show a close relationship between the prayer of the day and the appointed lections. The following three examples illustrate the way in which the crafting of new prayers gives expression to the central themes of the readings:

Epiphany 5 (Year C)
Isa. 6.1–8 (9–13)   *Isaiah's vision in the Temple*

Ps. 138
1 Cor. 15.1–11   *the gospel of the resurrection*
Luke 5.1–11   *from now on you will be catching people*

> Most Holy God,
> in whose presence angels serve in awe,
> and whose glory fills all heaven and earth:
> cleanse our unclean lips
> and transform us by your grace
> so that your word spoken through us
> may bring many to your salvation;
> through Jesus Christ our Lord . . . (*APBA*, p. 537)

Lent 3 (Year B)
Ex. 20.1–17   *the giving of the Ten Commandments*
Ps. 19
1 Cor. 1.18–25   *the Cross as the power and wisdom of God*
John 2.12–23   *the temple of his body*

> Lord our God,
> by your Holy Spirit
> write your commandments upon our hearts
> and grant us the wisdom and power of the cross,
> so that, cleansed from greed and selfishness,
> we may become a living temple of your love;
> through Jesus Christ our Lord. **Amen.** (*APBA*, p. 487)

Sunday between 23 and 29 October (Year B)
[Jer. 31.7–9   Ps. 126]   *a great company shall return*
Job 42.1–6, 10–17 Ps. 34.1–8,   *Job is comforted*
                   (19–22)
Heb. 7.21–8   *Christ our High Priest*
Mk 10.46–52   *healing of blind Bartimaeus*

> O God,
> you give light to the blind and comfort to the sorrowing,
> and in your Son you have given us
> a High Priest who has offered the true sacrifice for us
> and yet can sympathise with us in our weakness:
> hear the cry of your people
> and lead us home to our true country,

where with your Son and the Holy Spirit
you live and reign, one God, in glory everlasting. **Amen.**
(*APBA*, p. 596)

BCW only employed one prayer by Janet Morley, the one cited above; *APBA* expands that, using 20 prayers. In 14 of the 20, the Morley prayer is an alternative, probably because her arresting style might not suit all tastes. The texts for the Visitation of the Blessed Virgin Mary to Elizabeth illustrate the point:

> Father in heaven,
> by whose grace Mary was blessed among women
> in bearing your incarnate Son,
> and still more blessed in believing your promises
> and in keeping your word:
> help us, who honour the exaltation of her lowliness,
> to follow her in obeying your will;
> through Jesus Christ our Lord . . .
>
> *or*
>
> O God our deliverer,
> you cast down the mighty
> and lift up those of no account:
> as Elizabeth and Mary embraced
> with songs of liberation,
> so may we also be pregnant with your Spirit,
> and affirm one another in hope for the world;
> through Jesus Christ. **Amen.** (*APBA*, p. 630)

Common Worship (2000)

The approach of the Church of England Liturgical Commission to the question of the relationship between collect and lectionary is set out in its report to the General Synod in 1995:

> it is clear that we have wanted to move away from the ASB tendency to connect collect and scriptural theme. Indeed, because in using RCL we have had to make a choice between attaching collects either to Sunday names or to sets of lections (but not to both) we have

opted clearly for the former. Thus, for example, the collect for the Second Sunday after Trinity will always be the same, though the readings will change, depending not only on the stage of the three-year cycle, but also on the date on which Trinity 2 falls in a particular year. Any attempt to relate the collect to the readings would have ruled out attachment to particular named Sundays, and this we were not prepared to do.

It should be emphasised, however, that a resistance to thematic collects does not mean an arbitrary set of prayers that could be given in any order. The proposals we make are strongly *seasonal*, and intentionally so.[15]

The Synod, not without protest, accepted this principle, and so while the collects in seasonal time are related to the lectionary, the collects in Ordinary Time bear no relation to the readings; indeed, the use of a greater number of Prayer Book collects than in the *ASB* rather reverts to the generalist approach of the Prayer Book itself. However, there are one or two exceptions. The observation that *RCL* was not strong on creation-related lections led to the replacement of *RCL* readings for the Second Sunday before Lent with creation readings and thematic collect, while the treatment of the Sundays before Advent was adapted to enable celebration of 'All Saints' Sunday' and Remembrance Sunday.

Evangelical Lutheran Worship (2006)

The successor to the 1978 *Lutheran Book of Worship* was commended for use in 2006 for the Evangelical Lutheran Church in America and the Evangelical Lutheran Church in Canada. Like other non-Roman Churches in North America, it adopts the *RCL*, but provides collects for each of the three years of the lectionary cycle for Sundays.

Some of this work builds on 1978. For example, for Advent 1, the single collect of 1978 is adapted into a threefold pattern maintaining a common framework:

Years ABC   Stir up your power, Lord Christ, and come. By your merciful protection

       A   save us from the threatening dangers of our sins and enlighten our walk in the way of your salvation,

---

15 The Liturgical Commission of the Church of England, 1995, *Report on the Calendar, Lectionary and Collects, 2000* (GS 1161, 1995), p. 23.

> B awaken us to the threatening dangers of our sins, and keep us blameless until the coming of your new day,
>
> C alert us to the threatening danger of our sins, and redeem us for your life and justice,
>
> ABC for you live and reign with the Father and the Holy Spirit, one God, now and for ever. **Amen.** (*ELW*, p. 43)

Like the 1995 Australian Anglican book, the collects are related far more closely to one or more of the lections. The prayers for Sunday 31 July to 6 August provide good examples. The prayer for Year A takes up themes of generosity, bread and water from Isaiah 55, and alludes to the Gospel, the feeding of the five thousand from Matthew 14:

> Glorious God, your generosity waters the world with goodness, and you cover creation with abundance. Awaken in us a hunger for the food that satisfies both body and spirit, and with this food fill all the starving world, through your Son, Jesus Christ, our Saviour and Lord. **Amen.** (*ELW*, p. 43)

For Year B, the story of the giving of the manna from Exodus 16, and the part of the Bread of Life discourse from John 6 set for the Gospel, are reflected thus:

> O God, eternal goodness, immeasurable love, you place your gifts before us; we eat and are satisfied. Fill us and this world in all its need with the life that comes only from you, through Jesus Christ, our Saviour and our Lord. **Amen.** (*ELW*, p. 44)

The collect for Year C contrasts with the sense of vanity and futility in Ecclesiastes 1 and 2, and echoes the Gospel account of the rich man who built bigger barns, with its conclusion, 'So it is with those who store up treasures for themselves but are not rich towards God':

> Benevolent God, you are the source, the guide, and the goal of our lives. Teach us to love what is worth loving, to reject what is offensive to you, and to treasure what is precious in your sight, through Jesus Christ, our Saviour and Lord. **Amen.** (*ELW*, p. 44)

Conclusion

A very significant fruit of late twentieth- and early twenty-first-century liturgical renewal in the historic denominations has been the broad agreement about the *ordo* of the Sunday assembly. While in some traditions the main act of worship may or may not be eucharistic, rites of gathering including the collect or 'prayer of the day', followed by the celebration of the word of God, are virtually universal. This convergence has been further strengthened by widespread use of either the Roman Lectionary or the development of the Roman Lectionary in the RCL, resulting in a very high degree of shared Bible reading.

Structurally, the collect (or equivalent) forms part of or concludes the gathering rites. But the survey above reveals a mixture of approaches to the relationship between collect and lections. For example, the Church of England in *Common Worship* maintains a clear distinction between collect and lectionary. While there is a degree of congruence in seasonal time, there is a complete distinction in Ordinary Time. By contrast, Australian Anglicans and North American Lutherans in their most recent books show a more direct association by making provision for particular lection-related prayers in each of Years A, B and C.[16] The Presbyterian *BCW* is somewhere in the middle, often providing two or three prayers for a Sunday, but designating many of them to more than one year, and thus providing more choice and therefore a more generalist approach. Indeed, in Protestant Churches where there is an extempore or 'free prayer' tradition, there is by definition the freedom to extemporize or create one or more opening prayers around a theme or without recourse to a theme.

The widespread adoption of the *RCL* introduces yet more variation, especially in its provision in Ordinary Time for related tracks or continuous tracks. Where the latter provision is followed, all three readings are unrelated, and while priority may be given to the Gospel reading, the very nature of the tracks is to enable preachers to follow one particular book over a period of weeks for catechetical purposes. In such cases, the very concept of a 'thematic' collect becomes somewhat problematic. Moreover, the relationship between collect and lectionary is further affected by the status of lectionaries. A good example is the provision in *Common Worship* for modular and locally devised patterns of readings for part of the year. So for Holy Communion,

---

16 Australia does, of course, also make provision for prayers 'of the week' or seasonal prayers.

an authorized lectionary must be used from Advent 1 to Candlemas, from Ash Wednesday to the Day of Pentecost, and on All Saints' Day. In Ordinary Time, while authorized lectionary provision remains the norm, local churches may use other lectionary provision. Similarly, in 'A Service of the Word' (an authorized alternative to Morning and Evening Prayer), while one or more readings must be used from an authorized lectionary from Advent 3 to Epiphany 1, and from Palm Sunday to Trinity Sunday, there is freedom of choice for the rest of the year.[17] Where these permissions are used, a generalist approach to authorized collects becomes a necessity.

This diversity of approach serves to illustrate that the historic ambiguities about the relationship between collect and lectionaries are still very much with us, and that the exact relationship between the two is likely to continue to be a debated and disputed area of liturgical practice into the future.

---

17 The conventions are set out in Archbishops' Council of the Church of England, 2008, *New Patterns for Worship*, 2nd edn, London: Church House Publishing, pp. 103 and 104.

10

Special Collections

MICHAEL PERHAM

Until the loosening up of forms of liturgical prayer in the latter decades of the twentieth century, saying collects is what Anglicans did when asked to lead public prayer. Sometimes in response to a bidding, just occasionally in response to silent prayer, they said a collect. If it were not a collect from *The Book of Common Prayer*, it would very often be a prayer of pure collect form, drawn from one of many anthologies of prayers. From its first publication in 1967, Frank Colquhoun's *Parish Prayers*[1] became the standard anthology. By no means all its 1,800 prayers were in collect form, but a very large number were. They included many from the old sacramentaries and also from authorized Anglican Prayer Books outside England, and Colquhoun wrote a number in the same style himself.

Frank Colquhoun was an evangelical churchman, who served as a parish priest and as Editorial Secretary of the World Evangelical Alliance, before becoming a residentiary canon, first at Southwark Cathedral, then at Norwich. He was also Principal of the Southwark Ordination Course. His anthology of collects and similar prayers is a broad collection (he even includes prayers for the dead despite his own difficulties with them) and his own compositions are straightforward, but have a poetic quality. He later edited *Contemporary Parish Prayers*[2] and *New Parish Prayers*,[3] but these later volumes did not become classics on every clerical bookshelf and prayer-desk in the way that *Parish Prayers* had become, nor did they have so many examples of the collect form, as the 1970s and 1980s developed a more discursive and less structured style of prayer.

---

1 Frank Colquhoun, 1967, *Parish Prayers*, London: Hodder and Stoughton.
2 Frank Colquhoun, 1975, *Contemporary Parish Prayers*, London: Hodder and Stoughton.
3 Frank Colquhoun, 1982, *New Parish Prayers*, London: Hodder and Stoughton.

The most frequent use of Colquhoun's anthology was at Morning and Evening Prayer, according to the *BCP*. The set 'State Prayers', unchanging from day to day and season to season, had, in most places on most occasions, been replaced by sets of variable prayers. These drew initially and principally on the provision of 'Occasional Prayers' in the proposed Prayer Book of 1928, and were later broadened by material from a number of anthologies, most of which became redundant when Colquhoun, with the archiepiscopal commendation of Donald Coggan, published his collection in 1967.

By the time Colquhoun published his third volume, the key date of 1980 had been passed. The Church of England had brought into use its *Alternative Service Book 1980*, introducing a series of new collects of the day, together with the modernizing of some older ones and some moving of traditional collects to new places in the Christian year, mainly to conform the collects to Sunday eucharistic lectionary themes. The Church of England was entering a new liturgical era, in which it would need new prayers, collects included, written in contemporary English.

In support of the *ASB*, there appeared, at the same time as the new service book, *Prayers for Use at the Alternative Services*.[4] Its author was David Silk, then Archdeacon of Leicester and a member of the Liturgical Commission. Frank Colquhoun wrote the Foreword, though the book had a much more Catholic flavour than his own anthologies. The prayers were arranged in accordance with the *ASB* calendar and, to some extent, its themes. The collection was described as 'compiled and adapted from ancient, medieval and modern sources' and, again, collects abound. Silk's work is significant for having engaged with the important task of translation into the liturgical style of the *ASB*. 'You' replaces 'thee' and 'your' replaces 'thy', and a simple use of language, stark even terse, is adopted in very much the spirit of the age. Silk's prayers enabled those with a contemporary regard for liturgy to see that the traditional collect could have its place in the new order.

Silk himself wrote a number of new prayers in collect form and these are important because the compilers of *Common Worship* (CW), as well as *Lent, Holy Week, Easter* (*LHWE*) and *The Promise of His Glory* (*PHG*) before it, drew frequently on Silk's book and on his own compositions. As an example, here is a collect that Silk wrote as a Saturday devotion in honour of the incarnation.

---

4 David Silk, 1980, *Prayers for Use at the Alternative Services*, London: Mowbray.

Almighty and everlasting God,
you have stooped to raise fallen humanity
by the child-bearing of blessed Mary;
grant that we who have seen your glory revealed
   in our human nature,
and your love made perfect in our weakness,
may daily be renewed in your image,
and conformed to the pattern of your Son . . .[5]

That unofficial provision, written for an anthology, then reappears in the rather more official publication *PHG* as a prayer commemorating the Blessed Virgin Mary[6] and again in the authorized *Calendar, Lectionary and Collects* (*CLC*)[7] that is now part of *CW*. By this time, it had become the collect for the two feasts of the Birth and the Conception of the Blessed Virgin Mary. Other material from Silk followed a similar path. Indeed, whether from Silk or another source, much of the collect material in *CW* has its origins in private enterprise of one sort or another, normally in the use of material at first written for a particular place or a particular occasion.

The publication of the *ASB* was expected to bring a period of intensive liturgical writing to an end, at least for the ten years for which the new book was authorized. Two books, however, soon appeared that introduced new collects to the English Anglican world. The first was *The Daily Office SSF* (1981).[8] Published privately, it was described as 'a book of prayer and praise for use in the Society of Saint Francis'. It followed the calendar of the *ASB*, but supplemented the collect provision, mainly in relation to the saints' days, where the *ASB* made little provision beyond the 'red-letter days' and a series of 'commons'. It provides the earliest examples in the post-1980 era of collects for 'lesser festivals', but only the earliest, for there has been a proliferation of such collects in the years since. The 1981 Franciscan office book might not have been of such significance, had it not been the main source for

---

5 Silk, *Prayers for Use*, p. 11.
6 *The Promise of His Glory*, p. 360.
7 Central Board of Finance of the Church of England, 1997, *The Christian Year: Calendar, Lectionary and Collects*, London: Church House Publishing, pp. 198 and 218.
8 Society of Saint Francis, 1981, *The Daily Office SSF*, London: Becket Publications.

Celebrating Common Prayer,[9] itself a key source for *CW*, and this is discussed below.

Writing collects for these 'lesser' saints' days was not, of course, a new exercise. Bishop Walter Frere had set the trend in his *Collects, Epistles and Gospels for lesser feasts according to the calendar set out in 1928*,[10] and private enterprise prayer books, such as *The Cuddesdon Office Book*,[11] had added to the collects available for such days. But there had been no systematic provision of a collect for every such day in the calendar. The *ASB* itself was content to let the 'commons' be sufficient, except for a small number of days, such of that of Saints Timothy and Titus, for which the common provision did not seem to meet the need. *The Daily Office SSF* provided a collect for every festival in the *ASB*, together with collects for specifically Franciscan festivals. The compilers were brothers and sisters of the Society of Saint Francis, among them Brother Tristam Holland SSF, who was later to play a key role in the drawing up of the *CW* calendar and its collects.

They drew on collect provision from around the Anglican Communion, especially the Episcopal Church, and also expressed thanks to 'those many churches and institutions around the country for permission to use collects for holy women and men where there is a local connection'.[12] But many of the collects were new. One emphasis was on making connections with the writings of the person being commemorated. Thus, for George Herbert on 27 February, they wrote (alluding to his hymn 'Teach me, my God and King'):

> Almighty and merciful God,
> who called your servant George Herbert
> from the pursuit of worldly honours
> to be a priest in the temple of his God and King:
> give us also the grace to offer our talents,
> with singleness of heart,
> in humble obedience to your service . . .[13]

Augustine of Hippo on 28 August is given a collect that is a light revision of a popular prayer based on his writings:

---

9 Society of Saint Francis, *Celebrating Common Prayer*, 1992, London: Mowbray.
10 W. H. Frere, 1938, *Collects, Epistles and Gospels for lesser feasts according to the calendar set out in 1928*, London, SPCK.
11 *The Cuddesdon Office Book*, London: Oxford University Press, 1940.
12 *The Daily Office SSF*, p. 551.
13 *The Daily Office SSF*, p. 246.

Lord God,
the light of the minds that know you,
the life of the souls that love you,
and the strength of the hearts that serve you:
help us, after the example of your servant Augustine,
so to know you that we may truly love you,
so to love you that we may fully serve you,
whom to serve is perfect freedom.[14]

The collects in *The Daily Office SSF* are conventional. Few of them stray far from the classical collect form. They are well written and a large number of them (sometimes in an enriched and revised gender-inclusive form) have since found a place in more general and official provision.

In 1981, awareness in Britain of the issue of gender-inclusive language was only just beginning and the *ASB* in no way reflects its insights. Similarly, the collects in *The Daily Office SSF* employ language in a way that would now seem inappropriate. For the feast of Saint Hilary, for instance, on 13 January, using an ECUSA collect, it speaks of Jesus Christ as 'true God and true Man'.[15] When the same collect was included 11 years later in *Celebrating Common Prayer*, it took this form:

Everlasting God,
whose servant Hilary steadfastly confessed your Son Jesus Christ
to be both human and divine . . .[16]

The lack of gender-inclusive sensitivity was also a major reason for the failure of another set of collects from this period to find a permanent place in Anglican liturgical provision. This was the set to be found in *Cloud of Witnesses*.[17] *Cloud of Witnesses* was commissioned by the Alcuin Club and compiled by Martin Draper, then curate of Saint Matthew's, Westminster in London. It set out to provide, for each of the lesser festivals of the *ASB*, a brief hagiography, sentences, lections, psalm, biddings, a non-biblical additional reading related to the saint concerned and a proper collect. Although the compilation was Draper's work, the collects were written by George Timms.

---

14 *The Daily Office SSF*, p. 277.
15 *The Daily Office SSF*, p. 238.
16 *Celebrating Common Prayer*, p. 431.
17 Martin Draper, 1982, *Cloud of Witnesses*, London: Collins.

Timms was at the end of a long period of service in the Diocese of London, latterly as Archdeacon of Hackney. He was Chairman of the Alcuin Club[18] and also involved in the *New English Hymnal* project, for which he wrote a number of hymns. For *Cloud of Witnesses*, he created a complete set of collects for lesser festivals.

The book was widely used from the time of its publication until the arrival of *CW*, the compilers of which considered Timms's collects in drawing up their own provision, though in almost every case they rejected them. In some cases the cause was simply the existence of a richer text (often from *The Daily Office SSF*), though the stark simplicity of Timms's collects has much to commend them. The lack of sensitivity to the issue of gender-inclusiveness counted more strongly against their adoption. In the collect for Saint Francis de Sales, the prayer was that 'each may follow that path of devotion which is fitted to his calling' (*CoW*, p. 22). In the collect for George Herbert, it is that 'we may daily speak your praise, do all as in your sight, and strive to set the peace of heaven within the hearts of men' (*CoW*, p. 37). The collect for Thomas Ken celebrated the fact that he 'counted a good conscience of greater value than the praise of men' (*CoW*, p. 57). The collect for Anselm speaks of sending 'your only-begotten Son to bring to man the good news of your love' (*CoW*, p. 69). *Cloud of Witnesses* was not many years old before such language was becoming unacceptable and in 1989, in both *Making Women Visible*[19] and *Towards Liturgy 2000*,[20] the need for gender-inclusive language was given strong support in the Church of England.

A second problem with Timms's collection is a narrowness of request. However brief a collect is, it has to draw together the prayers of the Church for the Church, for the whole company of those united by prayer. A number of Timms's collects pray only for specific groups, usually the ordained. That for John Chrysostom prays that God will 'enlighten the ministers of your word with the spirit of prophecy that with courage they may expound the gospel' (*CoW*, p. 26). The collect for Saint David's Day asks that 'your Church in Wales may faithfully

---

18 Founded in 1897 to promote sound liturgical scholarship, it played an important role in the Church of England in the early twentieth century in the debate on the proposed revision of the *BCP*. Its aims have since broadened to include the liturgical traditions of other denominations, though its principal focus remains the Anglican Communion.

19 Liturgical Commission of the Church of England, 1989, *Making Women Visible*, London: Church House Publishing.

20 Michael Perham, 'Affirming the Feminine', in Michael Perham (ed.), 1989, *Towards Liturgy 2000*, London: SPCK/Alcuin Club, pp. 75–83.

preach the gospel which he proclaimed' (*CoW*, p. 40). On Saint Clare's Day the prayer is that those 'who forsake all for your name may be enriched by your Holy Spirit in this life and receive the reward of the blessed in the life to come' (*CoW*, p. 132). The collect for Saint Aidan prays that 'all ministers of your word and sacraments may strive to attain his zeal and holiness' (*CoW*, p. 42). The provision for Lancelot Andrewes asks that all whom God calls 'to the sacred ministry of your Church may follow him in holiness of life and in love of souls' (*CoW*, p. 154). There was a tendency for these collects too easily to become prayers for bishops, pastors and religious and this counted against their adoption as the collect of the day.

Only two of Timms's collects have found their way into official provision in the Common Worship series, though both have been marginally altered. His collect for Saint Ignatius, with the additional words in *Common Worship: Daily Prayer* bracketed, reads:

> Feed us, O Lord, with the living bread
> and make us drink deep of the cup of salvation that,
> following the teaching of your bishop Ignatius
> (and rejoicing in the faith with which he embraced a martyr's
>   death,)
> we may be nourished for that eternal life for which he longed . . .
> (*CLC*, p. 207; *CWDP*, p. 508)

His collect for Saint Nicholas reads:

> Almighty Father, lover of mankind, who chose your servant to be a bishop in the Church, that he might give freely out of the treasures of his grace: Make your people mindful of the needs of others, and as they have themselves received, so teach them also to give . . .
> (*CoW*, p. 205)

In *CW* this becomes:

> Almighty Father, lover of souls,
> who chose your servant to be a bishop in the Church,
> that he might give freely out of the treasures of his grace:
> make us mindful of the needs of others,
> and, as we have received, so teach us also to give . . .
> (*CLC*, p. 217; *CWDP*, p. 217)

Compared with the later collects, such as those in *CLC*, Timms's prayers, though his own original work, echo the simplicity of more ancient forms, often lacking very specific reference to the life or the writings of the saint whom he is commemorating. The mood in the 1990s was clearly against this simplicity and the tendency was to expand (as in the collect for Ignatius) and to draw heavily on what was specific to the person commemorated. Subsequent generations may come to appreciate Timms's directness. For instance, *CLC*'s somewhat complex collect for John Keble, drawing on his writings, may seem less appealing than Timms's less literary construction.

CLC, using a collect from Keble College Oxford, prays:

Father of the eternal Word,
in whose encompassing love
all things in peace and order move:
grant that, as your servant John Keble adored you in all creation,
so we may have a humble heart of love
for the mysteries of your Church
and know your love to be new every morning,
 in Jesus Christ our Lord. (*CLC*, p. 186; *CWDP*, p. 482)

Compare this with Timms's prayer:

Everlasting Father, who raised up your servant John Keble
to be an example of priestly devotion in your Church: Grant that we, like him, may hold firmly to the faith we have received, and show forth in our lives the good works of your Spirit . . .
(*CoW*, p. 63)

The first depends for its affectiveness on a knowledge of Keble's writing; the second is more immediately accessible. Although Timms's set of collects are uneven in their quality and in some ways dated, despite being crafted in 'contemporary' English, many of them deserve reconsideration and it would be a pity if only two survived.

It was another decade before more collects for the *sanctorale* appeared, and by then the intention was not to supplement the *ASB*, but to begin to move towards its successor. Meanwhile *LHWE* was published in 1986, with new and rich provision for Lent and Easter, still very much an enriching of the *ASB* and using its collects. Its provision of additional collect material (none of it allocated to particular days) was minimal. By the time *PHG* followed in 1991, the days of the *ASB* were seen to be numbered and new patterns for calendar and seasons were emerging. *PHG* included a large compendium of prayers, the majority of them in collect form, allocated by season and theme, but not to particular days. There was a variety of sources, but the majority of collects, not already part of official provision, came from Silk's *Prayers for Use at the Alternative Services*, with several from Colquhoun's *Parish Prayers* and a number from the old sacramentaries. Neither *LHWE* nor *PHG* was authorized by synodical process, but both were commended by the House of Bishops.

In 1992 *Celebrating Common Prayer* (CCP) was published, commended by the Archbishop of Canterbury, but compiled by private enterprise. It was the fruit of collaboration between a number of religious (chiefly, but not entirely, Franciscans) and some members of the Church of England Liturgical Commission. Prominent among the former were Brother Tristam Holland SSF, and, among the latter, David Stancliffe, at the time Provost of Portsmouth. The aim was a new daily office book, usable by the whole Church, but rich enough also to provide for the needs of religious communities. Indeed, when published, it came in two editions, *CCP* for general use and a new *Daily Office SSF* for use by the Franciscans. This was an immensely creative and formative book, among other things, deeply influencing the shape of *Common Worship Daily Prayer*, which appeared in 2005. Collects were, of course, quite a small part of its provision.

As far as the *temporale* was concerned, it reflected the changes advocated by *PHG*, which necessitated some new collects for seasons that had been given a different emphasis. There was a greater use of collects from the *BCP*, with some careful modernizing, the rearrangement of the days on which a number of *ASB* collects were used, and five Sunday collects (Kingdom 1, Advent 2, Christmas 2, Epiphany 4 and Pentecost 5) drawn from the collection of collects not allocated to dates in *PHG*.[21] But the intention, at this stage, was simply to modify existing provision for a calendar that had given a new shape to the period from All Saints' Day to Candlemas.

The *sanctorale* of *CCP* was in the main drawn from the *ASB* as far as the festivals were concerned, and from the 1981 *Daily Office SSF* for the lesser festivals, though there was gentle editing and enriching of those texts. The exceptions were new collects for John Keble, provided by Keble College (see above), for Bede (*CCP*, p. 447), provided by Durham Cathedral, for Oswald (*CCP*, p. 458), provided by St Oswald's Church, Durham, for Lucy (*CCP*, p. 479), by David Silk, for Richard

---

21 *The Promise of His Glory*, pp. 337–67.

Hooker (*CCP*, p. 474), by Kenneth Stevenson, and for Joseph (*CCP*, p. 439) and George (*CCP*, p. 443), by Michael Perham.

Stevenson's collect for Richard Hooker reflected the move towards more elaborate collects drawing on the writings of the person commemorated. There were to be further examples in *CWDP*. Whereas the 1981 *Daily Office SSF* had used the common collect for a teacher for Hooker, Kenneth Stevenson, at the time Rector of Holy Trinity, Guildford, in Surrey wrote:

> God of peace, the bond of all love,
> who in your Son Jesus Christ have made the human race
> your inseparable dwelling place:
> after the example of your servant Richard Hooker,
> give grace to us your servants ever to rejoice
> in the true inheritance of your adopted children
> and to show forth your praises now and ever . . .[22]

It was to find its way unamended into *CWDP* (p. 514), as were Perham's collects for Joseph and for George, the former being the one case of replacing an *ASB* collect with something thought to be more fitting. The *ASB* collect for Joseph of Nazareth was composed by the Liturgical Commission:

> Almighty God,
> who called Joseph to be the husband of the Virgin Mary,
> and the guardian of your only Son:
> open our eyes and ears to the messages of your holy will,
> and give us the courage to act upon them . . . (*ASB*, p. 760)

Michael Perham was, at that time, Team Rector of Oakdale in the Diocese of Salisbury. His collect strengthens the prayer by reference to Joseph's ancestry and his trade, to the incarnation, to grace and to faithfulness:

> God our Father,
> who from the family of your servant David
> raised up Joseph the carpenter
> to be the guardian of your incarnate Son
> and husband of the Blessed Virgin Mary:
> give us grace to follow him

---

22 The collect alludes to Hooker's *Laws* V, 54, 5; V, 59, 5.

in faithful obedience to your commands . . .
(*CW*, p. 428; *CWDP*, p. 458)

CCP marked the end of writing on the national level for the *sanctorale* until much of the material described acquired official status in *CLC*, which was authorized in anticipation of its inclusion in *CW*. *Exciting Holiness*,[23] compiled by Brother Tristam SSF, has proved a very helpful resource in celebrating the saints of the *CW* calendar, but its collects and post-communion prayers are entirely the authorized collection from *CW*.

Three sets of unofficial collects for the *temporale* are discussed below. They are *All Desires Known*,[24] *Opening Prayers: Collects in Contemporary Language*[25] and *Prayers for an Inclusive Church*.[26] Each of these also provides new collects for the *sanctorale*, but, because their principal interest lies in what they provide for Sundays and feasts of the Lord, they are explored below in that context.

Before moving to the *temporale*, it is important to look at collects for local festivals. Throughout the period and up to the present day, there have been local calendars of saints, some of which have included provision of collects. The *ASB* stated that 'diocesan, local or other commemorations may be added' to the national lesser festivals and commemorations.[27] *CLC* encouraged local initiative in similar fashion, when it states that 'in the calendar of the saints, diocesan and other local provision may be made to supplement the national calendar'.[28] The majority of these diocesan calendars do not include sets of collects, though some reproduce a limited number that have had long use in cathedrals, sometimes drawing on medieval sources. But there have been a number of more imaginative diocesan compilations.

---

23 Tristam SSF (ed.), 1997, *Exciting Holiness*, Norwich: Canterbury Press.
24 Janet Morley, 1992, 3rd edn, 2005, *All Desires Known*, London: SPCK.
25 International Commission on English in the Liturgy, 1997, *Opening Prayers: Collects in Contemporary Language*, Norwich: Canterbury Press.
26 Steven Shakespeare, 2008, *Prayers for an Inclusive Church*, Norwich: Canterbury Press.
27 *Alternative Service Book 1980*, p. 18.
28 Central Board of Finance of the Church of England, 1997, *The Christian Year: Calendar, Lectionary, Collects*, p. 12. This encouragement is carried over into *CW*. The Archbishops' Council of the Church of England, 2000, *Common Worship: Services and Prayers for the Church of England*, p. 530 ('Rules to Order the Christian Year').

Probably first in the field was the *Chichester Diocesan Kalendar*,[29] issued in 1997 at the same time as the new national calendar. Edited by Jeremy Haselock, the Diocesan Liturgical Consultant, it included collects from the Roman Missal and from various Anglican provinces, together with new compositions, some of them by Bishop Eric Kemp. It follows *CLC* wherever possible.

The year 2000 saw the publication of a substantial booklet by the Diocese of Lincoln. Entitled *Furthering Holiness*,[30] it provides collects for each of 21 local saints and worthies. Some are collects that were already in circulation and, in some cases, authorized; others were newly written, but without any attribution of authorship.

Probably the latest in the field is the Diocese of Gloucester's *Companions in the Faith*,[31] with 24 new collects, the majority of them written by the Bishop, all in the style of the *CW* provision. The collect for William Laud, Dean of Gloucester from 1616 to 1621, reflects the trend (previously seen in *CW* in the collects for Anselm, Alcuin, Richard of Chichester, Lancelot Andrewes and Alfred) of modifying a prayer of the person commemorated to create the collect:

Grant, Lord,
that, following the steps of your bishop William,
we may live in your fear,
die in your favour,
rest in your peace,
rise in your power
and for ever worship you in the beauty of holiness;
for your beloved Son Jesus Christ's sake.[32]

These three very full diocesan collections remain faithful to the conventional shape of the collect and, though in contemporary English, have a traditional, and even timeless, style. Perhaps inevitably there is little overlap between them. In general they commemorate local heroes, whose festivals are not celebrated more widely. But, even where they do have names in common, local enterprise has produced a local collect. Chichester and Lincoln both have Gilbert of Sempringham, but the collects are entirely different. Chichester and Gloucester both have

---

29 Jeremy Haselock (ed.), 1997, *Chichester Diocesan Kalendar*, Chichester: Chichester Board of Finance.
30 *Furthering Holiness*, 2000, Lincoln: Lincoln Diocesan Trust and Board of Finance.
31 *Companions in the Faith*, 2008, Diocese of Gloucester.
32 *Companions in the Faith*, p. 9.

Blaise and Bridget, but there is no overlap of collects. It remains to be seen whether other dioceses will respond in the course of time to the *CLC* and *CW* invitation to make local provision.

Much of this chapter has focused on the collects for the *sanctorale*, simply because that is where there has been most opportunity for creativity. We turn now to three major sets of collects for Sundays and feasts of the Lord. This means going back first to 1992 and the publication of Janet Morley's *All Desires Known*. In fact this was an expanded version of her earlier book under the same title, published in 1988 by the Movement for the Ordination of Women and Women in Theology.[33] Janet Morley was emerging then as the most impressive writer of feminist prayers. The style was poetic, biblical in its imagery, refreshing and sometimes disturbing. *ADK* was quite conventional in its set of what it calls 'lectionary collects', in the sense that the prayers really are in collect form, but utterly unconventional in its feminist emphasis, though the freshness of the material cannot be entirely attributed to that.

For those used to traditional addresses to God at the beginning of the collect, Morley was breaking new ground with the opening words of the prayer. 'O God from whom we flee' (*ADK*, p. 4 [p. 36]), she began on the Fifth Sunday before Christmas; 'O God our disturber' (*ADK*, p. 5 [p. 17]) on Advent 2; 'Spirit of energy and change' (*ADK*, p. 7 [p. 29]) on Epiphany 1; 'Christ our lover' (*ADK*, p. 17 [p. 23]) on the Sunday after the Ascension; 'God of intimacy' (*ADK*, p. 22 [p. 21]) on Pentecost 14.

The feminine is made more visible than in many traditional collects. 'God our mother', she begins on Mothering Sunday, 'you hold our life within you, nourish us at your breast, and teach us to walk alone' (*ADK*, p. 11 [p. 25]). Her collect for Christmas Eve addresses 'God our beloved, born of a woman's body' and prays that 'we so cherish one another in our bodies that we may also be touched by you; through the Word made flesh, Jesus Christ' (*ADK*, p. 6 [p. 20]). On Epiphany her collect reminds us that God's coming 'was revealed to the nations not among men of power but on a woman's lap' (*ADK*, p. 7 [p. 13]). On Easter 5, she asks the God 'for whom we long as a woman in labour longs for her delivery' to 'give us courage to wait, strength to push, and

---

33 References are to the 1992 edition: London, SPCK. The collection has more recently been substantially revised in conformity with the *RCL*, and was republished by SPCK in 2005. Page references to the 2005 edition are given here in square brackets.

discernment to know the right time; that we may bring into the world your joyful peace' (*ADK*, p. 16 [p. 15]).

The prayers reflect a wider concern with liberation. They champion the causes of the poor, the dispossessed and the marginalized, but always with a beauty rather than a harshness of language and nearly always drawing closely on Scripture, with biblical references included. The God 'whose holy name defies our definition' is asked on the Sixth Sunday before Christmas to 'make us to be one with all who cry for justice; that we who speak your praise may struggle for your truth' (*ADK*, p. 4 [p. 19]). On the Eighth Sunday before Easter, when the *ASB* Gospel was the story of the Syro-Phoenician woman, the collect asks for 'faith like the Syro-Phoenician woman, who refused to remain an outsider: that we too may have the wit to argue and demand that our daughters be made whole' (*ADK*, p. 9 [p. 35]).

In their theology, Morley's collects sometimes rejoice in a gentle and vulnerable God. But at other moments, God is a God of terror, arising to shake the earth. While adopting the collect form, she is also ready quite often to address her prayers to the second and third persons of the Trinity.

Twenty years on from their first publication, most of these prayers would not offend or shock most Christian people. Addressing God in a wider variety of ways, reclaiming feminine imagery from Scripture and putting an emphasis on the vulnerability of God have all become more commonplace. When they first appeared, however, alongside some other collects of a similar kind in *Women Included*,[34] to which Janet Morley was also a contributor, they were well received and their literary quality admired, but they were thought too radical and overtly feminist to find their way into official or commended material.

Just one of Morley's collects was included in *Enriching the Christian Year*.[35] It was her collect for Trinity Sunday and appeared in *Enriching the Christian Year* as a post-communion prayer for that feast:

O God our mystery,
you bring us to life,
call us to freedom,
and move between us with love.
May we so participate
in the dance of your trinity,

---

34 St Hilda Community, 1990, *Women Included*, London: SPCK.

35 Michael Perham (ed.), 1992, *Enriching the Christian Year*, London: SPCK.

that our lives may resonate with you,
now and for ever.[36]

Similarly, a single collect from *ADK* found its way into the official provision of *CW*. In *ADK* (1992) it is the collect of Epiphany 3, but in *CW* it appears as the post-communion prayer for Trinity 3:

O God, whose beauty is beyond our imagining
and whose power we cannot comprehend:
show us your glory as far as we can grasp it,
and shield us from knowing more than we can bear
until we may look upon you without fear . . . (*CW*, p. 409)

Both these prayers show Janet Morley to be an accomplished and sensitive wordsmith, writing with a haunting and disturbing depth. *All Desires Known* bears frequent revisiting.

In 1999, two years after the Church of England had authorized its new collects to complement its calendar and the *Revised Common Lectionary*, the Joint Liturgical Group of Great Britain commended another set of collects, *Opening Prayers: Collects in Contemporary Language*, which had been prepared originally by the International Commission on English in the Liturgy for use within the Roman Catholic Church with the Roman Lectionary itself. This was, of course, the lectionary from which the *RCL* had been derived. It is an interesting collection, beautifully written, but lacking authority. There is a certain irony that, just as the Church of England and its sister Churches in Great Britain abandoned thematic collects, tied to lectionary themes, and returned to an approach that saw the collect as the concluding prayer of the Gathering, rather than as the opening prayer of the Liturgy of the Word, a Roman Catholic source should embrace an approach to the collect that draws heavily on the lections of the day. Because it does that, it provides a three-year cycle of prayers, with a different one for each year to reflect the changing readings. They are rightly described as 'dramatic in their imagery, richly biblical in their language and skilfully connecting the bible readings of the day'.[37] Because they engage with the lectionary, there is a case for their use later in the liturgy, once the readings have been heard and as part of a response to them.

The collect form is just about maintained, although these are longer and more discursive prayers. They are very different from the stark

---

36 Perham, *Enriching the Christian Year*, p. 73.
37 Publisher's cover endorsement.

SPECIAL COLLECTIONS

prayers of the Missal in the manner of their address to God, in their rich scriptural allusions and in their sheer length. In terms of address, they reflect some of the same concern shown in *ADK* to get away from an over-use of 'Almighty' and indeed 'Father'. We are given here 'God of glory and compassion' (Advent 3, *OP*, p. 6), 'O God of mystery' (Advent 4, *OP*, p. 8), 'God of Abraham and Sarah' (Christmas Day, *OP*, p. 10), 'God of the covenant' (the Baptism of the Lord, *OP*, p. 18), to mention only some of those that occur in the first weeks of the liturgical year. Later, God is called eternal, merciful, faithful, compassionate and boundless, but never vulnerable; sometimes father, never mother. Indeed, other than in some beautiful wording relating to Mary, feminist concerns do not receive treatment.

Two examples must suffice to give the flavour of this material. Both illustrate the quality of the writing, the first drawing as fully as any collect on the Scriptures, the second highly theological, with profound teaching expressed succinctly.

The collect for Easter afternoon, when the Emmaus story (Luke 24.13–35) has formed the Gospel reading, is as follows:

O God, worker of wonders,
you made this day for joy and gladness.
Let the risen Lord abide with us this evening,
opening the Scriptures to us
and breaking bread in our midst.
Set our hearts aflame and open our eyes,
that we may see in his sufferings
all that the prophets spoke
and recognize him at this table,
the Christ now entered into glory, first-born from the dead,
who lives with you now and always
in the unity of the Holy Spirit,
God for ever and ever. (*OP*, p. 36)

The collect for the Feast of the Holy Trinity in Year C is this:

O God,
your name is veiled in mystery,
yet we dare to call you Father;
your Son was begotten before all ages,
yet is born among us in time;
your Holy Spirit fills the whole creation,

yet is poured forth now into our hearts.
Because you have made us and loved us
and called us by name,
draw us more deeply into your divine life,
that we may glorify you rightly, through your Son,
in the unity of the Holy Spirit,
God for ever and ever. (*OP*, p. 53)

The sets of unofficial collects for the *temporale* are completed by *Prayers for an Inclusive Church* (*PIC*).[38] Its author is Steven Shakespeare, an Anglican priest who is Lecturer in Philosophy at Liverpool Hope University. His set of collects, every single one a new composition, is in a line of succession from both *ADK* and *OP*. They are successors of Janet Morley's work in that they seek new ways of addressing God, affirm the feminine, lay emphasis on a God of the marginalized drawing people into inclusive relationship, have real literary quality in many of the prayers and are a little too much on the edge of orthodoxy to find their way, at present at least, into official provision. They are similar to *OP* in being longer than conventional collects, while maintaining, in most cases, the collect form, and in being based on the *RCL* and therefore providing different sets of prayers for each of the three years.

To engage with the style and radicalism of the prayers, it is helpful to note that, in the opening weeks of Year A, God is addressed as 'holy Thief' (Advent 1, *PIC*, p. 1), 'God of the keen blade' (Advent 2, *PIC*, p. 2), 'God of the burning sand' (Advent 3, *PIC*, p. 2), 'God of David's fragile house' and 'God of rough hands and hardened feet' (Christmas, *PIC*, pp. 3 and 4), 'Foolish God' and 'Lover of the vineyard' (Epiphany 4, *PIC*, p. 8). In terms of social justice and the cry of the marginalized, he is the 'inviting God', laying open his table 'to the deviant and deranged, setting a place for the foreign and unwanted', whom we ask to 'overturn our tables of power and teach us to receive bread from strange and wounded hands' (on one of the Sundays after Trinity in Year C, in relation to Luke 14.1, 7–14, *PIC*, p. 104). He is also 'the God of the dirtied hands, the wandering feet' and we ask him to take us with him 'into the abandoned places to find a new community outside our fortress walls' (on another of the Sundays after Trinity in Year C, in relation to Luke 15.1–10, *PIC*, p. 105).

---

38 Steven Shakespeare, 2008, *Prayers for an Inclusive Church*, Norwich: Canterbury Press.

In order to catch the flavour of Steven Shakespeare's prayers and to compare them with what has gone before, it is instructive to read his collect in response to the Emmaus story and also his Year C Collect for Trinity Sunday:

> Lord of the gathering feast,
> you walk with us on the shadowed road:
> burn our hearts with scripture's open flame;
> unveil our darkened eyes as bread is torn and shared
> and from the broken fragments
> bless a people for yourself;
> through Jesus Christ the host of the world. (*PIC*, p. 22)

> Holy Trinity,
> you are neither monarch nor monologue
> but an eternal harmony of gift and response:
> through the Uncreated Word
> and the Spirit of Truth
> include us and all creation in your extravagant love;
> through the Wisdom of God,
> who raises her voice to call us to life. (*PIC*, p. 96)

The extent to which this collection will be used as the collect of the day will depend on whether people welcome a return to lection-based collects, which many have thought to be a twentieth-century aberration, and on whether these prayers are judged sufficiently orthodox for mainstream use. Many of them are undoubtedly beautiful and the imagery striking.

As a footnote to the issue of contemporary collects, a word needs to be written about post-communion prayers. Many of these are constructed in collect form. Many indeed are interchangeable with the collect of the day. In the Church of England their arrival is recent. The Rite A Eucharistic Rite in the *ASB*, alongside two set texts after communion, noted that 'other suitable prayers'[39] might be used, but provided none. The emphasis was on a post-communion sentence, which was provided, rather than on a post-communion prayer, which was not provided. It was not long before private enterprise entered the scene in a little book by Charles MacDonnell, entitled *After Communion*.[40] MacDonnell, then Curate of Westbury-on-Trym, provided a

---

39 *Alternative Service Book 1980*, p. 144.
40 Charles MacDonnell, 1985, *After Communion*, London: Mowbray.

post communion for every Sunday and holy day. Some of his prayers found their way into *PHG*, alongside a limited number of other post communions, allocated by season. *Enriching the Christian Year* took matters a stage further, incorporated some of MacDonnell's texts, but also drew heavily on the Canadian *Book of Alternative Services*[41] and *A New Zealand Prayer Book*.[42] At this stage, there was little fresh writing in England of post-communion prayers, other than MacDonnell's, although this was all to change when the Liturgical Commission turned its attention to post-communion prayers for *CW*, when, especially for the *sanctorale*, there was a flowering of new texts. These, of course, were official prayers, falling outside the compass of this chapter. Five of MacDonnell's post communions were included in *Common Worship*, notably his fine prayer for Ascension Day:

> God our Father,
> you have raised our humanity in Christ
> and have fed us with the bread of heaven:
> mercifully grant that, nourished with such spiritual blessings,
> we may set our hearts in the heavenly places . . . (*CW*, p. 404)

It is encouraging that, with so many anthologies of prayers being published and fresh styles of praying taking root in the life of the Church, the collect form still attracts liturgical wordsmiths, even those wanting to push at the boundaries of theology. The adaptability of the collect, allowing its form to be extended and stretched without loss of form and clarity, has helped. In the end its stark simplicity will frequently draw people back to it as a timeless art form when more discursive forms of prayer wear thin.

---

41 Anglican Church in Canada, 1985, *Book of Alternative Services*, Toronto: Anglican Book Centre.

42 Anglican Church in Aotearoa, New Zealand and Polynesia, 1989, *A New Zealand Prayer Book*, Auckland: Collins.

11

The Collect: A Roman Catholic Perspective

ALAN GRIFFITHS

Context

This collection of essays has demonstrated how fundamental the collect is to Christian liturgy in the 'Western' tradition. In the twentieth century, many liturgical communities have attempted to 'update' this form of prayer, both by writing new prayers and translating older texts.

In this chapter, written from a Roman Catholic perspective, I hope to outline the history of translation of the collect into English in the Catholic community during the twentieth century and since. I will attempt to explain how the collect form has been a vehicle for theological expression in the Church's tradition both past and present. I shall ask what recent developments may or may not contribute to a common Christian collect 'heritage' in the future. Lastly, I hope to argue the case for the retention of the collect as a still vital member of a diversity of prayer forms reflecting Scripture and theological intelligence.

The term 'collect' in the Roman liturgy

In older editions of the Roman Missal the first prayer of each Mass Formulary is referred to as the *Oratio*. This is true of the Tridentine Missal, its predecessor the *Editio Princeps* of 1474, the Sarum Missal and, further back, the *Ordo Romanus Primus*, and the more remote sources of the Roman Mass Liturgy in the Gelasian and Gregorian Sacramentary traditions. The recent (2001) Third Edition of the Missal employs the term *Collecta*.[1]

---

1 I use the term 'Roman Missal' in this essay to refer to the *Missale Romanum*,

Collecta seems originally to have meant the place of assembly before a procession into church for Mass. It appears as the designation of the first prayer in the Mass formularies of the *Missale Gothicum* and *Missale Gallicanum Vetus*.

The collect is one of three short prayers in the Roman Mass, the second being the prayer 'Over the Offerings' and the third the prayer 'After Communion'. These three prayers are perhaps the feature most characteristic of the Roman Mass. They have two things in common: they close a stage in the rite and open the next stage; and they vary according to the feast or season.

Learning from ourselves

English-speaking Catholics have worshipped in their own tongue at Mass for over forty years. Looking back, we may review what we have been exposed to and what we have learnt.

The English Catholic priest and writer John Gother (d. 1704) seems to have produced the first English translation of the Mass for congregants to follow. His work was continued by Richard Challoner (1691–1781), the great eighteenth-century English missionary bishop. They tried to render both the Latin sense and form into English. Their method was followed also by translators in the earlier twentieth century. Vernacular liturgical books such as the *Manual of Prayers* for use at Benediction of the Blessed Sacrament and books for the sacraments, as well as 'missals' for the laity, all translated both the shape and syntax of Latin collects into English. But change was on the way.

The Second Vatican Council (1962–65) mandated a reform of the Roman liturgy. The reformed liturgical books that resulted were the fruit of many years' research into the ancient sources of the Roman rite. The revised *Missale Romanum* contained material dating from the fourth century and from every period up to the time of the Council itself, whose documents are also echoed in its texts.

In the English-speaking world, the International Commission on English in the Liturgy (ICEL) was set up in 1965. Its brief was to translate the Latin liturgical books into English. In 1969, the Holy See issued *Comme le prévoit* (*CLP*), translation guidelines to help ICEL and the other translation commissions that were set up at the same

---

Editio Typica Tertia, Rome: Librariae Editricis Vaticanae, 2002. Older forms of the Missal are referred to by date or as such.

time.[2] These guidelines represented a radical departure from previous practice.

Bruce Harbert, formerly the Executive Secretary of ICEL, has traced the origin of *CLP* to academic theories of translation from the 1960s known as 'Dynamic Equivalence'.[3] Put simply, this meant determining the 'kernel' of meaning in a text in the 'donor' (the Latin) language and representing it in the 'receptor' (vernacular) text.

CLP maintained that the meaning of a passage must be determined by the whole passage, not by individual words. It claimed that syntax and rhetoric were culturally conditioned. It implied that what was elegant and sonorous in Latin might sound fussy in a modern vernacular and should not be imitated.

The ICEL translation of the Missal appeared in 1973.[4] It seems to have taken full account of *CLP*'s provisions. The collect for the Second Sunday of Ordinary Time in the Roman Missal exemplifies this approach. This text is found in the Missal of 1962 and in its predecessors, including the Sarum Missal, for the Second Sunday after Epiphany:

Omnipotens sempiterne Deus,
qui caelestia simul et terrena moderaris,
supplicationes populi tui clementer exaudi,
et pacem tuam nostris concede temporibus.
Per Dominum Nostrum Iesum Christum Filium tuum,
qui tecum vivit et regnat in unitate Spiritus Sancti,
Deus per omnia saecula saeculorum, Amen.

It is a prayer for peace composed according to the form of the *Oratio*. The opening address in line 1 has *Deus* qualified by *omnipotens* and *sempiterne* – 'almighty' and 'everlasting'. The relative pronoun names God as having governance (the verb *moderor* has the sense of one who

---

2 *Comme le prévoit* is the French title of an 'instruction' on translation devised by Consilium, the group appointed by the Vatican to oversee the liturgical changes after the Council. (Father McManus was a member of the Consilium.) The translation guidelines in *Comme le prévoit* advocate the dynamic equivalency translation principles which have governed all English-language liturgical translation until the recent review of a massive revision of the Roman Missal (lectionary and sacramentary).

3 Bruce Harbert, 2005, 'The Roman Rite and the English Language', *Antiphon* 9.1, pp. 16–29.

4 The English translation of *The Roman Missal* © 1973, *International Committee on English in the Liturgy*.

holds everything in its proper place and order) over things in heaven and earth (line 2). The petition follows in line 3, where God is asked to hear his people's prayer. Those offering the prayer are conscious of the need for due modesty before the Almighty. They bend low as suppliants (*supplicationes*) and ask a merciful (*clementer*) hearing. The petition is defined in line 4 by a motive, that God may give peace in our times. The lengthy conclusion in lines 5–7 sums up the prayer as both the action of the Trinity in the worshipping assembly and the giver of what is sought by that assembly.

In addition to a richness of content and the relating of ideas and images one to another, the text also exhibits a certain rhythm. This is particularly so in the last line before the conclusion, which resembles the second half of a Latin hexameter. It acts as an aurally satisfying closure to the collect's main section.

Superficially, the 'kernel' meaning seems simple: 'God, you are always in charge. Give us peace all the time.' ICEL 1973 expressed it thus:

Father of heaven and earth,
hear our prayers
and show us the way to peace in the world.
We make this prayer through our Lord Jesus Christ your Son
who lives and reigns with you in the unity of the Holy Spirit,
one God, for ever and ever.

This gets part of the 'kernel' meaning across. If that were all that mattered, then it would have partly succeeded. Yet it lacks the shape, grace and theological literacy of the original. Five comments are appropriate.

First, the address to God is changed. God is no longer the 'moderator', but simply 'Father of heaven and earth'. The familial has replaced the transcendent. Second, the restraint of the language found in the Latin *supplicationes* and *clementer* is absent. Third, 'show us the way to peace' represents a diminished theology when compared to 'grant us your peace'. Fourth, the shape of the collect has not been caught at all. The *CLP* point about form being culturally conditioned and not a necessary part of translation has apparently been taken to its extreme. Fifth, the conclusion has created a clumsy ending. The Latin begins *per Dominum* . . . ICEL adds 'We make this prayer . . .'. ICEL justified this by arguing that it represented the Latin *quaesumus*, often found in these texts.

Compare the version of this collect from *The Book of Common Prayer*:

> Almighty and everlasting God,
> who dost govern all things in heaven and earth:
> Mercifully hear the supplications of thy people,
> and grant us thy peace all the days of our life.
> Through Jesus Christ our Lord.

The Prayer Book captures not just the 'core' meaning but also the shape of the Latin. This gives it a dynamic lacking in the ICEL version. The strong rhythmic line 4 creates an English *cursus* inspired by (though not reproducing) the *cursus* of the original.

The ICEL 1973 translations rejected elaborate syntax and did not employ relative or final clauses. They concentrated on expressing one aspect of the meaning while ignoring the sophisticated relationships of ideas expressed in the Latin.

Throughout the 1970s and 80s there was criticism of the ICEL translation. Some critics focused on its literary quality, some on its 'secular' language. Others pointed to a lack of modesty in speech. God, it was said, was being harangued.

Another kind of criticism was more theological. Archbishop Eric D'Arcy of Hobart, writing in *The Tablet* in April 1984, demonstrated how, in the prayers over the offerings and after communion, ICEL collapsed a rich Latin theological vocabulary of sacrifice and communion into single, repeated English terms such as 'Eucharist'.

Was ICEL tilting at the theology and spirituality of the Roman tradition? An example of this tendency is the *Oratio* for Ash Wednesday. In Latin, it reads:

> Concede nobis, Domine,
> praesidia militiae christianae sanctis inchoare ieiuniis,
> ut, contra spiritales nequitias pugnaturi,
> continentiae muniamur auxiliis.

Even those with little Latin will spot the military character of this text. *Praesidia militiae christianae* means an armed campaign. Line 3 specifies this as a battle against spiritual wickedness, for which (line 4) weapons are required. Scripturally the text echoes Ephesians 6.10–20 and a long tradition of viewing Christian life as a battle. Such a bold metaphor was apparently not acceptable to ICEL:

Lord,
protect us in our struggle against evil.
As we begin the discipline of Lent,
make this day holy by our self denial.
We make this prayer . . .

This English rendering excises the military metaphor, introduces a new focus on 'this day' and alters the syntactical form of the prayer.

The forthcoming translation[5] gives full weight to meaning, metaphor and shape:

Grant us, Lord,
to begin with holy fasting
this campaign of Christian service,
that as we enter the fight against spiritual evils
we may be armed with weapons of self-restraint.
Through our Lord Jesus Christ your Son . . .

Clearly, lessons have been learnt about what is required in translation for the liturgy. Some of these lessons have been drawn from experience, others from a change in the approach adopted by the legislators of the Church.

In fact, it had become clear well before work began on the English translation of the 2002 *Missale Romanum* that spoken prayer does not have to be as plain as the 1973 translation made it. ICEL admitted as much in its second edition of the English Missal, entitled *The Sacramentary*, which appeared in 1998 after many years' patient work. In this book the collects had largely abandoned the simple language of 1973. Relative and final clauses were employed and a serious attempt had been made to convey something of the Latin syntax.

The Sacramentary was rejected by the Holy See, which itself had prepared new guidelines for translators in two documents. The first, known as *Liturgiam Authenticam*, appeared in 2001,[6] the second,

---

5 Since the issuance of the *Missale Romanum* in 2002, ICEL has been engaged in providing an English translation for the consideration of the Conferences of Roman Catholic Bishops. The process calls for each section to be sent to the Conferences for study and comment (Green Book) and after the comments are incorporated into the texts reissued for Canonical vote (Grey Book).

6 Holy See, 2001, *Liturgiam Authenticam: Vernacular Languages in the Books of the Roman Liturgy*, London: Catholic Truth Society.

the *Ratio Translationis* (English language version), in 2007.[7] Without going into a detailed analysis of these, it would be fair to say that they insisted that the Latin text in both sense and form should be regarded as a model that the translated prayer should take. It was not going to be sufficient to convey a simple 'core' meaning. Texts must retain the particular shape of the *Oratio*, as well as conveying the full meaning of the Latin. 'Dynamic Equivalence' had given way to 'Formal Equivalence'.

One view of this change would be that the new rules represent a break with ICEL's 1973 practice. In fact, the norms return to the long-established usage of attempting to create a shape of English collect that resembles its Latin original. The stream of tradition has been rejoined.

Liturgiam Authenticam was criticized as mandating, word for word, literal translation. The charge was levelled that the new prayers would be hard to speak and harder to understand. Some critics saw a more sinister context. Was the Church trying to turn the liturgical clock back?

Those who favour the new rules point out that *Liturgiam Authenticam* does not mandate literal translation. It asks for prayers that are faithful to the Latin original and exhibit a flow and rhythm proper to a people's prayer. It asks for a language that is worthy of the sacred nature of the liturgical act. It can be argued that since these prayers are repeated with different degrees of frequency, they will have the chance to become embedded. Certainly, experience proves that complexity does not necessarily hinder understanding or memorability.

This approach amounts to an attempt to capture something of a more 'sacred' language in the Church's public prayer. Such terminology is difficult to define. What is 'sacred'? One answer might be that our contemporary popular culture takes a great interest in the past and in the revival of the 'retro' – older forms of design, music and so on. Are we locating 'sacred' in the past? Or is it more the case that exercises in solemn public speaking naturally tend to be informed by a tradition, to be more ritualized, formal and archaic?

Collects: God and human beings

The origins of the Latin *Oratio* lie in the early fifth-century Roman Church and a movement towards the comprehensive use of Latin in her liturgy. Such a development was inevitably influenced by contemporary

---

7 Holy See, 2007, *Ratio Translationis for the English Language*, Vatican City: Congregation for Divine Worship and the Discipline of the Sacraments.

theological preoccupations. In our own time, too, the collect has been influenced by theological reflection. The following three instances are noteworthy.

First among the ideas that shape the Latin collect is that God is supreme, the author and sustainer of all that is. This may reflect the anti-Pelagian debates of the fifth century, and there is a certain Augustinian tone in the collect genre. Typical of this is the collect now assigned to the Thursday after Ash Wednesday in the Roman Missal. Anglicans will know a version of this prayer as the fourth of the collects to be said after the offertory when there is no communion in the Prayer Book Order for Holy Communion.[8]

Actiones nostras, quaesumus, Domine,
aspirando praeveni et adiuvando prosequere,
ut cuncta nostra operatio a te semper incipiat
et per te coepta finiatur.
Per Dominum . . .

God is asked to inspire our actions and encourage them, so that everything we do may always begin from God and through him be brought to conclusion. The use of *cuncta* and *semper* emphasizes this.

Other collects speak of God being the sole hope of his household, his 'familia, quae in sola spe gratiae caelestis innititur' – 'who rely solely on the hope of heavenly grace' – (Fifth Sunday of Ordinary Time), or of God as the One without whom 'nihil potest mortalis infirmitas' – 'mortal weakness can do nothing' (Eleventh Sunday of Ordinary Time).

The collect for the Third Sunday of Ordinary Time understands good works as themselves motivated by God and gifts of grace, through the use of the verb *mereor*, which indicates the reception of something as wages or reward. God is asked to reward what God has inspired:

Omnipotens sempiterne Deus,
dirige actus nostros in beneplacito tuo,
ut in nomine dilecti Filii tui
mereamur bonis operibus abundare.
Per Dominum . . .

---

8 The *BCP* collect reads, 'Prevent us, O Lord, in all our doings with thy most gracious favour, and further us with thy continual help; that in all our works begun, continued, and ended in thee, we may glorify thy holy Name, and finally by thy mercy obtain everlasting life . . .'

[Almighty, everlasting God, direct our actions in your good pleasure, that in the name of your beloved Son we may be rewarded by being abundant in good works.]

A second theme found in the collects is that the celebration of the sacred liturgy enacts the work of our salvation here and now. Such an immediate connection between liturgy and saving event is expressed succinctly in this prayer over the offerings, used at the Holy Thursday Mass of the Lord's Supper and on the Second Sunday of Ordinary Time. God is asked to permit the Church a worthy celebration of the Mass: 'quia, quoties huius hostiae commemoratio celebratur, opus nostrae redemptionis exercetur' – 'because, whenever the commemoration of this Victim is celebrated, the work of our redemption is accomplished'.

The collect for Easter Day as found in the Roman Missal takes up the theme:

Deus, qui hodierna die, per Unigenitum tuum,
aeternitatis nobis aditum, devicta morte, reserasti,
da nobis, quaesumus,
ut qui resurrectionis dominicae sollemnia colimus,
per innovationem tui Spiritus
in lumine vitae resurgamus.
Per Dominum . . .

[O God, who on this day, through your Only Begotten Son, opened to us, with the vanquishing of death, the entry to eternal life: grant to us, we pray, that we who keep the solemnity of the Lord's resurrection may, by renewal of your Spirit, rise in the light of life.]

Here, it is those who celebrate the rising of the Lord liturgically on *this* Easter feast, 'qui resurrectionis dominicae sollemnia colimus', who ask to be renewed by the same Holy Spirit in whom Christ has been resurrected. Saving event and liturgical event are one.

The highlighting of the work of the Holy Spirit is a more contemporary theological theme appearing in the reformed Roman Liturgy. The 'new' Eucharistic prayers of the Roman Rite focus on the Spirit as the sanctifier both of the bread and cup and the whole liturgical assembly. Collects, too, are drawn into this, as the Easter Day example makes clear.

The Collect for the Nineteenth Sunday of Ordinary Time adds the phrase 'docente Spiritu Sancto' to an ancient prayer:

Omnipotens sempiterne Deus,
quem, docente Spiritu Sancto,
paterno nomine invocare praesumimus,
perfice in cordibus nostris spiritum adoptionis filiorum,
ut promissam hereditatem ingredi mereamur.
Per Dominum . . .

[Almighty, everlasting God, whom by the prompting of the Holy Spirit we dare to invoke under the name of Father, perfect in our hearts the spirit of adoption of sons, that we may be given entrance to the promised inheritance.]

The new English Missal: its effects

I have tried to demonstrate above how the new English translation of the Missal will, comparatively speaking, amount to a complete change in the sound of our liturgy as well as a considerable augmentation in its theological content. The mandate of the Holy See that translators should stay close to the sense as well as to the shape of our historic collects, prayers over the offerings and post-communion prayers will certainly be noticed in other Christian communities.

One aspect of the 1973 ICEL collect translations found many echoes in the work of other liturgical drafters. This is the treatment of the Latin relative pronoun 'Qui' with its second-person-singular address at the opening of the collect.

In Latin and sixteenth-century English, the second person singular, 'thou art', 'thou hast', 'thou dost' and so on, is used with the relative pronoun. This form, already changing in the seventeenth century, remained standard for the collect. A debate took place in the 1960s about how to render this in modern English. Is it 'O God, you . . .', or, 'O God, you who . . .', or 'O God, who . . .'? Of these options, the second was ruled out, since the hornlike sound that it creates, resembling 'yoo-hoo', would have a comic effect.

The first option was the one favoured by ICEL. Typical is its 1973 version of the collect for the Fourteenth Sunday of Ordinary Time:

Father,
through the obedience of Jesus,
your servant and your Son,
you raised a fallen world.

Free us from sin
and bring us the joy that lasts for ever.

This device had its critics. It was argued that to address God with 'you . . .' necessitates a strong stop before anything can follow, a stop that fragments the unity of the collect. In the example given above, it is an actual full stop. The short sentence that follows it ('Free us . . .') lacks any connection with what precedes.

Another disadvantage was that the 'you' form was sonically too strong. As a result, the texts seemed to be telling God something God already knows.

In fact, by adopting this style of address, ICEL was in subtle ways shifting the register of the collect as a whole, making its tone more hortatory than euchological. An example is the post-communion prayer in the Roman Missal for the Sixth Sunday of Ordinary Time. ICEL's text sounds like a political speech:

Lord,
you give us food from heaven.
May we always hunger
for the bread of life.

It is not over-critical to suggest that, along with so many others in the 1973 collection, this text is easy to 'ham up'.[9] The new text will read:

Having feasted on heaven's delights
we pray, O Lord,
that we may always hunger
for the food by which we truly live.

Here, 'hunger' is retained (the Latin is *appetamus*, which recalls 'appetite'), but it is softened by being included in a longer sentence with a more complex rhythmic conclusion than before.

The radical change that awaits Catholic congregations and clergy is the return to a relative pronoun structure at the opening of the collect and the reinstatement of the syntactical form of the prayer as a whole. For example, the proposed new translation of the collect for the Fourteenth Sunday of Ordinary Time, whose 1973 version I gave above, will now retain the single sentence structure of the Latin, and reproduce the second-person-singular construction of the Latin address:

---

9 I am told that it is best read in an exaggerated Midwest accent.

> O God, who in the abasement of your Son
> raised up a fallen world,
> grant your faithful people a holy joy,
> so that those you have snatched from the slavery of sin
> you will bring to enjoy eternal happiness.

Despite the possible aural confusion of 'abasement' (the *basement* of your Son?), this construction restores to the collect its unity, form and flow.

ICEL used the third option, the relative pronoun, but little. In Anglican circles it achieved greater popularity. Where an attribute of God is invoked it is not uncommon. This is the *Common Worship* collect for the Fifth Sunday before Lent:

> Almighty God,
> by whose grace alone we are accepted
> and called to your service . . . (CW, p. 387)

It occurs also where the sound of the second person singular and the third person singular of the verb are identical, as in the *Common Worship* collect for the Fourth Sunday of Epiphany:

> God our creator,
> who in the beginning
> commanded the light to shine out of darkness . . . (CW, p. 385)

As will be clear in previous essays, the 'you' form of collect opening has had many imitators. In the *Alternative Service Book 1980* of the Church of England, the Prayer Book's great Ash Wednesday collect was adapted in this way, as were others. The American Episcopalian *Book of Common Prayer* (BCP 1979) and the *Lutheran Book of Worship* (1978) display many examples of similar treatment.

The collect for the Fourteenth Sunday given above also tackles a second issue. The Latin construction has a relative pronoun in the accusative case ('those you have snatched') as the object of a verb which also has a second object ('you will bring to enjoy eternal happiness'). In Latin this is a terse and elegant construction.

There are two ways of dealing with it in English, if one wishes to retain something of the Latin shape. Close translation, as in this example, is one. The other is a version employed by *The Book of Common Prayer* using 'as' and 'so'. A further example of this is the collect said at the Angelus, which in the older Roman Missals was the post communion for the Annunciation. In the Roman Missal it is the collect for the Fourth Sunday of Advent. The English version probably dates back to the fifteenth century and, with modifications, is retained in the new English Missal. It translates literally:

> Pour forth, we beseech thee, O Lord, thy grace into our hearts,
> that we to whom the incarnation of Christ thy Son
> was made known by the message of an angel,
> may by his passion and cross be brought into the glory of his resurrection.

The Book of Common Prayer (in which it is the collect for the feast of the Annunciation of the Lord) replaces the construction 'we to whom . . . may by his passion . . .' with 'as' and 'so'. ICEL 1973 adopts the same solution:

> Lord, fill our hearts with your love,
> and as you revealed to us by an angel
> the coming of your Son as man,
> so lead us through his suffering and death
> to the glory of his resurrection . . .

I commented earlier on the phenomenon of 'learning from ourselves'. This illustrates a parallel and equally positive willingness in the ecumenical community to learn from each other.

The collect: alive or dead?

Between 'Friends, Romans, countrymen, lend me your ears' and 'Okay now, people, listen up!' there is more than just four centuries – there is a significant difference in the perception of what is appropriate public speech. Modern culture seems to prefer the familial and intimate to the formal and the public.

The Latin collect evolved in a different culture. Here, rhetoric and elaboration in public speech were prized as artifice and effective as tools of communication. Its English equivalent evolved in a similar culture. The collect was intended to be heard and to teach by hearing. In an elegant and memorable form it taught grand theological themes of the Faith.

Our own age finds a conflict between elegant speaking and ease of hearing. We think that truth is not served by complexity of expression. This raises questions about the possibility of the collect form in our own day. How are we to speak publicly in the presence of God?

The question demands more than a simple answer. Modern evangelicalism has challenged traditional prayer models with its breezy worship styles and (allegedly) more spontaneous and intimate modes of prayer. Some Christian groups find that traditional prayer forms exclude minorities and ignore their sensitivities. Those who value more traditional prayer forms accuse evangelical prayer styles of lacking reverence. They find such forms manipulative, attempting to induce particular emotions in the hearers.

So has the collect had its day? Is this tight and sophisticated prayer too contrived for our 'laid back' contemporary liturgies? I would like to present three arguments for the retention of the collect form: that collects with great formal integrity are still being written; that the collect is above all a biblical form of prayer; that the collect stands for diversity in the types of prayer form appropriate to different moments in the liturgy.

That collects are still a living liturgical form is illustrated by a brief examination of two collections of collects, that of the Anglican Janet Morley in *All Desires Known* and that of ICEL in its 1998 *Sacramentary* project. These two collections have several features in common. Both attempt to find alternative ways to speak of God. Both find their inspiration in sacred Scripture. Both are conscious of the need to be as inclusive in worship as the gospel is in its invitation to all men and women.

Janet Morley's first collection was published in 1988.[10] It is a collection of different sorts of prayers including a set of collects to accompany the lectionary of the *Alternative Service Book*. This lectionary was themed, unlike the lectionaries that have succeeded it in *Common Worship*.

In her introduction, Morley questions the male terminology traditionally used of God. While rejecting the simplistic substitution of feminine for masculine, she goes looking in Scripture and elsewhere for suitable, more inclusive, modes of address. She employs the many and

---

10 Janet Morley, 1988, *All Desires Known*, London: Movement for the Ordination of Women and Women in Theology; republished in 1992, with a 3rd edn in 2005, London: SPCK. References are to the 1992 edition, with page numbers of the 3rd edition, 2005, given in square brackets.

sometimes unusual ways God is imaged in the Bible. These lines, from her collect for Advent 2, are typical:

> O God our disturber,
> whose speech is pregnant with power
> and whose word will be fulfilled . . . (*ADK*, p. 5 [p. 17])

Here the combination of the idea of God as 'disturber' and the 'pregnant' nature of divine speech recalling Genesis 1 is striking. Both are thoroughly biblical, and the second makes a subtle allusion to God's femininity. The text allows the richness of sacred Scripture to speak.

Morley retains the traditional collect form with tenacity. She seems to revel in encouraging the relative pronoun without stretching the syntax too far. Often this will be in the genitive, something to which I have referred above as a feature of other Anglican writing, as in her collect for Pentecost 19:

> O God, before whose face
> we are not made righteous
> even by being right . . . (*ADK*, p. 24 [p. 22])

Here too the pun on 'righteousness' and 'being right' is clever and arresting, though perhaps such a device might only yield its qualities on repetition or reflection.

Perhaps the most striking feature of Morley's collects is that they display a sense of interiority that is not afraid to speak of the spiritual life in sometimes quite vivid imagery. A good example, among many, might be the collect for Easter Eve, with its echoes of Saint John of the Cross:

> O God,
> you have searched the depths we cannot know,
> and touched what we cannot bear to name:
> may we so wait,
> enclosed in your darkness,
> that we are ready to encounter
> the terror of the dawn,
> with Jesus Christ, **Amen.** (*ADK*, p. 14 [p. 31])

This particular focus in the collect is both new and welcome. The Latin tradition is more objective. It relies more on sonority than on imagery.

Is this because of its antiquity? Is it because it was addressing the liturgical needs of large assemblies in huge buildings? Or has it something to do with a (presumed) male authorship?

Janet Morley's collects demonstrate that life remains in this form of ritual speech. She shows how one might still work successfully within the traditional shape of the collect, the vocabulary of sacred Scripture and ecclesial requirements. I can testify that even on a 'blind' hearing in a crowded Sunday Mass, Morley's collects are thought-provoking.

During the 1980s, ICEL was also working on a series of English collects, described as 'Opening Prayers', which were related to the Scripture readings of the Roman Lectionary. Prayers were to be provided for each of the Sundays and major festivals of the three-year lectionary cycle.[11] As with Morley's work, these prayers are developments, rather than imitations, of the traditional form. Like Morley's collects, they search for new ways of addressing God and find them in Scripture. Here is the prayer for the Fourth Sunday of Lent, in Year B of the Lectionary (cf. Eph. 2.4–10 and John 3.14–21):

O God, rich in mercy,
you so loved the world
that when we were dead in our sins,
you sent your only Son for our deliverance.
(*OP*, p. 26)

Sometimes the reference is lengthy and striking, as in the prayer for the first Sunday of Advent, Year A:

God of majesty and power,
amid the clamour of our violence
your Word of truth resounds;
upon a world made dark by sin
the Sun of Justice casts his dawning rays. (*OP*, p. 2)

This is (arguably too) highly coloured and elaborate; it certainly echoes the day's Scripture readings (Isa. 2.1–5, Rom. 13.11–14).

The petitions, too, call upon the readings that are to be heard, as here, in the prayer for the Second Sunday of Easter, where the Gospel is that of Doubting Thomas. The image of God as refiner of faith is intriguing:

---

11 International Commission on English in the Liturgy, 1997, *Opening Prayers: Scripture-related Collects for Years A, B & C from The Sacramentary, The ICEL Collects*, Norwich: Canterbury Press.

Day by day refine our faith,
that we who have not seen the Christ
may truly confess him as our Lord and God,
and share the blessedness of those who believe. (*OP*, p. 37)

The ICEL opening prayers share Morley's interest in the expression of the interiority of Christian faith. Like Morley, they name the trials of Christian spiritual life with frankness, as in this petition from the prayer for the First Sunday of Lent, Year C:

When we walk through the desert of temptation,
strengthen us to renounce the power of evil.
When our faith is tested by doubt,
illumine our hearts with Easter's bright promise. (*OP*, p. 21)

A second significant defence of the collect form is that it reproduces and maintains one of the basic patterns of prayer found in sacred Scripture. Those familiar with the psalms will recall their often employed sequence of remembering what God has done, and on that basis asking for a furtherance, or renewal, of those *mirabilia Dei*. This sequence is found both in psalms of praise and of lament. Jewish liturgical prayer patterns have been formed in the same way. In longer prayers, blessing God for his deeds leads into supplication for continued divine action.

The Latin collect takes over this basic form and re-expresses it with Roman elegance and brevity. It seems to have been the deliberate invention of a new prayer genre. In the fullest forms of this prayer, God is addressed, God's actions are remembered and God is besought. The doxology characteristic of Jewish prayer is transformed into the expression of Christ's mediation in all prayer by virtue of the divine and human nature which are perfectly united in him.

Lastly, the collect stands for diversity in the styles of liturgical prayer. In the tradition of the Roman liturgy, the terms *Oratio* and *Prex* respectively define the collect and the longer prayers such as the Canon of the Mass or the consecratory prayers at ordination, the dedication of a church or the consecration of virgins. The term *Praefatio* rendered in English (to the confusion of many) as 'Preface', describes the first section of the *Prex Eucharistica*.

Each of these genres has its own character, though all of them, in different ways, are thoroughly scriptural in origin and shape. They also serve different functions. The *Prex* is often the principal verbal articulation of the sacrament or rite being celebrated. The *Oratio* is a subsidiary prayer. It often serves as the introduction to a *Prex*, as at Mass and ordination. At Mass it is, like the more elaborate and lyrical *Praefatio*, the vehicle for an objective, ongoing and liturgically contextual reflection on seasons and feasts.

A style of worship that deliberately sacrificed tradition and did not recognize the distinctions between prayer forms would quickly become amorphous and unable to function in anything but the most primitive way. It would lose all possibility of theological literacy. It would forfeit any pattern or shape. Shape is important. It marks the difference (for the congregant at least) between the experiential assurance of 'This is what we are doing' and the chaos of 'Whatever are they going to get up to next?'

Conclusion

In this chapter I have tried to identify how recent experience of praying the collect in English has influenced the changes about to take place in English Catholic liturgical speech. I have tried to demonstrate that these changes touch on the ability of the collect form to express orthodox tradition in a terse and well-organized manner. I have indicated that we are shortly to return to more traditional lineaments of this form, after the experience of the novel translation styles of ICEL 1973. Throughout, I have tried to express my own conviction that the collect form remains a living way of speaking prayer and asserting the diversity of prayer forms which offer differentiation and assist participation in the sacred liturgy.

Reviewing the principal considerations raised in this chapter in relation to the significant changes forthcoming in the English liturgy of the Roman Catholic community, it is appropriate to ask what consequences there might be ecumenically. Will our new liturgical prose style set a new trend?

I have suggested that the rules informing the forthcoming translation of the Roman Missal into English are not new at all. Indeed, the opposite is true – they appear to return to the practice of earlier translators (and authors) in English. Some aspects of the new English Roman Missal, such as the restoration of the response 'And with your spirit'[12] and the abandonment of the common texts of the Ordinary of

---

12 In mandating this change, the Holy See took the view that 'And also with you' does not convey the theological weight of the response, which is the

the Mass, may be seen as out of step with other Christian communities. One certainly cannot say the same about the new versions of the collects, however. In reconnecting with translation usages common to both Anglicans and Catholics, and increasingly adopted in the revised worship books of other Churches of the Reformation, it is clear that this is a very ecumenical approach.

---

naming of the ordained minister as the one equipped with spiritual gifts to serve the Church.

Index

Abridgement 69, 70, 85, 86 *see also* Sunday of Service of the Methodists in North America
absolution 22, 94n, 126, 127 *see also* forgiveness
Advent 17, 33, 58, 60, 81, 158, 160, 162, 169
Advent Sunday 50, 158, 171
Africa 83, 113
agenda 110, 111
Albright, Jacob 97
Albright's People 97
Alcuin Club 62, 182, 183
All Saints' Day 186
Ambrose of Milan 109
America *see* United States
American Declaration of Independence 68
American Revolution 111
Amsterdam 140, 141, 142
Anglican 3, 50, 53, 55–6, 58, 63, 65, 67, 71, 72, 78, 85, 143n, 160, 161, 178, 180, 182, 194, 208, 210, 211
Anglican Church in Aotearoa New Zealand and Polynesia 61n
A New Zealand Prayer Book 1989 61, 196
Anglican Church of Australia 60n

A Prayer Book for Australia 1995 60, 168–73, 175
An Australian Prayer Book 1978 60, 65, 168
Anglican Church of Canada 59, 168
Book of Alternative Services 1983 59, 168, 196
Book of Common Prayer 59n
Anglican collect 1, 27, 50–66
Anglican Communion 2, 50, 54, 55, 56, 59, 62, 64, 181, 181, 183n
Anglican Provinces *see* Anglican Communion
Anglo-French 10
ante-communion 85, 86, 112
anti-Pelagian 204
antiphon 36
Aquinas 58
Arianism 107, 132
Arminianism 75, 139
Ascension Day 17, 68, 92, 196
Ash Wednesday 17, 68
assembly 1, 4, 6, 118, 124, 125, 127, 128, 129, 130, 140, 141, 176, 200, 205, 211
Assembly of Divines *see* Westminster Assembly
Asia 83
Aubrey, M. E. 152

217

INDEX

Augustine of Hippo 39, 75
Australia 60, 65, 161
Ave Maria 13
Awakening(s) 83, 97

baptism 3, 25, 28, 85, 86, 101, 107, 140, 152, 153
Baptist 4, 5, 139, 140, 142, 147–56
Baptist Union of Great Britain 149, 152, 153
Praise God 153
Barkley, John 126n, 135
Becket, Thomas 13
Bedford, England 143, 146
believer churches 140
Benediction of the Blessed Sacrament 198
Benedictus 12, 170
Berry-Bailey, Barbara 117
Beza, Theodore *see* de Bèze
Bible 4, 13, 25, 28, 35, 39, 43, 48, 49, 161, 176, 210
bishop(s) 83, 85, 86n, 87, 90, 92, 101, 117, 184
Blessed Virgin Mary *see also* Mary 39, 180
Boehm, Martin 97
Bonner, Henry 151
books of hours 9, 12, 13
Bowie, Walter Russell 95
Brand, Eugene L. 116
Bright, William 55, 88, 94, 97, 102, 114
Brightman, F. E. 14, 24
British Baptist Church 2, 4, 139
Bromhead, Anne and Hughe 141
Brook, Stella 19
Bucer, Martin 24, 126, 127, 128, 130, 135
Bunyan, John 143–7

burial 3, 17, 55, 85, 86, 87, 90, 94n, 97, 100, 107, 152n
Burk, Michael 117

calendar 38, 56, 68, 70, 76, 95, 108, 109, 117, 119, 159, 160, 179, 180, 181, 186, 188, 189, 192 *see also* Christian year, church year
Calvin, John 1, 4, 126, 127, 128, 129, 130, 131, 132, 133, 134, 135
Calvinist 139, 140, 142
Canada 65, 162, 168
canticles 12, 170
Caribbean 73, 79
Catholic Apostolic Church 134
Challoner, Richard 198
chanting 5
Chapman, David 69
charismatic renewal 149, 150, 154
Charlemagne 32
Chichester Diocesan Kalendar 189
Christ Seminary-Seminex 116
chorale 108
Christian year 95, 136, 145, 152, 157, 158, 162, 165, 179 *see also* calendar, church year
Christmas 55, 58, 62, 68, 160
Chrysostom, John 39, 94n, 101, 102
Church in Wales 183
Church of England 2, 3, 6, 50, 53, 56, 57, 62, 84, 132, 140, 160, 179, 183, 192, 195, 208
Alternative Service Book 1980 58, 59, 61, 62, 63, 64, 160, 163–4, 168, 174, 179, 180, 181, 182, 185, 186, 187,

INDEX

188, 191, 208, 210
Additional Collects 2003 64
Book of Common Prayer 1662
see also *Prayer Book* 1662 2,
3, 4, 5, 52, 57, 60, 62, 63, 64,
67, 68, 69, 70, 71, 84, 99, 103,
114, 121 141, 144, 146, 155,
158, 169, 178, 179, 186, 204n,
208, 209
*Calendar, Lectionary and
Collects* 180, 184–5, 188–90
Common Worship 3, 20, 62,
63, 64, 65, 173–174, 176, 179,
180, 181, 183, 184, 188, 189,
190, 196, 208
General Synod 62, 63, 173
*Lent, Holy Week and
Easter* 179, 185, 186
Liturgical Commission 57, 58,
62, 63, 64, 74, 173, 179, 186,
187, 196
Prayer Book 1549 (First Prayer
Book of Edward VI) 9, 10, 12,
16, 17, 18, 19, 21–2, 23, 24,
25, 26, 27, 50, 51, 52, 53, 158
Prayer Book 1552 (Second
Prayer Book of Edward VI)
52
Prayer Book 1559 52
Prayer Book 1604 52
Prayer Book 1662 20, 52, 55,
56, 57, 59, 61, 62, 84, 85, 89,
92, 94, 98, 101, 158, 169
Prayer Book 1928 53
Promise of His Glory 179, 180,
185, 186, 195
Church of Ireland 62
Church of the Province of
Southern Africa (The
Anglican Church of Southern
Africa)

An Anglican Prayer Book
1989 61, 65
South African Prayer Book
1972 58
Church of Scotland 2, 114, 130,
132, 134, 135
Church of South India 56, 58,
71
Book of Common Worship 56,
71, 79
Church of Sweden 1, 3, 6, 28–49
Breviarium Lincopense 35
Breviarium Scarense 35
Breviarium Strengense 35
Breviarium Upsaliense 35
Church Assembly 31, 41, 42,
46
Church Service Book 39, 41,
42, 44
Governing Body 31, 45, 46
General Synod 31, 45, 48, 49
Gospel Book 3, 30, 31, 32, 36,
37, 38, 39, 40, 41, 42, 43, 44,
45, 46, 47, 48
Swecana Missa 28
Skara Diocesan Missal 32
Skara Diocesan Breviary 32
Church of the United Brethren in
Christ (New Constitution) 97,
98
Church of the United Brethren in
Christ (Old Constitution) 97
church orders, German 5, 109,
111, 112, 114
Church Service Society 134
church year 68, 69, 70, 92n,
103, 104, 108, 109, 111, 112,
117, 135, 136 *see also* calendar,
Christian year
Churches of Christ in
America 95

INDEX

collecta 30, 36n, 39, 197, 198
Colquhoun, Frank 55, 58, 76, 178, 179
  Parish Prayers 178, 186
  Contemporary Parish Prayers 178
  New Parish Prayers 178
common collect 39, 180, 181, 187
Common Service (Lutheran) 112
communion 3, 11, 63, 79, 99, 195, 201, 204
  of the sick 28, 85, 86
compline 35, 116
confession 73, 81, 86, 126, 127, 135, 148, 150, 163
confirmation 3, 80, 107
Congregational 71
Congregationalists 140
Constitution on the Sacred Liturgy (*Sacrosanctum Concilium*) 160, 161n
Consultation on Common Texts 61, 119, 161
Cooke, R. J. 87
Cosin, John 52, 58
covenant 128, 146
Covenant Service 79
creed 11, 13, 111, 112, 163
cremation 3
Cranmer, Thomas 9, 14, 15, 16, 17, 18, 22n, 23, 24, 25, 27, 50, 51, 52, 53, 54, 57, 58, 59, 75, 115, 119
Cranmerian *see* Cranmer
Cromwell, Thomas 13
Cuddesdon Office Book 1940 181
culture, cultural 5, 107, 153, 161, 203, 209

Cumberland Presbyterian Church 165
Cuming, Geoffrey 9, 15, 16, 17, 23, 26, 53
cursus 201

daily office(s) 3, 66, 158, 163, 169 *see also* Matins, Morning Prayer, Evening Prayer, Evensong, Vespers
deacon(s) 80, 85, 86, 90, 97, 98, 152
dead, prayers for 178
Dearmer, Percy 53
de Bèze, Theodore 130
Declaration as to the Forgiveness of Sins 69 *see also* absolution, forgiveness
Dieter, Cheryl 117
Dietrich, Viet 109, 111
Directory for the Publick Worship of God *see* Westminster Assembly
Dissenters 52
Draper, Martin 182
  Cloud of Witnesses 182, 183–5
Duffy, Eamon 26
Durham Cathedral 186
Durham (England), St Oswald's Church 186
dynamic equivalence 199, 203

Easter 17, 34, 55, 62, 160, 161, 166, 185
ecumenical 7, 70, 72, 74, 137, 139, 153, 155, 156, 159, 174–5, 209, 215
elders 85, 86, 91, 97, 98, 101
Ellis, Chris 2, 4, 5, 153n
England 2, 10, 11, 32, 135, 168, 178

INDEX

English (language) 13, 15, 16, 19, 25, 114, 118, 179, 197, 198, 206, 208, 214
English Missal *see* International Commission on English in the Liturgy
entrance rite 3, 72, 124, 125, 157 *see also* opening rite, gathering
Epiphany 68, 115, 118, 119, 162, 163
Episcopal Church in the United States of America (ECUSA) 54, 88n, 89, 92n, 96, 114, 116n, 163, 181, 182
  Book of Alternative Services 119
  Book of Common Prayer 1789 54
  Book of Common Prayer 1892 55
  Book of Common Prayer 1928 55
  Book of Common Prayer 1979 55, 56, 58, 65, 114, 116, 163, 208
  Forward Movement 96
Epistle 38, 44, 45, 54, 55, 86, 111, 112, 114, 158, 161, 169
Eucharist 3, 24, 58, 63, 65, 66, 72, 81, 163, 169, 201
Evangelical Association 97, 98
Evangelical Church 97, 98, 99, 101
Evangelical Lutheran Church in America 1, 3, 6, 103, 106, 116, 117, 174
  Evangelical Lutheran Worship 2006 5, 106, 115–21, 174–5
  With One Voice 116
  This Far by Faith 116

Libro de Liturgia y Cántico 116
Evangelical Lutheran Church in Canada 1, 3–4, 6, 106, 117, 174
Evangelical United Brethren Church 83, 98, 101–2
Evening Prayer 9, 44, 51, 72, 85, 86, 87, 89, 92, 93, 94, 110, 116, 158, 177, 179 *see also* Evensong, Vespers
Evensong 17, 22, 26, 27, 51 *see also* Evening Prayer, Vespers
extempore (extemporaneous, extemporary, ex corde, spontaneous) 3, 4, 67, 69, 85, 98, 111, 129, 139, 140, 142, 143, 146, 147, 148, 150, 151, 154, 156, 165, 176

feminine 191, 210
feminism 61
feminist 190, 191, 193
forgiveness 73, 80, 81, 86 *see also* absolution
free church 139, 144, 146, 147, 148
Free Churches 2, 57, 154
free prayer 99, 143, 149, 150, 151, 156, 176
French language 10, 11, 131, 132
Frere, W. H. 181
funeral 87, 101, 152 *see also* burial

Galbreath, Paul 2, 3, 4, 5
Gallican 50, 107, 118
Gardiner, Stephen 24
gathering 3, 136, 137, 159, 176, 192 *see also* entrance rite, opening rite

Gaunt, Alan 72
Gealy, Fred 103
Gelasius 39
gender-inclusive 116, 182, 183
 see also inclusive language
gender-specific 117 see also
 gender-inclusive, inclusive
 language
General Baptists 139, 154
General Instruction on the
 Roman Missal 1969 65
Geneva 2, 123, 126, 130, 131,
 138
George, A. Raymond 70, 71, 74
German language 32, 97, 106,
 108, 109, 110, 111, 126, 130
Germany 125, 137
Gill, John 142
Gloria in excelsis 11, 111, 124,
 126, 135
Gloria patri 89, 124, 132
Gloucester, Diocese of 189
 Companions in the Faith 189
Good Friday 17, 68
Gospel reading 38, 44, 45, 54,
 55, 86, 111, 112, 126, 158,
 161, 166, 169, 176
Gother, John 198
grace 21, 22, 23, 51, 75, 187
gradual 36, 114
Grantham, Thomas 154
Gray, Donald 2, 3, 4
Gregory, A. S. 77
Gregory the Great 39–40, 75
Griffiths, Alan 7
Guilbert, Charles 55

Hampstead Road Baptist
 Church 151–2
Harbert, Bruce 199
Harrower, Charles S. 87

Haselock, Jeremy 189
Hatchett, Marion 55, 157
Helwys, Thomas 140
hexameter 200
Holland, Tristam SSF 181, 186
 Exciting Holiness 188
Holy Communion 24, 51, 52,
 55, 72, 73, 75, 81, 89, 90n,
 94n, 99, 101, 112, 113, 120,
 152, 155, 158, 164, 176, 204
Holy Roman Empire 32
Holy See 7, 198, 206
 Comme le prévoit 198–9, 200
 Liturgiam Authenticam 202
 Ratio Translationis 203
Holy Spirit 23, 36, 77, 78, 123,
 127, 128, 130, 133, 138, 141,
 142, 143, 144, 145, 146, 148,
 154, 184, 205
Horn, Edward Traille 112
Humble Access, Prayer of 99
Huntington, William Reed 55
hymnal 5, 33, 34, 39, 106, 108,
 110, 111, 112, 147 see also
 hymnody, hymns
hymnody 5, 75, 148, 149, 154
 see also hymnal, hymns
hymns 28, 36, 54, 84, 85, 102,
 103, 108, 109, 111, 126, 149,
 154, 155, 181 see also hymnal,
 hymnody

illumination, prayer for 4, 126,
 128, 129, 131, 132, 133, 134,
 135, 136, 138
incarnation 179, 187
inclusive language 46, 61, 71,
 72n, 75, 116, 168, 210
Independents 140
India 113
Institution, Words of 34

INDEX

Institution Narrative 35
Inter-Lutheran Committee on Worship 114, 115, 116, 162
International Commission on English in the Liturgy (ICEL) 7, 61, 118, 192, 198, 199, 200, 201, 202, 206, 207, 208, 209, 210, 212, 213, 214
  Opening Prayers 118, 188, 193–4, 212–13
  The Roman Missal (English Translation 1973) 7, 60, 61, 199, 200, 201, 202, 203, 206, 207, 209, 214
  The Roman Missal (English Translation of 2002 Missale Romanum) 206–9
  The Sacramentary 115, 118, 202, 210
International Committee on English Texts 114, 115
introit 36, 114
invocation, prayer of 97, 101, 148, 149
Iona 71
Ireland 65, 160

Japan 113
Jacobs, Henry Eystser 114
Jeanes, Gordon 25
John of the Cross 211
Joint Commission on Church Federation and Union 101
Joint Liturgical Group (JLG) 4, 6, 56, 57, 62, 70, 71, 72, 74, 76, 159, 160, 163
Jones, K. Vaughan 77
Joye, George 12
Jungmann, Josef 107
justification 24, 108
Justin Martyr 39

Katrina, Hurricane 121
Keble College, Oxford 185, 186
Kemp, Eric 189
King's Primer 1545 13
Kingdomtide 95
Knox, John 130, 132, 134
Krauth, Charles Porterfield 112
Kyrie eleison 108, 124, 126

Lampard, John, 1, 3, 5
Latin 2, 3, 7, 9, 10, 11, 13, 14, 15, 17, 18, 19, 20, 21, 22, 23, 25, 27, 28, 29, 31, 32, 33, 34, 35, 36, 37, 40, 41, 42, 43, 46, 47, 48, 49, 50, 54, 57, 63, 73, 106, 107, 108, 109, 114, 118, 119, 120, 130, 158, 198, 199, 200, 201, 202, 203, 204, 206, 207, 208, 209, 211, 213
Lay Folks' Mass Book 11
lectionary 3, 4, 6, 29, 45, 56, 57, 61, 62, 70, 71, 72, 74, 115, 120, 121, 137, 159, 160, 161, 162, 163, 164, 165, 173, 174, 176, 177, 190, 192, 210, 212
  Common Lectionary 1983 61, 159, 161
  Revised Common Lectionary 1992 4, 60, 62, 74, 117, 118, 159, 160, 161, 164, 169, 176, 192
  Roman Lectionary (*Ordo Lectionum Missae*) 1969 2nd edn 1981 115, 118, 159, 161, 162, 163, 166, 169, 176, 192, 212
Lee, Jesse 85
Lent 17, 58, 60, 68, 69, 169, 185
lesser festivals 61, 117, 119, 180, 182, 183, 186, 188

223

INDEX

Lincoln, Diocese of 189
Linköping 32
litany 3, 9, 12, 14, 15, 16, 17, 22, 110, 111, 137, 156
Little Hours of the Virgin 12, 16
Liturgical Movement 70, 150, 152, 159
liturgical renewal 155, 159, 176
Liturgy of Comprehension 1689 4, 52, 54
Lord's Prayer 11, 51, 86, 115
Lord's Supper 68, 85, 87, 89, 91, 97, 153
love-feast 84
Luther, Martin 1, 28, 108, 110, 119, 120, 125
  Formula Missae et Communionis 1523 108, 109, 125
  Deutsche Messe 1526 108, 109, 125
Lutheran 1, 2, 12, 30, 32, 33, 37, 40, 83, 97, 104–22
Lutheran Church in America 113
  Lutheran Book of Worship 1978 61, 116, 117, 118, 119, 121, 162–3, 174, 208
  Service Book and Hymnal 1958 113, 114, 115
Lutheran Church-Missouri Synod 113, 114, 121

MacCulloch, Diarmaid 12, 15
MacDonnell, Charles 62, 195, 196
  After Communion 195
McGrath, Alister 147
McNutt, Francis 55
Magnificat 12
Marot, Clement 130
marriage 3, 91, 98, 101 *see also*

Solemnization of Matrimony
Marshall, William 12
Marshall's Primer 15
Maundy Thursday 68
masculine 6, 75, 210
Mass 11, 13, 24, 26, 28, 29, 32, 33, 34, 35, 36, 37, 44, 48, 51, 107, 108, 109, 110, 113, 119, 124, 125, 126, 132, 137, 157, 158, 159, 160, 197, 198, 205, 212, 213, 214
Matins 22, 26, 27, 35, 51, 110, 112, 116 *see also* Morning Prayer
Mennonite 83, 97, 139
Mercersburg Movement 134
merit 21, 51
metaphor 7, 201, 202
Methodist Church of Great Britain 1, 5, 67–82
  Book of Offices 1936 70, 72
  Methodist Service Book 1975 71, 72, 73, 74, 76, 79, 81
  Methodist Worship Book 1999 5, 74–81
  Methodist Prayer Handbook 81, 82
Covenant Service 79
Local Preachers 80
Methodist Liturgical Sub-Committee 74, 76, 79, 80
Methodist Sacramental Fellowship 77
Methodist Church in the United States 2, 83–105, 164, 165 *see also* United Methodist Church
Methodist Episcopal Church 83, 84–90
Methodist Episcopal Church, South 84, 91–3

Methodist Protestant
  Church 84, 90–91, 93
*Sunday Service of the
  Methodists in North
  America* 68, 69, 85, 86, 88n,
  87, 89, 91, 93, 94, 95
metrical psalms, metrical
  psalter 126, 127, 128, 148,
  154
Meyer, F. B. 152
Midlane, Albert 77
Ministerium of
  Pennsylvania 110, 111
Ministry to the Sick 95, 96 *see
  also* communion of the sick
Missale Gallicanum Vetus 198
Missale Gothicum 198
Missale Romanum see Roman
  Missal
Morley, Janet 6, 61, 62, 72, 76,
  170, 173, 190–2, 194, 210–
  12
  All Desires Known 6, 61, 188,
    190–2, 194, 210–3, 214
Morning Prayer 9, 51, 68, 69,
  70, 72, 73, 85, 86, 87, 89, 92,
  93, 94n, 110, 115–16, 158,
  177, 179 *see also* Matins
Movement for the Ordination
  of Women and Women in
  Theology 190
Mueller, Craig 117
Muhlenberg, Henry
  Melchior 110, 112, 113, 121

Nässelqvist, Dan 32
Nevin, John 134
New Testament 12, 39, 51, 161,
  162, 163, 168, 171
Nichols, Bridget 2
Nilsson, Nils-Henrik 3, 5, 107

Nunc Dimittis 12
Nuremberg 109, 111

offerings, prayer over 198, 201,
  205, 206
offertory 3, 107, 108, 120, 204
Old Testament 56, 159, 160,
  161, 162, 166, 168, 169
opening rite 86, 124, 125, 126,
  126n, 127, 130, 132, 133,
  135, 135n, 136, 137 *see also*
  entrance rite, gathering
oratio 16n, 30n, 36n, 125, 197,
  199, 201, 203, 213
ordination 29, 85, 86, 87, 89,
  90, 91, 92, 94n, 97, 98, 101,
  213
Ordo Lectionum Missae see
  lectionary
Ordo Romanus Primus 124
Otterbein, Philip William 97

Particular Baptists 139, 150,
  154
Payne, E.A. *see also* Winward,
  Stephen 152, 153
  *Orders and Prayers for Church
    Worship* 152, 155
Perham, Michael 2, 3, 6, 187,
  189, 191, 195
Petri, Laurentius 28, 34, 35, 36
Petri, Olaus 28, 29, 32, 34
Pfatteicher, Philip 116
post-communion 81, 108, 120,
  163, 188, 191, 192, 195, 196,
  206, 207, 209
Presbyterian Church (USA) 1, 6,
  123, 124, 135, 136, 168
  Book of Common Worship
    1993 5, 118, 119, 165–8, 169,
    170, 171, 173, 176

INDEX

Presbyterian Church in the Republic of Korea 137
Primitive Methodist Church 70
Protestant Episcopal Church in the United States 54, 89
psalms, psalmody 3, 12, 115, 166, 120, 124, 126, 130, 132, 133, 154, 158, 161, 163, 182 *see also* metrical psalms
psalter collects, psalm collects, psalter prayers, psalm prayers 115, 116, 120, 131, 132
primers 9, 12, 13, 14, 16, 17, 19
printing 12, 23

Quinquagesima 17, 22

Ramshaw, Gail 117
red-letter days 38, 51, 180
Redman, Robert 12
Reformed 1, 83, 97, 123–38, 158
Regan, Patrick 124
Regnault, François 12
relative clause, relative pronoun 59, 62, 64, 114, 199, 201, 201, 206, 208
rhythm, rhythmic 5, 7, 15, 19, 200, 203
Robinson, Armitage 55, 58
Robinson, Ian 15
Roman Catholic 7, 13, 28, 61, 104, 107, 114, 115, 116, 119, 127, 129, 140, 159, 161, 197–215
Roman Missal 60, 61, 113, 157, 164, 169, 189, 192, 197, 199, 202, 204, 205, 206, 209, 214 *see also* International Commission on English in the Liturgy
Rome 7, 12, 65, 124

Sacramentary, sacramentaries 96, 106, 107, 114, 120, 147, 178, 186
Gelasian Sacramentary 106, 107n, 110, 113, 197
Gregorian Sacramentary 106, 107n, 113, 197
Verona [Leonine] Sacramentary 106, 113
St Hilda Community 19n
Women Included 191
saints' days 16, 22, 29, 39, 51, 180, 181
Sanctorale 52, 76, 185, 186, 188, 190, 196
Sarum Horae 12
Sarum Missal 16, 17, 18, 19, 21, 23, 26, 50, 51, 53, 73, 157, 158, 197, 199
Sarum rite 9, 15, 158
Sauer, Christopher 111
Schaff, Philip 134
Schmucker, Beale Melanchthon 112
Schwarz, Diebold 126
Scotland 134, 135
Scripture 4, 6, 7, 13, 22, 51, 52, 73, 81, 84, 90, 117, 123, 126, 127, 128, 129, 130, 133, 134, 135, 136, 148, 155, 159, 160, 191, 193, 197, 210, 211, 212
seasonal time 157, 162, 169, 174, 176
Second Vatican Council 7, 65, 102, 114, 198
Seltz, Martin 117
Seltzer, George Rise 114

INDEX

Senn, Frank 3, 4, 5, 116
Separatists 140, 147
sermon 38, 44, 45, 51, 92, 94n, 110, 126, 127, 130, 133, 135, 136, 137, 147, 149, 163
Shakespeare, Steven
 Prayers for an Inclusive Church 188, 194–5
Shepherd, Massey H. 55
Silk, David 62
 Prayers for Use at the Alternative Services 179, 180, 186
singing, song, sung 5, 37, 39, 48, 65, 126, 127, 129n, 130, 132, 133, 154
Smyth, John 140
Society of Saint Francis 78, 180, 181, 186
 Celebrating Common Prayer 78, 181, 182, 186, 187, 188
 The Daily Office SSF 180, 181, 182, 186, 187
Solemnization of Matrimony 85, 91 *see also* marriage
Spirit *see* Holy Spirit
spirituality 6, 82, 139, 140, 143, 144, 145, 147, 148, 153, 201, 211, 213
Spurr, F. C. 151
Stancliffe, David 186
Stevenson, Kenneth 62
Stoldt, Frank 117
Stookey, Laurence Hull 103
Storey, William G. 116
Strasbourg 2, 24, 123, 126, 127, 130, 138
Summers, Thomas O. 92, 93
Sweden 2, 28–49
Swedish language 28, 29, 35, 36, 49

Taizé 71
Taylor, John V. 76
Temporale 52, 186, 188, 194
Ten Commandments 13, 126
Tertullian 39
Theme (lectionary), thematic, thematically 40, 41, 43, 44, 45, 46, 48, 49, 56, 58, 61, 62, 71, 73, 157, 160, 163, 165, 173, 174, 176, 192
Thirkield, Wilbur P. 87
Thompson, Bard 126
Timms, George 182–5
Trinity (Holy) 40, 200
Trinity season 17, 19, 95
Tyndale, William 12

United Church of Canada 161
United Evangelical Church 97, 98, 99
United Lutheran Church in America 113
United Methodist Church 1, 2, 5, 83, 84, 97, 98, 102–5, 164
 Book of Worship 164–5
United States 2, 67, 83, 124, 134, 161, 162
Uniting Church in Australia 61
 Uniting in Worship 61
University of Lund 32, 46
University of Notre Dame, Indiana 116
Uppsala 28, 32

Vadstena Articles 33
vernacular 2, 5, 10, 11, 13, 14, 16, 24, 28, 29, 33, 36, 59, 198, 199
versicles 36
Vespers 35, 110, 112, 116 *see also* Evening Prayer, Evensong

INDEX

Visitation of the Sick 1 *see also* communion of the sick, Ministry to the Sick

Wakefield, Gordon S. 70, 71
Wales 65, 135
Wallwork, Norman 77, 82n
Watchnight 79, 84
Watts, Isaac 5, 79, 142, 143, 148, 150, 151
Webb, Pauline 71
weddings 86 *see also marriage*, Solemnization of Matrimony
Wenner, George Unangst 112
Wesley, Charles 5, 76, 77, 78. 79, 84, 85
Wesley John 2, 67, 68, 69, 75, 76, 77, 78, 79, 80, 84, 85, 86, 87, 89, 93, 97
Wesleyan Methodist Church 69, 79
Westerfield Tucker, Karen 2, 3, 5
Westminster Assembly 132
Directory for the Publick Worship of God 1645 132, 133, 134, 135
White, James F. 96, 125
Winward, Stephen see also Payne, E. A. 152, 153
women 5, 6, 61
Wright, Milton 97–8

Yelverton, Eric Esskildsen 34

Zeller, Paul 108n, 114

Index of Collects

Temporale (arranged according to the Church's Year)

Advent, Sunday next before 75
Advent 1 17, 22, 44, 50, 72, 75, 92, 119, 158, 162, 171, 174, 186, 194, 212
Advent 2 17, 22, 44, 50, 72, 109, 119, 158, 186, 190, 194, 210–11
Advent 3 44, 52, 72, 119, 158, 193, 194
Advent 4 52, 55, 72, 119, 169, 170, 193, 209
Christmas, Sixth Sunday before 191
Christmas, Fifth Sunday before 190
Christmas Eve 190
Christmas Day 68, 92, 115, 145, 193
New Year's Day 40
Christmas 2 186
Epiphany 69, 71, 190
Epiphany 1 55, 94n, 190
Epiphany 2 199
Epiphany 3 192
Epiphany 4 186, 194, 208
Epiphany 5 55, 171–2
Epiphany 6 52, 158
Epiphany 8 55
Presentation of the Lord (also Candlemas, the Purification of the Blessed Virgin Mary) 39
Lent, Fifth Sunday before 208
Quinquagesima 17, 22, 158
Easter, Eighth Sunday before 191
Lent, Sunday next before 22
Ash Wednesday 17, 22, 75, 84, 117, 201–2, 208
Ash Wednesday, Thursday after 204
Lent 1 17, 22, 33, 34, 92, 158, 213
Lent 2 165
Lent 3 121, 172
Lent 4 55, 76, 212
Mothering Sunday 76, 190
Palm Sunday 38, 117
Holy Week, Monday in 55
Maundy Thursday 117
Good Friday 17, 22, 38, 47, 54, 92, 117
Holy Saturday 76
Easter Vigil 117
Easter Eve 55, 211
Easter Day until Easter Dawn 76
Easter Sunday 34, 38, 40, 92, 145, 205
Easter afternoon 193
Easter Monday 40

INDEX OF COLLECTS

Easter week, Thursday in 55
Easter 2 17, 22, 59, 158, 170, 212–13
Easter 3 54
Easter 4 52
Easter 5 190
Ascension Day 92, 196
Ascension, Sunday after 17, 158, 190
Pentecost (Whitsunday) 16, 54, 92, 103
Whit Monday 40, 55
Trinity Sunday 16, 92, 191, 193, 194
Pentecost 4 168
Pentecost 5 186
Pentecost 14 162–3, 190
Pentecost 15 164
Pentecost 19 211 (others?)
Trinity 2 17, 52, 54, 174
Trinity 3 7 note 1, 35
Trinity 4 17, 33
Trinity 7 40
Trinity 8 40
Trinity 9 40, 54
Trinity 10 21
Trinity 11 52, 54
Trinity 12 21–22, 69
Trinity 15 40
Trinity 16 19–20
Trinity 18 52
Trinity 19 35
Trinity 20 55
Trinity 21 55
Trinity 24 94n
Trinity 26 38
Trinity 27 38
Christ the King 164
Kingdom 1 186
Proper 1 (week of the Sunday closest to 11 May) 55
Proper 9 (Sunday closest to 6 July) 55
Proper 18 (Sunday closest to 7 September) 55
Proper 20 (Sunday closest to 21 September) 55, 166
Proper 29 (Sunday closest to 23 November) 55
Sunday between 23 and 29 October 172
Second Sunday in Ordinary Time 199
Third Sunday in Ordinary Time 204
Fifth Sunday in Ordinary Time 204
Eleventh Sunday in Ordinary Time 204
Fourteenth Sunday in Ordinary Time 206–8
Nineteenth Sunday in Ordinary Time 205–6
Sundays 9, 17, 33, 51, 52, 57, 60, 63, 76, 89, 112, 125, 136, 157

Sanctorale

Aidan 184
Alcuin 189
Alfred the Great 189
All Saints' 38, 71, 76, 114
Andrew the Apostle 22, 37, 52
Andrewes, Lancelot 184, 189
Annunciation 16, 37, 39
Anselm 183, 189

INDEX OF COLLECTS

Augustine of Hippo 181–2
Baptism of the Lord 193
Bartholomew the Apostle 37
Bede 186
Birth of the Blessed Virgin
  Mary 180
Blaise 190
Bridget 190
Clare 184
Conception of the Blessed Virgin
  Mary 180
David, Patron of Wales 183
Francis de Sales 183
George, Patron of England 187
Gilbert of Sempringham 189
Herbert, George 181, 183
Holy Innocents 37
Hooker, Richard 186–7
Ignatius of Antioch 184
James the Apostle 37
John Chrysostom 183
John the Baptist 37, 39
John the Evangelist 17, 37
Joseph, Guardian of the
  Lord 119, 187
Keble, John 185, 186
Ken, Thomas 183
Laud, William 189
Lucy 186
Mark the Evangelist 22
Matthew, Apostle and
  Evangelist 37
Matthias the Apostle 37
Michael and All Angels 17, 37, 39
Nicholas 184
Oswald 186
Paul, Conversion of 37
Peter and Paul, Apostles 37
Philip and James, Apostles 37
Richard of Chichester 189
Saints' days 16, 17
Simon and Jude, Apostles 38
Stephen 37
Thomas the Apostle 37, 55
Timothy and Titus 181
Transfiguration 40, 55
Visitation of the Blessed Virgin
  Mary to Elizabeth 173
Visitation of the Blessed Virgin
  Mary to Elizabeth 37, 173
Wesley, John and Charles 76, 78

Other Commemorations

Hurricane Katrina 121
Tsunami (26 December
  2004) 121
September 11, 2001 121
Incarnation 179

Pastoral/ Occasional

Admission and Commissioning
  of Methodist Local
  Preachers 80
Baptism 3, 101, 86, 101
Burial 17, 90, 91, 100, 101, 107
Church anniversary 76
Confirmation 107
Confirmation and Reception
  into Membership
  (Methodist) 80

INDEX OF COLLECTS

Form of Laying the Corner Stone
   of a Church 92
Funeral *see* Burial
Harvest 76
Marriage 91, 98, 101, 107

Ministry to the sick 96
Ordination 87, 90, 91–2, 98,
   101
Welcome Service for Ministers,
   Deacons and Probationers 80

Fixed Collects

After sermon 92
Angelus 209
Before Lessons and sermon 92
Evensong 17
For aid against all perils 51,
   72–3, 89, 92
For grace 51, 68, 89, 92, 97, 110
For peace 51, 68, 72, 92, 94n,
   110
For purity 51, 58, 68, 86, 87, 90,

   91, 94, 97, 99, 100 n. 39, 101,
   102, 103, 104, 135, 164
King, the 9, 68
Prayer of St Chrysostom 94n,
   101, 102
Supreme rulers of these United
   States, the 68
To be said when there is no
   communion 3, 204n

Thematic and Intentional Collects

Christian Unity 76
Creation 121
For illumination 127, 131, 132,

   133, 134, 135, 136, 138
Global warming 121

COMING SOON

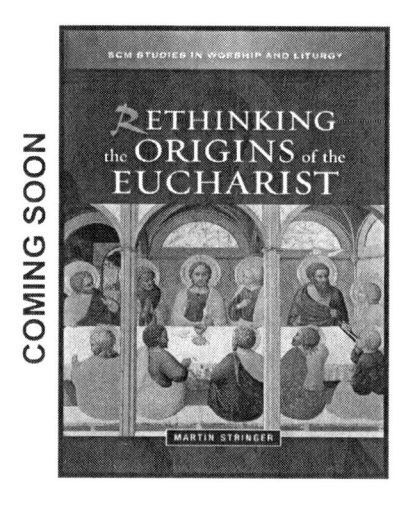

SCM STUDIES IN WORSHIP AND LITURGY:
RETHINKING THE ORIGINS OF THE EUCHARIST
MARTIN STRINGER

978 0 334 04214 3   paperback   300pp   £40.00

Available in all good bookshops
Alternatively order direct from the publisher:
Tel: 01603 612 914   Online: www.scmpress.co.uk

In the USA?
Refer to our US distributor Westminster John Knox:
Tel: 1-800-523-1631   E-mail: orders@wjkbooks.com

www.scmpress.co.uk

THE NEW SCM DICTIONARY OF LITURGY AND WORSHIP
PAUL BRADSHAW
978 0 334 02883 3   hardback   512pp   £50.00

Available in all good bookshops
Alternatively order direct from the publisher:
Tel: 01603 612 914   Online: www.scmpress.co.uk

In the USA?
Refer to our US distributor Westminster John Knox:
Tel: 1-800-523-1631   E-mail: orders@wjkbooks.com

www.scmpress.co.uk

LaVergne, TN USA
26 January 2011
214046LV00001B/3/P